Opera in Paris, 1800–1850

Opera in Paris, 1800–1850

A Lively History

by Patrick Barbier

translated by Robert Luoma

AMADEUS PRESS
Reinhard G. Pauly, General Editor
Portland, Oregon

First published in the French language as *La vie quotidienne à l'Opéra au temps de Rossini et de Balzac: Paris, 1800–1850* by Hachette, Paris. Copyright © Hachette 1987.

English-language edition copyright © 1995 by Amadeus Press
(an imprint of Timber Press, Inc.)
All rights reserved.

ISBN 0-931340-83-7

Printed in Singapore

AMADEUS PRESS
The Haseltine Building
133 S.W. Second Avenue, Suite 450
Portland, Oregon 97204, U.S.A.

Library of Congress Cataloging-in-Publication Data

Barbier, Patrick.
    [Vie quotidienne à l'Opéra au temps de Rossini et de Balzac, Paris, 1800–1850. English]
    Opera in Paris, 1800–1850: a lively history / by Patrick Barbier; translated by Robert Luoma.
            p.   cm.
    Includes bibliographical references (p.   ) and index.
    ISBN 0-931340-83-7
    1. Opéra de Paris. 2. Opera—France—Paris—19th century.
I. Luoma, Robert Gust. II. Title.
ML1727.8.P2B313   1995
782.1'0944'36109034—dc20   94-26952
                                                                      CIP
                                                                      MN

Contents

Introduction

"I like what I see in this city—the best musicians and the best opera in the world." Chopin was not the only one to love Paris and be spellbound by the dazzling musical climate that reigned from the beginning of the nineteenth century to the romantic period. From the time of Gluck, in prerevolutionary France before 1789, numerous composers chose Paris as a second home. A first wave brought Cherubini, Spontini, Blangini, and Paër; and a second, even more prestigious, led to the installation of Rossini, Meyerbeer, Bellini, Donizetti, Liszt, and Chopin.

Paris's cosmopolitanism is by no means a modern phenomenon: as early as 1799, at the end of the Revolution, foreigners of all nationalities flocked to the capital. The political, economic, and cultural radiance of Paris was so great that in the space of thirty years the population doubled, from 550,000 to over one million. *La musique lyrique*, musical theater, survived the Napoleonic Wars and two revolutions (in 1830 and 1848) undamaged. It spanned three political regimes—the Empire*† (1804–1814), the Restoration* (1814–1830), and the July Monarchy* (1830–1848)—yet succeeded in uniting two

---

†Words marked by asterisks are briefly explained in the Glossary, p. 235

generations in a shared thirst for entertainment, a shared passion for singing and its new idols. To be seen at the theater, to argue the respective merits of the Opéra or the Théâtre-Italien, to have Rossini or Meyerbeer at the center of sophisticated conversation, became more and more common in daily Parisian life.

This pivotal era, the first half of the nineteenth century, justified such an infatuation. In the space of a few years the art of singing made great strides: *tragédie lyrique** and *opera seria** were dropped in favor of *grand opéra** and romantic drama. The musical arts were no longer the prerogative of the aristocracy, but the indispensable pastime of the upper middle and middle classes.

Seen close up, however, Paris was not the resplendent city that one would like to imagine today. It was little changed from the time of Louis XIV: a poorly lit maze of narrow, dirty streets. The Right Bank, according to Balzac, was "revoltingly filthy and decayed."

But in Paris's topography, as in its cultural life, opposites intermingled: aristocrat and pauper lived side by side, tragedy competed with bawdy vaudeville every evening, and slums bordered the cultural heart of the capital, which was situated within the boundaries of the Rue de Richelieu and the Boulevard des Italiens. And what a district this was, with all the finest musical venues within a square kilometer! Music lovers could pass from an opera house on the Rue de Richelieu to one on the Rue le Peletier, from the Salle Favart to the Salle Feydeau, from the Théâtre Louvois to the Salle Ventadour.

Let us accompany the theater-goer who, whether once or several times a week, frequented the major theaters of Paris, attended the great spectacles, and applauded burlesque as well as works of propaganda. With our Parisian companion we will follow the reactions of governments to musical theater, rub shoulders backstage with the composers and the singers who so stirred the emotions, and peer over a shoulder to scan the frequent reviews in the music press.

Following the flow of the theatrical seasons, the pages that follow will attempt to throw light on the daily life of this early nineteenth-century Parisian. Thus today's music lover may join the thousands of professionals and spectators of that era who placed opera at the center of their lives.

The Empress Josephine in her salon at Malmaison. Portrait by François Gerard. Courtesy National Museum of Malmaison.

CHAPTER 1

Rulers and Music

The operas of Lully had come to symbolize the artistic radiance of the reign of Louis XIV, but neither Louis XV nor Louis XVI shared the Sun King's passion for *tragédie lyrique*. The former attended only when duty required, and the latter was far from sharing the enthusiasm of his wife for entertainment of this genre. Curiously, and unlike the rulers in Germany and Italy, the two Bourbons gave much more support to the completely new *opéra comique**, which was lighter, more entertaining, and paradoxically less "aristocratic" than the formerly popular tragic operas. A frequently told story had Louis XV walking through the salons of Versailles humming, "in the worst voice in the world," the air "J'ai perdu mon serviteur" (I have lost my servant) from *Le devin du village* (The Village Soothsayer) by Jean-Jacques Rousseau.

By the time of Rameau's death in 1764, opera and the art of French song were already in decline, and even the innovations of Gluck, between 1774 and 1779, could not halt the decline. The future kings Louis XVIII and Charles X showed no more love for art in general or for opera in particular than had their brother Louis XVI. Neither Versailles nor exile had fired their interest, and although their reigns were not without musical events, Louis and Charles were more or less indifferent spectators. Louis-Philippe, like his cousins, exhibited no particular taste for music; only the concrete and the useful, the palpable and the profitable, interested him. That did not prevent him, fortunately, from supporting artists and promoting opera, which reached the high point of the first half of the century during his reign.

Napoleon's approach was quite different. Without doubt he had no more musical knowledge than the Bourbons, and had not even had the exposure of the festivities at Versailles. Yet this man, self-made, without the benefit of the influences of a royal court and with no artistic family heritage, had the deep-seated conviction that the arts would further the glory of the empire he had founded. He pursued an active and substantial policy of favoring grand, prestigious musical events in Paris, in which the Opéra played an important part. The curtain now rises on Napoleon and his politics, on the man and his work.

The Emperor's Tastes and Shortcomings

The first to come to power in the period in question, Napoleon was also indisputably the ruler most involved in music in general and opera in particular. Initially, he did not have any particular taste for music: in his eyes, only classical tragedy merited wholehearted approval, and throughout his reign the Théâtre-Français (today the Comédie-Française) remained the premier theater of the nation, the only one authorized to bear the name Théâtre de l'Empereur. In fact, his passion for tragedy (and especially for Corneille) was such that he required all the members of his family and the grand dignitaries of the crown to retain a box at the Théâtre-Français, setting an example by paying 21,000 francs* per year for his own box, and never failing to appear there upon his return from a campaign, by way of an official homecoming in view of his subjects.

Beyond that, Napoleon had scant artistic knowledge. It could be said that he was limited in outlook, and certainly he had trouble forming even a basic judgment on a work of art or a piece of music. Concerning the plastic arts, his interest was even more restricted. Chaptal wrote that

> he was so narrow-minded in this regard that he could not conceive of anyone being enthusiastic over a picture or a statue since, he said, all were copies of nature and there was no great merit in copying and imitating.[1]

Nevertheless, Napoleon brought back from his conquests incredible quantities of works of art that still grace French museums. Likewise, he did all he could to encourage artists. Their social situation improved appreciably, and they found themselves less subject to censorship than the literati.

In terms of music, the emperor revealed somewhat more personality: he may not have been a connoisseur, but at least he clearly asserted what he did or did not like. In 1797 he declared that "of all the fine arts, music is the one that has the most emotional influence, the one that a legislator should encourage the most."[2] Should one see in this assertion an acknowledgment of his own escapades? As well as his special friendship with Mlle George, an actress at the Comédie-Française, Napoleon enjoyed a liaison with Caroline Branchu—destined to become the greatest French singer of his reign—before allowing himself to be seduced, in Milan, by the singer the Italians nicknamed the "tenth muse," Giuseppina Grassini.

Beyond this quite specific approach to music, the emperor's knowledge of the subject was virtually nonexistent. In 1805 he asked, "What is this piece *Don Giovanni* that they want to do at the Opéra?"[3] And when he attended a performance of the same work in Stuttgart some months later, he merely wrote that "the music seemed very nice."[4] Nonetheless, he tirelessly backed the Opéra, attended its performances as often as possible, and intervened directly in its administration—even in the choice of works to be given—without hiding his enthusiasm for certain operas such as *Ossian; ou, Les bardes* (Ossian; or, The Bards) by Le Sueur.

What was his favorite musical genre? The answer is simple: Italian opera. This was his real weakness, and his Théâtre de la Cour, or Court Theater, was comprised almost exclusively of Italian singers and composers. Napoleon detested anything with "too many notes" or "too much noise," and for this reason Italian music, with its lightness, graceful tunes, and sublime vocal lines, appealed to him. His most intense emotions were stirred, and it astonished those around him that a man as combative and virile as he, accustomed to the field of battle, relished only pretty or sad melodies.

Laws Regulating the Theaters

That the emperor sang out-of-tune and had no particular knowledge of opera was of no great importance. No ruler was more concerned about the life and problems of the theaters—even to the point of being over-protective. His sole intention was to make Paris "the capital of the civilized world," hence his sometimes excessive guardianship of the more prestigious theaters.

The end of the Consulate* in 1804 and the beginning of the Empire* constituted a time of some disorder, arising from the Parisians' extravagant passion for spectacles and indeed any type of entertainment. By liberalizing the dramatic arts and other forms of artistic expression, the Revolution had facilitated a spontaneous growth of theaters—at the beginning of the century more than thirty venues shared the applause of a population of about 550,000 inhabitants!

Strict regulations governed all these venues, but they affected only essential matters of security and order, not the freedom to open new theaters. Laws stipulated standards in the construction and fitting out of the buildings, with requirements for a minimum amount of tanked water and the good working order of fire hoses. Ticket scalping was illegal, as was loitering in the foyers and lobbies; one law even banned the wearing of hats during performances.

These details failed to halt the worrisome proliferation of theaters in the capital and new venues sprang up like mushrooms. The number of theatrical and operatic performances multiplied, dispersing and squandering talents and contributing to the spread of mediocrity, not to say vulgarity. The artists themselves, contemptuous of the minimal discipline that prevailed, followed their own whims. In this atmosphere of growing competition and anarchy, the most prestigious and costly theaters inevitably suffered a slump.

Napoleon issued a decree in June 1806 in an attempt to check this decline. Broadly speaking, no theater could be established in the capital without special authorization from the emperor, following a proposal from the minister of the interior. Moreover, no venue could stage a work from the repertoires of the Opéra, the Comédie-Française, or the Opéra-Comique without paying a fee to the management of the theater concerned. Finally, the decree stipulated that only the Opéra could perform certain ballets of a historic or mythological nature, thus penalizing several companies, including the Théâtre de la Porte-Saint-Martin. The press and the knowledgeable public were manifestly relieved by this demonstration of the emperor's refusal to dedicate public money to the advancement of histrionics.

Alas, in spite of these strong measures, the situation, far from being improved, worsened each day. Three months after the decree, a journalist from the *Journal des Dames et des Modes* painted, not without humor, a vivid picture of Parisian theatrical life:

> Every evening I go to a different show, but the show is always the same. At the Théâtre-Français opening nights are like farewell performances, because by the time the curtain comes down, the actors are already has-beens. At the Opéra, nothing changes— the singing is always bad, and the dancing is always good. Women go there to be seen, and men to enjoy the dual spectacles on the stage and in the boxes. The evening ends in considerable boredom, and when the habitués of the theater leave, they look like schoolchildren who have just been scolded. At the Opéra-Comique, I see crowded foyers but few watching the performance. At the Louvois, where even the braggarts inspire

melancholy, I see a few sorry specimens. Ever since the Comédie-Française took it into its head to perform vaudeville, the
Vaudeville Theater claims to stage nothing but comedy. Formerly we enjoyed sharp, witty vaudeville, today the performances make us weep. The Montansier is, they say, the one theater that will soon be presenting plays in better taste. And then
there are the boulevard theaters, where so many good plays, distinguished actors, and new or original things can be seen that
the crowds are deserting the theaters at the city's heart. Boxes
are reserved eight days in advance, and the tickets are gone by
five o'clock.[5]

The crisis was very real, with the widespread confusion favoring
the offbeat over the mainstream. Small neighborhood theaters continued to draw spectators, while the big theaters were so empty they
were forced to contemplate partial closure. Action by the emperor
could not be long in coming, and this time it would be the inevitable
authoritarian act of a statesman afraid of being overwhelmed by a situation he could no longer control.

On 8 August 1807, Napoleon decided that henceforth only
eight theaters would be allowed in Paris; all others, without exception, were to close their doors and dismiss their artists and personnel
by 15 August. In one week, twenty-five flourishing theaters had to
cancel productions and lower their curtains permanently without
hope of obtaining the slightest compensation from the government.
The eight surviving theaters were, of course, the four official venues—
the Opéra, Opéra-Comique, Théâtre de l'Empereur, and Théâtre de
l'Impératrice—for plays, the Théâtre de la Porte-Saint-Martin for
great spectacles and melodramas, the Théâtre des Variétés for plays of
a "licentious, vulgar, or rustic" nature, the Théâtre du Vaudeville for
short plays mixing light songs and satire, and finally the Théâtre de la
Gaîté for pantomimes, farces, and harlequinades. These theaters
would operate under the auspices of the government, and no new
venues could be constructed. Thus competition from the boulevard

theaters would end. This gesture, which favored the large national stages, could be perceived by some as a suppression of liberties.

Napoleon and the Opéra

We have already mentioned the emperor's dislike of French opera and his ignorance of music. One thing is certain, these short-comings never undermined his desire to implement a significant musical policy. The attention and largesse Napoleon lavished upon the major Parisian stages illustrates his steady awareness that the prestige of his reign depended upon their fame.

Napoleon, who knew Italy and its theaters well, certainly wanted to make the Paris Opéra the foremost musical stage of Europe, and he considered it a beacon of French music. Moreover, he saw the Opéra as becoming a focal point for a new, rich, and elegant society that would resemble that of the *Ancien Régime**, the world of prerevolu-tionary France. One of his ministers confirmed this aim.

> Through the union of art and talent, this unique spectacle pro-vides a useful impetus to the fashion and luxury goods trades, at-tracts a throng of foreigners to Paris, and adds to the brilliance of this great city and—as befits it—to the genius and taste of the nation.[6]

The Opéra thus had a double significance: it was a springboard for creative activity and at the same time a luxury product that stimu-lated business. Through it, the names of Napoleon and Paris gained international prestige.

Napoleon intervened in the life of the Opéra frequently—un-doubtedly more frequently than at the other theaters. One of his pri-mary concerns was to highlight the great events of his reign by his ap-pearance at the Opéra, and one can imagine what the presence of such a man, whose mere return to the capital caused a rise at the stock ex-change, could do to benefit a theater such as the Opéra.

Was attending a musical performance such a dreadful ordeal for a man who cared so little for opera? Probably not, because his knowledge of the subject grew during his reign, and very quickly the duty of attending performances was tempered by the pleasure of judging them. Although it was much easier for Napoleon to get about and participate fully in Parisian theatrical life when he was consul, Napoleon the emperor was nonetheless able to attend twenty-six operas and ballets at the Académie Impériale de Musique. With two or three attendances most years, and up to seven in 1810, he put himself well ahead of any of the other sovereigns of the first half of the century who deigned to appear at the Opéra. In general, Napoleon sought to combine an important event in his reign (a military victory, the presentation of Marie-Louise at court, the birth of Napoleon II and his subsequent proclamation as King of Rome) with one of the highlights of French opera—a new work by Spontini, perhaps, or a revival of an opera by Gluck or Sacchini.

Napoleon paid considerable attention to composers, and many profited from his generosity. Le Sueur (along with the Italian Paër at the Court Theater) was always his favorite composer. It was he who wrote the Coronation March after having triumphed with *Ossian,* which the emperor considered a visual and musical masterpiece. Le Sueur received the Légion d'Honneur (an exceedingly rare award for an artist of this period), 6,000 francs, and a snuff-box engraved with the words "From the Emperor of the French to the Composer of the Bards."

The Empress Josephine, if Mme de Rémusat is to be believed, "was certainly not a person of elevated mind," but she at least had the merit of wanting to encourage artists. She was undoubtedly more of a musician than her august husband, and in addition to the musical soirées that she organized at Malmaison, like every lady of good society she played the harp, an instrument that had the enormous advantage of showing off her pretty arms. According to witnesses, she played it mainly "to pass idle time, and always the same tune."

Josephine knew how to use her position to reward certain

singers, dancers, and composers with recommendations, titles, or financial aid. "How many have been helped by her!" exclaimed Mlle Avrillon; "how many have received encouragement, and always with the most exquisite delicacy!" Among those who profited from this high-ranking patronage were the ballerina Mlle Aubry (whose misadventures will be related later), and in particular the young Italian composer who arrived in Paris in 1803 and prospered at the Opéra for more than fifteen years: Gaspare Spontini. Josephine quickly linked herself to him by making him Special Composer of Music to the Empress, thus rewarding him for *Milton*, his first triumph at the Opéra-Comique. She soon increased her advocacy in order to speed her protégé's entry into the Opéra and allow the production of his opera *La vestale* (The Vestal Virgin). Without the constant and effective help of the empress, *La vestale* would perhaps never have seen the light of day, though it was the greatest musical masterpiece created in Paris during the Empire.

Another example of the emperor's intervention in the arts was the introduction of the Decennial Prize, which, as we will see, was to pit Napoleon's favorite, Le Sueur, against the empress's, Spontini. As early as 1804 the emperor had the idea of distributing prizes once a decade on the anniversary of 18 Brumaire (Napoleon's coup d'état of 9 November 1799, which took place during the second month of the new Republican calendar). The different branches of the Institute would assign the prizes to artists, writers, or scholars.

The Decennial Prize was first presented in 1810. The idea was to reward the best opera and the best *opéra comique* mounted between 1799 and 1809 at the two theaters concerned. Twenty-nine operatic works had been produced, but only three attracted the jury's attention: Catel's *Sémiramis*, Le Sueur's *Le triomphe de Trajan* (The Triumph of Trajan), and Spontini's *La vestale*. All three had to be restaged in early 1810 to refresh the memories of the judges and ensure a fair and thoughtful choice. In selecting *Trajan*, the jury must have believed they would please the emperor, since the opera is nothing more than a solemn concert of praise to Napoleon. On the contrary, the jury, in its effort to flatter the sovereign, had simply not taken into consideration Napoleon's own preferred opera: *Ossian; ou, Les bardes* by the same composer, Le Sueur. This flagrant injustice had to be rectified as soon as possible: the director of the Opéra received an order from the emperor requiring the immediate preparation of *Ossian* for participation in the competition. Despite this, the members of the jury did not yield to Napoleon's pressure, and it was to *La vestale* that they awarded the Decennial Prize for opera, with a sum of 10,000 francs for the composer and an equal amount for the librettist, Jouy. There is no doubt at all that Josephine, who was divorced in 1809, rejoiced in the victory of her composer, whom she continued to receive as a friend at Malmaison until her death.

As for the Decennial Prize for *opéra comique*, it was awarded to Méhul for *Joseph*, one of the rare operas in the history of music to have no female role (another is Massenet's *Le jongleur de Notre-Dame* [The Juggler of Notre-Dame]). *La vestale* and *Joseph* were the only operas awarded the prize, for the Restoration quickly put an end to a tradition that so clearly represented the usurper Napoleon.

Napoleon continually issued directives concerning the good administration of the Opéra and the Opéra-Comique. As though the conduct of political, economic, and military affairs was not enough for him, he was also omnipresent in the management and organization of the theaters—from the greater issues of finance to such lesser business as the replacement of an usher. He was the one who required all secondary theaters, from 1811 on, to present touring shows, balls, and concerts. Profits from these shows helped to expand the Opéra's finances, which were a constant preoccupation. This measure remained in force until the end of the Restoration. In the end though, Napoleon struggled in vain to stem the flow of complimentary tickets, one of the principal causes of the deficit at the Opéra.

It was in the realm of programming that his presence was most strongly felt. Just as he was capable of modifying the casting of *Le Cid* at the Théâtre-Français, he always supervised the Opéra's offerings. On one occasion he wrote, "I do not want *La vestale* to play. I think that *La mort d'Adam* (The Death of Adam) should be staged, since it is ready."[7] And at another time:

> It will be necessary to mount *La mort d'Abel* (The Death of Abel) on the 20th of March, the ballet from *Persée et Andromède* on Easter Monday, *Les bayadères* two weeks later, *Sophocle* and *Armide* during the summer run, *Les danaïdes* in the autumn, and *Les sabines* at the end of May.[8]

Apropos of *La mort d'Abel*, he did not hesitate to impose certain very personal points of view:

> Since the opera *La mort d'Abel* has been produced, I consent that it play. Henceforth, no opera may be staged without my authorization. In general, I do not approve of any work taken from the Holy Scriptures; these subjects should be left to the church.[9]

Finally, when the field-marshal of the palace, Duroc, proposed to transfer the projected cost of producing Gluck's *Armide* (10,000 francs) to Catel's *Sémiramis*, Napoleon retorted bluntly: "Refused. If *Armide* is not produced, I shall not give the 10,000 francs."[10]

Between Saint Cecilia and Saint Goulifar

The royal families of the Restoration were never particularly skilled in musical matters. The only exception was the young Duchess of Berry, the daughter-in-law of Charles X, who had a definite love of music and who practiced the piano and the harp (undoubtedly due to the same social considerations as Josephine), took voice lessons from Paër, and patronized the arts. In the atmosphere of austerity that surrounded the Bourbons, with the inartistic Louis XVIII and Charles X, and with a husband who labored to get a few notes out of his hunting horn, Marie-Caroline was the only member of the Tuileries court who was playful, laughing, dynamic, and artistic—a charming and effervescent spirit.

Louis XVIII's and Charles X's major problem was surely that

they neither set the tone for a musical policy nor went to any effort to encourage one by attendance. Encouragement for artists certainly existed, but only in the form of kind words, presents, pensions, decorations, and titles. These kings never cultivated a rich and brilliant theatrical and musical life by means of their own glittering presence at performances. They never tried to launch an art form that would give their reigns a distinctive mark. For example, Louis XVIII happily retained Napoleon's distinctively styled furniture, which occupied the places of honor among all the rooms in the Tuileries. After the Hundred Days* of Napoleon's return to power from March to June 1815, Louis was content merely to remove from the palace furnishings the *N*, star, and bee emblems that reminded him a little too much of his predecessor.

Louis had a taste for precious stones and miniatures painted on enamel or porcelain, his only true artistic interests. His literary taste remained essentially classical, and he placed Racine above all others. He did not know how to cultivate the young, rising generation of writers such as Chateaubriand, Lamartine, and Hugo, writers who nevertheless supported him. Of all the "arts," he preferred gastronomy. Rather than proving himself to be a disciple of Saint Cecilia, the patron saint of music, Louis XVIII, in the words of the Duchess of Berry, revealed himself as "a follower of Saint Éboudiche and Saint Goulifar, the patron saints of gluttony." As for Charles X, his reign emphasized religion over the fine arts. It is a pity that although in his youth he was a patron to many artists, the final years of his life were nearly devoid of artistic influence.

Opera was not totally excluded from the public life of the Restoration sovereigns, but it served mainly as a showcase for the royal family and as a point of contact with the populace, even though the opera-going public was a select group entirely devoted to the Bourbons. On his accession in 1814, Louis XVIII attended a performance at the Opéra with the Tsar of Russia and the King of Prussia. The audience buzzed with excitement in the huge hall lavishly decorated with fleurs-de-lys and white cockades. After the Hundred Days of

1815 and just before the return of his brother Louis, Charles showed up in the royal box, paid a visit to the box of the allied sovereigns during the first intermission, and was visited by them in turn during the second intermission, to the applause of an audience flattered to see its prince so honored. At the time of his return, Louis XVIII attended the Opéra for a performance of Sacchini's *Oedipe à Colone* in the company of the Duchess of Angoulême (the daughter of Marie-Antoinette), who delighted the audience when, in accordance with court etiquette at Versailles, she bowed three times before the king.

Opera during the Restoration functioned as a sanctuary for the monarchy, a high-society display case where the court and the Saint-Germain aristocracy could spend an evening together. If Louis XVIII did not often attend, it was chiefly because his awkward body did not permit the stately bearing and gestures that made Napoleon so dashing. Louis's obesity, the malformation of his hip, and the incessant attacks of gout that restricted his walking meant he had nothing in common with the lively dandy who loved social events for the pleasure of making an appearance.

Alas, Charles X was hardly more responsive to the arts, even though he ruled during a period that witnessed the extraordinary rise of the Opéra and the Théâtre-Italien. When he attended a performance of Rossini's *Il viaggio a Reims* (The Journey to Reims), composed specially for the coronation (and probably the only opera with any genius that was written for a special occasion), Charles X was bored to death before so much beauty. Castil-Blaze observed:

> King Charles X, who was fêted in the most brilliant and sumptuous manner, did not have a good time at all. Sitting in one of the front boxes between the Duchesses of Angoulême and Berry, His Majesty at first endured the extravaganza patiently, but, like Dido at the stake, soon raised his eyes to heaven, sought the gaslight, and groaned. This expressive pantomime was evidence of royal boredom. I saw the monarch lean toward the Duchess of Berry and ask if the drudgery was still far from ending. Without

a word, the princess responded by showing him the open libretto. One-third was done, two-thirds remained to be endured: he had to take his medicine in three doses![11]

Like his brother, Charles preferred to surround himself with music in the intimacy of the Tuileries, since that way the musicians had to travel, not the king.

The Pleasures of Love

The musical tastes of Louis-Philippe were no more innovative than those of his predecessors, although from time to time he did enjoy the little musical soirées organized at the Tuileries and Fontainebleau by his sister and daughter-in-law, the only members of his entourage who were at all musical. As in his youth, the king particularly appreciated the *opéra comique* of the eighteenth century, particularly the works of Grétry, whose famous *Richard coeur-de-lion* he caused to be revived in an arrangement by Adam. As for opera, it was not surprising that Louis-Philippe's enthusiasm was for Gluck, the most popular composer of the eighteenth century, though the king was familiar with his work mostly through excerpts heard at private concerts.

Louis-Philippe, who was criticized for his bourgeois tastes, liked nothing better than the *romance*, a musical form that was no less bourgeois for being fashionable in the intimate salons of affluent Parisian society. The uninterrupted success of the *romance* extended from the end of the *Ancien Régime* in 1789 to the monarchy established by the July Revolution of 1830, and professionals and amateurs (among them Queen Hortense) wrote them by the thousands. With simple, pleasant, even naive melodies, accompanied by piano or harp, the melodies of the *romance* were set to couplets and short refrains usually expressing the torments of love. The *romance* corresponds to a certain extent to today's popular song. Indeed, it touched all levels of society, including the fashionable women of the aristocracy or bourgeoisie, who were delighted to be able to shine in their salons without too much effort. A wonderfully intimate art, the *romance* was also extremely accessible, easily learned by adolescents, and a good introduction to music even for relatively uneducated families. The celebrated "Plaisir d'amour" (Love's Pleasure) by Martini remains one of the flowers of this art, and those close to Louis-Philippe recognized it as one of the pieces the royal family never tired of hearing.

Still, the tastes of the Orléans family were not limited to the *romance*. The bel canto of Italian opera was currently blossoming in Paris and arousing widespread admiration, and the presence of the king and his family at the Théâtre-Italien was an undeniable sign of their interest in this style of singing. The Orléans kept three boxes with six seats each at the Opéra and the Théâtre-Italien, and boxes with six seats at both the Odéon and the Opéra-Comique. In 1831, for example, the king appeared with his whole family at the Opéra once, at the Opéra-Comique once, and at the Théâtre-Italien twice. Queen Marie-Amélie and her daughters attended the Théâtre-Italien four times, and the young Dukes of Orléans were seen in their box at the Opéra three times—notably for the premiere of *Robert le diable* (Robert the Devil)—and at the Théâtre-Italien once. Some years later, the king attended a performance of *La juive* (The Jewess) and wanted to personally introduce the composer, Halévy, to the queen and all his family. If the king appeared less and less often, it was because every visit to the city generated so much criticism and so many pamphlets, his bourgeois dress was the source of so much sarcasm that Louis-Philippe preferred to take refuge in the Tuileries and to send his children to the royal box in his place.

When it came to the frequent benefit concerts and performances, the king's generosity exceeded even that of his predecessor. Tradition required that whenever an artist organized such a concert, he requested the honor of the king's presence. Neither capable nor desirous of attending all these performances, Louis-Philippe would usually send money instead. The sum varied greatly, with such celebrities as Giuditta Pasta, Harriet Smithson, or Luigi Lablache receiving

1,000 francs, and little-known artists (performing for their own benefit or for charity) receiving only 50 to 200 francs. If the queen attended a performance, the sum would be slightly higher. Louis-Philippe was always generous in these matters. In 1831 alone, he made ninety-six donations, all between 50 and 1,000 francs, whereas Charles X never gave more than 200 francs. Similarly, when Rossini organized a subscription to finance the funeral of Bellini, the embalming of the young composer's body, and the erection of a monument to his memory, Louis-Philippe and Marie-Amélie were among the principal donors.

A Castrato at the Court Theater

The Court Theater constituted a connecting thread between the four reigns of the half-century between 1800 and 1850. It was at the Tuileries—known, to be precise, as "The Palace" under the Empire and "The Castle" under the Monarchy—that the royal stage was erected, though this was the one theater that could be transported to follow the movements of the court, whether to Saint-Cloud, Compiègne, Fontainebleau, or other royal residences. Moreover, this theater was reserved for the royal family, for carefully selected foreign guests, and, before 1830, for nobility formally presented to the king. Formal presentation meant, as at Versailles, approaching in elaborate court dress, ceremoniously greeting the monarch with triple bows, and departing backwards, still facing the king. The Court Theater was the only one to have a succession of comedies, tragedies, operas, ballets, and even vaudevilles on its stage. This eclectic repertoire, generally of excellent quality, was presented exclusively in private, this being the primary function of the royal venue.

At the beginning of Napoleon's reign, no theater could have served in this capacity, because the *Ancien Régime*'s former theater, the Salle des Machines, which was transformed during the Revolution into a meeting place and was used for the Counsel of Elders and the State during the Directory (1795–1799), could not be used in this way. In 1806 the emperor constructed a luxurious theater to remedy the situation. He inaugurated it in 1808 with a production of Paër's *Griselda.* The stage was situated directly behind the Marsan Lodge, so the audience had the "court side" (of the Louvre) to its right, and the "garden side" (of the Tuileries) to its left, appellations which henceforth substituted for the *Ancien Régime*'s traditional "king's side" and "queen's side." By producing an *opera seria* Napoleon continued the custom dating from the time of Louis XIV of allowing only the Court Theater to present this type of opera. The Théâtre-Italien, which was open to the general public, obtained the right to mount repertoire of this kind only with the emperor's authorization of June 1810.

The organization of the theater was entrusted to the superintendent of entertainment, M. de Rémusat, a busy man since Napoleon was not easy to satisfy and was very demanding as to the quality and staging of operas, concerts, ballets, and plays taking place at the Tuileries. Talleyrand often pitied Rémusat for being charged "with amusing the unamusable." In fact, in creating the prestigious atmosphere of a court theater, the emperor's sole purpose was to recapture the splendor of the *Ancien Régime.* The words *luxury* and *elegance* appeared constantly in his orders, and he meant a formal luxury—an "explosion of regulated magnificence." The new audience at the Palace did not always possess the education or the literary and artistic culture of the old aristocrats. Except for some rare initiates, this fashionable society was bored by the performances, though they were compensated by their pleasure in the unparalleled elegance of the spectators. As Mme de Chastenay wrote, "Nothing surpassed the good taste of the surroundings, the richness of the adornments, the brilliance of the lavish lights. Women sparkling with diamonds filled the lower balcony and first row of the gallery."[12] General Durand echoed these reflections:

> The theater offered a dazzling view. Women had to wear the most elegant finery, and men would be admitted only if they were wearing formal evening-dress with swords at their sides.

During the intermissions the emperor's liveried footmen would liberally distribute ices and other refreshments throughout the hall.[13]

But Mme de Chastenay could not help specifying that "the court was very formal, and in spite of the magnificence of its festivities, one did not go there for amusement."[14] To this lack of general enthusiasm was added the not very encouraging tradition of never applauding in this theater.

Then from 1806 to 1812 the Court Theater enjoyed an extraordinary singer, the veritable jewel of the emperor's private musicians and his favorite artist: the castrato* Girolamo Crescentini. After an international career performing in the principal cities of Italy, then in London and Lisbon, Crescentini came to Napoleon's attention in Vienna during its occupation by French troops. Immediately conquered by the indescribable, almost supernatural charm of his voice, the emperor invited him to Paris.

The singer rapidly became the idol of the Court Theater, and though opinions were mixed—understandable for French listeners unaccustomed to the voices of castratos—he nevertheless produced an unprecedented impression that is difficult to imagine today. Crescentini was not particularly attractive physically, but his angelic voice and the emotion that emanated from his whole person when he interpreted Zingarelli's Romeo were enough to conquer his audiences. The emperor's valet spoke of him in these terms:

> Movements full of grace and dignity, great theatrical awareness, restrained gestures complementing the dialogue perfectly, a face that reflected every emotional nuance with marvelous reality: all these rare and precious qualities endowed this artist's enchanting voice with a magic impossible to imagine without experiencing it. With each scene the interest he inspired intensified, until by Act 3 the audience became almost delirious with emotion and delight. In this act, played almost exclusively by Crescentini, the admirable singer caused his audience to suffer the heartbreak of

love through a captivating melody, and all the sadness and despair that can be expressed in sublime song.[15]

Certainly, Crescentini was the only singer who succeeded in moving
to tears the emperor and the courtiers who attended the performances
of *Giulietta e Romeo* (Romeo and Juliet). Another witness confirms
that one evening, when the sopranist stopped singing, "people were
no longer listening, but weeping."

Napoleon, literally mad for Crescentini, went so far as to pay
him the exorbitant salary of 30,000 francs. In addition, not suspect-
ing the scandal the gesture would provoke, he bestowed upon him
the Lombardy Cross of the Crown of Iron, until then an award reserved for military prowess. "What?" exclaimed the military men,
"Give this honor to a singer, and what is more, to a castrato?" This
minor affair of state led Mme Grassini, the great Italian singer who
shared the reign of the Court Theater with the castrato, to make an
oft-repeated quip. When a group of officers and civil servants in a
salon were raging at this inadmissible gesture that so humiliated the
military and reduced the value of the decoration, Mme Grassini,
shocked to hear such talk about her friend Crescentini, cried, "But
gentlemen, you forget *his* wound!"

In 1812, Napoleon had to be reluctantly separated from his favorite singer, for the sopranist, whose health suffered in the French
climate, requested a return to his native Italy, where he died in 1846
at the age of eighty-four. With his disappearance and that of Velluti in
1861, the glorious period of the Italian castrato ended.

The Court Theater after the Empire

After Napoleon's departure from power, the reinstated Bourbon court was unable to restore an atmosphere of gaiety and vigor. Because of Louis XVIII's and Charles X's ages when they came to power
(sixty-three and sixty-seven respectively), because of the austere and
sour omnipresence of the Duchess of Angoulême, daughter of Louis

XVI, and because of a return to strict etiquette in an effort to recreate both materially and in spirit the epoch of the royal martyrs (Louis XVI and Marie-Antoinette), the large Restoration courts developed a cold and formal atmosphere and a routine life of official presentations, elaborate Sunday masses, and just a few enjoyable soirées. Furthermore, this court was not as open as Napoleon's had been to new blood from the bourgeoisie. From 1816 to 1822, of the 421 people presented at court (of whom three-quarters were women), 38 percent belonged to the old court nobility, and 44 percent to nobility never before presented at Versailles (essentially provincial nobility); a mere 18 percent were commoners.

Added to this return to the grand and noble style of former times—a style that was very elegant and distinguished, but often anachronistic at the beginning of the nineteenth century—were the insistent moral and religious rigors imposed by Charles X. Convinced of the divine origin of his power and possessing a resolutely mystical concept of the monarchy, he imposed on the court a quiet and austere life geared essentially toward religious practice and the avoidance of all extravagance. Even the spontaneity and the vivacity of "the little one"—as Louis XVIII called the Duchess of Berry—could not dissipate the leaden cloud hanging over the Tuileries. The Duchess of Broglie made her feelings plain when she wrote, "The day before yesterday I went to court and was somewhat afraid to find myself alone in the midst of all those old faces."[16] This is one illustration among many of the gulf between a France with 67 percent of its population younger than forty years old, and an aged and formal court.

This official severity led to the hypocritical state of affairs whereby one would go to the Court Theater to see what one would not dare see elsewhere. Ladies who displayed a certain piety and would refuse to go to a play in the city would nevertheless attend the same production by the same actors if it was given at the Tuileries; the blessing of conscience made an exception of entertainment at the Court Theater. As the Countess of Boigne observed,

Young ladies who were not permitted to see *Polyeucte* at the Théâtre-Français were taken, with clear conscience, to see a licentious vaudeville from the small boxes of the royal theater. Moreover, it offered a glittering scene, and the court was always very grand on such occasions.[17]

It was the royal chapel in which the most important musical events took place. There, in the works of Le Sueur or Cherubini, the finest singers of the Académie Royale de Musique or the Opéra-Comique—Lays, Martin, Mmes Branchu, Albert, and Armand—performed, and all were extremely well remunerated for their obligatory Sunday's work. Of about forty orchestral musicians, half belonged not to the Opéra, but exclusively to the court; of more than forty choristers, thirty-three to thirty-six were in the permanent service of the chapel. All received far higher salaries than performers at the other royal theaters. The popularity of the chapel music was such that Parisian high society snatched up the famous tickets that guaranteed attendance, in the presence of the royal family, at the Sunday afternoon festivities.

It is impossible to describe adequately the extent to which the fall of the Bourbons upset the Parisian musical climate. Until 1830 the royal chapel constituted a place of recruitment and privileged opportunities for the students of the conservatory. Not only did the chapel cease to perform its formative role, but religious music was soon relegated to a marginal, secondary role. The demise of the Choron Institute (which will be discussed in Chapter 5) at the beginning of the July Monarchy is clear proof of this.

Outside the chapel musical activity at court consisted, as under Napoleon, of excerpts from operas and *opéras comiques*, often just arias and duets, given sometimes at court and sometimes (before 1820) at the Élysée residence of the Duke and Duchess of Berry. The Court Theater did not have a resident company and called on singers, dancers, and musicians of the Académie Royale. Occasionally the troupe would mount an entire opera, such as the occasion when

Auber's *La muette de Portici* (The Mute Girl of Portici) was presented during the 1829 Carnival. Opera no longer enjoyed the preferred status it had during the Empire with Grassini and Crescentini. Only the festivities for the coronation of Charles X and the Renaissance Ball for the 1829 Carnival, where princes and princesses paraded and danced in the sumptuous court costumes of François II, restored any panache to court life.

The atmosphere of the Tuileries changed entirely again with the arrival of Louis-Philippe and the demise of the royal court in the old sense of the word. The king had no squires, huntsmen, grand masters-of-ceremony, or pages, and was content with a semblance of a court. (The funding of this semi-bourgeois and semi-military court nonetheless required no less than a fiftieth of France's total budget.) In deference to modernism, but also due to personal conviction, the sovereign abolished all traces of Bourbon-style etiquette. Practically anyone could enter the Tuileries, which was filled from one end of the year to the next, and anyone who visited could see that the king and queen shared the same apartment and maybe even slept in the same bed!

The Tuileries took on the bourgeois character of its occupant, and industrialists, financiers, and merchants were admitted there as easily as imperial, or legitimist, nobles (those who supported rule by hereditary right). Its doors wide open, the Tuileries became a place of constant comings and goings. Even when the Bourbons were able to arrange for a private suite of rooms inaccessible to common mortals, Louis-Philippe had to lock the doors himself to obtain a few moments of tranquillity. Queen Marie-Amélie was as bourgeois as her royal spouse: her only pleasures were taking care of the children, advising her husband, and managing the house. One day she went so far as to confide to a visitor, who was amazed by the sumptuousness of the salons, "You can't imagine the staff we need, Monsieur, to keep all this clean!" This is certainly not the language of a Marie-Antoinette, or even a Josephine de Beauharnais.

The disappearance of the royal chapel and of music specifically performed for the king led to a clear decline in court performances, a state of affairs that seriously concerned the Parisian musical community. Louis-Philippe and his family continued to use the Court Theater for evening concerts at which the great names of the Opéra or the Théâtre-Italien appeared: the tenors Adolphe Nourrit and Gilbert Duprez, the soprano Giulia Grisi and bass Luigi Lablache, and the ballerina Fanny Elssler. Often performances took place at Fontainebleau, one of the royal family's favorite residences. In these cases the artists would receive generous traveling expenses in addition to their regular salaries. At the Tuileries the pomp that had marked the first thirty years of the century had disappeared. Now small, informal gatherings were held at the residence of the king or Mme Adélaïde, his sister, in the presence of the leaders of finance and a great number of foreign, especially English, guests. In this unaffected, intimate ambiance, they ate succulent ices while listening to select arias by Gluck, Grétry, Rossini, or Bellini.

Even the court balls had a total change of appearance: though less frequent than previously, they were considerably larger. The Orléans rarely received fewer than three thousand at their great winter balls and numerous gala dinners. Not only had court etiquette and elaborate dress disappeared, but the old court's good manners had given way to a certain lack of polish among the new guests, and to the unceremonious ways of the nouveau riche. This delighted some, astonished others, and made the old legitimist nobility—more often than not absent from such soirées—roar with laughter. Among countless witnesses to this strange atmosphere, the intractable Alphonse Karr offered this unflattering description:

> What a ball, and what a court! A third-rate masked ball at the theater never produced a more horrible mob of people. They pushed, jostled, and knocked things over, especially at the buffet, which they pillaged. The salons were strewn with ribbons, epaulettes, and gloves; boots stepped on satin shoes which feet could no longer find. Women were worn, rumpled, mottled, and striped from pokes of the elbow.[18]

After the brief euphoria of the "Three Glorious Days" of the 1830 Revolution, Louis-Philippe was to become the most criticized, insulted, laughed at, and satirized king in history, condemned relentlessly by the Bonapartists and the legitimists as well as by the advocates of the Republic. This John Doe, who dressed simply, shook hands in the street, addressed the queen with the familiar *tu* instead of *vous*, and showed little taste for military adventures, had the misfortune of reigning during the birth of romanticism, an epoch that took no interest in the antihero.

The opera house on the Rue le Peletier on opening day in 1821.
Courtesy Bibliothèque Nationale de France.

CHAPTER 2

Managing the Opéra and the Opéra-Comique

The Paris Opéra went through no fewer than five names and two venues in little more than a half-century. It was known as the Théâtre National in 1793, the Théâtre de la République et des Arts in 1797, the Théâtre de l'Opéra in 1802, the Académie Impériale de Musique in 1804, and the Académie Royale de Musique from 1814 until the 1848 revolution. It occupied two locations, an unremarkable record compared to the many venues of the Théâtre-Italien, which positively toured Paris. From 1793 to 1820, the Opéra was situated on the Rue de Richelieu, from which it moved a few hundred meters to the Rue le Peletier.

The Opéra-Comique also remained in the vicinity of the Boulevard des Italiens, and in 1801 reopened in the Salle Feydeau, which today no longer exists. From 1829 to 1832 it moved to the Salle Ventadour, a few steps from the present-day Avenue de l'Opéra. For the following eight years it occupied the Théâtre des Nouveautés, on the Place de la Bourse. Finally, in 1840, the Opéra-Comique moved into the Salle Favart, which had been completely rebuilt after the destructive fire of 1838.

The Opéra-Comique and the Opéra had similar names and occupied neighboring theaters, but they were completely different institutions and attracted completely different audiences. The Opéra-Comique had to struggle constantly to establish a popular genre of its own and to win the right, year by year, to sing verses and to present spoken dialogue, to produce new works, and to present plays in one act, then two, then three. The battle was vindicated when Napoleon classified the Opéra-Comique as one of the four greatest theaters of the capital.

The dawn of the nineteenth century saw the Opéra thriving on its long, aristocratic past, still decorated with the glory accumulated over the years by Lully, Rameau, and Gluck. Indeed, the Opéra's inauguration in 1669 makes it the oldest operatic institution in the world. Just as the Théâtre-Français was known for plays and classical tragedies, the Opéra became a prestigious symbol of the Empire and the Monarchy, representing the brilliance of French music in Europe. It epitomized a society that was in constant evolution but that remained passionate about *art lyrique*. We will enter this fascinating closed world, which the Duchess of Abrantès named, though not without some exaggeration, the "marvel of Europe."

The Venues of the Opéra

The pedestrian who today strolls along the Rue de Richelieu, in the vicinity of the National Library, is probably unaware that the small Louvois Square, opposite the library, was the exact site of the Paris Opéra from 1793 to 1820. The streets surrounding the garden are the same that bordered the Académie de Musique and were filled with elegant, animated crowds on the evenings of performances.

The architect Louis had built the theater inexpensively and with no great regard for aesthetics in order to house Mlle Montansier's acting company. Unfortunately, with the change in political regime, Mlle Montansier's former ties to the *Ancien Régime* quickly led to her imprisonment, and she had to give up her theater to the state, which, having compensated her, located the Opéra there.

Visiting this location today, one can see that the Opéra was not huge, and engravings of the period show an unimaginative square structure. It comprised three stories with many windows (more than 130, not counting those at the back) and eleven gated arches on the street level of the facade. The building contained recessed boutiques, and one could obtain refreshments at the Opéra Café or buy librettos and musical scores as well as opera glasses at shops near the café. The Opéra resembled an opulent apartment building rather than a prestigious theater, and its facade, which was completely smooth for forty meters, overlooked the entrance to the National Library. The street was so narrow that it presented the constant danger that a fire at the Opéra would spread to the library. For the music lover who had known the beautiful Palais-Royal, the new theater did not have either a breathtaking exterior or interior.

After passing through the open gates and the foyer, members of the audience entered an auditorium with seating for about 1,700. It was the largest in Paris, and—in spite of the beauty of its red draperies and blue boxes—posed enormous technical problems. In 1804 its director gave the following description:

> The present theater is too small and is badly located. We are crowded together, and we lack auxiliary space. We need better lighting and have to struggle against the accumulation of breaths, odors, and candle smoke that deprives the air of the elasticity necessary for the transmission of sound. The wings are minuscule. We suffocate, can see little, and hear even less. The actors exhaust themselves in vain efforts, and the spectator leaves overwhelmed by heat, lassitude, and boredom.[1]

The above explains why the emperor demanded the construction of a new, better designed theater that would be more worthy of its name. Several projects came into existence on paper, but only on paper, and those concerned had to be content with redecorating and refurbishing the entire theater in 1808 and reinforcing the building itself in 1811.

Audiences and visitors certainly admired the magnificence of the refurbishment. The borders of the balconies were adorned with gold motifs on a white background that contrasted with the solid green of the boxes beyond. For gala evenings these borders were decorated with garlands and draperies that were enhanced by the brightness of the crystal chandelier. The ceiling panels alternated designs of crowns, stars, and bees, with, in the center, a head of Apollo encircled by perforated rays that permitted the discreet and ingenious ventilation of the auditorium.

It appeared that this theater would be permanent, since it was preserved during the Restoration exactly as it had been during the Empire. On 13 February 1820, however, it was the scene of an event that brutally interrupted its activity. The Duke of Berry, son of the future Charles X and heir to the throne, attended a one-act opera, *Le rossignol* (The Nightingale), and two ballets, *Le carnaval de Venise* (The Carnival of Venice) and *Les noces de Gamache* (The Wedding of Gamache). During the interval, he escorted his wife, the beautiful and vivacious Marie-Caroline, who was tired from a ball the previous evening, to her carriage at the side door on the Rue Rameau. Protection for the royal family was reduced to a minimum that evening, because all the officers of the guard and the garrison were attending a ball. As the prince was taking leave of his wife, Louvel—a thirty-seven-year-old Parisian saddle-maker who was faithful to the memory of the emperor and who had sworn to exterminate the Bourbon race—threw himself on the duke and stabbed him in the chest. The duke was quickly carried first to a small room next to his box and then to the director's office. It was there, while the theater roared with laughter at Polichinelle's buffooneries, that he spent his last hours, dying at about half past six the next morning.

Dismayed by this gratuitous violence, which was the prelude to numerous acts of political unrest, Louis XVIII decided to stop all performances at the Académie Royale immediately. Soon afterward he ordered the complete destruction of the theater. A memorial chapel was planned, honoring the life and death of Charles-Ferdinand de Berry, but the 1830 revolution put an end to that project, and a simple fountain, which can still be seen today, was built on the site instead.

For sixteen months the Opéra was in exile, moving from the Salle Favart to the Salle Louvois while the construction of a new theater on the Rue le Peletier was being completed. Material from the old building was reused, and a much more aesthetic facade was added. It was single-storied, in the style of Palladio's Basilica in Vicenza, Italy, and had seven high, wide, central windows that were crowned with pediments and arches and framed by eight columns topped by statues of the Muses. The ground floor had two small projections linked by a long porch that allowed members of the audience to descend from their carriages under shelter during storms.

In spite of the marked improvement of this facade over that of the old building, Parisians criticized the new Opéra from the time of its inauguration on 16 August 1821. Some compared its facade to a stable, and others were quick to observe that there were only eight Muses on the columns and that the missing one could only be the Muse of Architecture! The Opéra ballerinas lamented that the door connecting their greenroom with the boxes of season ticket holders had been omitted (an oversight that was quickly corrected!). Finally, a journalist from the *Journal des Débats* criticized the varnish used in the decoration because it irritated the throat and made "the singers so hoarse that they vied with each other to see who was the most out-of-tune." It is true that the surroundings were not very luxurious, with a stark, uninteresting auditorium and an unimposing wooden staircase with iron banisters. This was far from the studied refinement of the Théâtre-Italien, and even farther from the solemn formality of the staircase of the future Palais Garnier.

Nonetheless, significant improvements were made at the new venue. Ancillary areas, such as flies, greenrooms, and backstage corridors, acquired much more space. Thanks to the wooden structure, the acoustics were excellent, and the auditorium's decor—gold and white on the lower levels, blue and gold on the balconies—bewitched even the most critical Parisians.

A member of the audience sitting in the orchestra could look around and see an interior that was in all respects identical to the old one, since the framework of the stage and the boxes was that of the theater on the Rue de Richelieu. For an approximate idea of the auditorium's configuration, one has merely to look at the present interior of the Palais Garnier, which is almost an exact copy of the theater on the Rue Peletier, itself a copy of its predecessor. The auditorium is practically the same (except for color and decor) as that of 1793. The dimensions of the new stage were a clear improvement over those of the Salle Richelieu: the depth increased by only two meters, from twenty-four to twenty-six meters, but the width increased from twenty-four to nearly thirty-three meters. Even that is far from the Palais Garnier's stage measurements of twenty-seven by forty-eight meters.

The Salle le Peletier, though it was initially vilified, had a surprisingly long existence, until a fire destroyed it in 1873. Two years later the Palais Garnier opened.

Personnel and Financing

The backstage area of the Salle le Peletier was a labyrinth of administrative offices, rehearsal rooms, workshops, and studios. The crowd of workers there on the day of a performance surprised visitors, for the Opéra operated with a staff of 350 to 400. This huge work force resulted in a ponderous and complex administration under the direct supervision of the head prefect of the palace during the Empire and the minister of the king's household during the Restoration—aided by a special director, a general secretary, and an inspector general. After the exile of Charles X, the Opéra became a special institution operating under the auspices of the minister of the interior.

It is difficult to cite exact figures, as staff numbers were naturally subject to variation from one regime to the next, and sometimes even from one year to the next.

Let us take two examples. In 1807, in addition to the directors already mentioned, the Académie Impériale included one cashier, 5 office clerks, 4 stage managers, 76 singers (from leads to chorus members), 103 dancers (including ballet masters and students), 75 orchestra members (including 2 conductors), one librarian-copyist, 6 painters and designers, and 56 people in charge of stage draperies and the general upkeep of the auditorium. In 1831 the total strength was increased slightly to over 80 musicians, about 70 chorus members, 80 supernumeraries (not counting children), 100 or more dancers, and about 60 stagehands.

One can appreciate the heavy expense of such a large staff in a theater that did not always command a full house and that routinely included a fair number of nonpaying members among the audience. In addition to the salaries of all these people were the costs of making costumes, maintaining stage machinery, renovating the decor, providing lighting (candles remained expensive until 1830), and many other costly provisions. The Académie had the largest work force and highest expenses of all the Parisian theaters.

In fact, apart from a few rare years, the Opéra always proved to be a financial nightmare. A succession of bad administrations was not the only cause, for each new production only reinforced the traditional, and inevitable, gap between expenses and box office receipts and subsidies. Has any theater, one hundred years ago or today, escaped the financial imbalance inherent to musical productions?

During the Empire, the government provided a monthly subsidy of 50,000 francs (a sum it considered to be very generous), to which were added annual receipts of 700,000 francs and fees imposed on all secondary theaters, traveling shows, exhibitions, curiosities, circuses, balls, and concerts under the guise of obligatory aid. Despite that, Bonet de Treiches, head director of the theater during the Empire, wondered "why, with receipts of 700,000 francs and a subsidy of 600,000 francs, the Opéra is always in arrears, always living by its wits."[2] In 1805 a friend of Mme de Rémusat's expressed bewilderment: "The Opéra is the only theater that is usually filled, so I cannot understand why, being so popular, it has so many debts."[3] The deficit for 1810 alone reached 160,000 francs, yet the government always met the Opéra's needs, because the emperor believed the Opéra was indispensable in "maintaining an establishment that enhances the national vanity."

During the Restoration the Opéra was financed by 1,300,000 francs from the ministry of the interior, 300,000 francs from secondary theaters and productions, and additional money assigned by the king from a fund intended to support theaters in financial trouble. Thus, in 1829 alone, Charles X gave nearly 970,000 francs to the royal theaters. The following year, when the July Monarchy came to power, the new regime was the "beneficiary" of a 1,200,000 franc deficit. Fortunately, the Opéra succeeded in recovering some financial soundness under the direction of Dr. Véron, who, before coming to the aid of the Académie de Musique, had become a celebrity in Paris by marketing a much-appreciated chest ointment. A government subsidy permitted Véron to keep the theater going, exposed to the same perils and vagaries of fortune as before. This proved particularly costly initially since the subsidy had to offset the ending of tax support from the secondary theaters. Each year the subsidy was cut back, from 810,000 francs the first year, to 760,000 the second, 710,000 the third, and so on. Thanks to his excellent administration, and thanks also to the triumphs of Meyerbeer's *Robert le diable* and Halévy's *La juive*, Véron made a fortune during his term as director, a unique achievement during the first half of the nineteenth century.

During the preceding regimes, one of the worst problems for the Opéra was without a doubt the loss of revenue resulting from complimentary tickets. As early as 1802 the prefect of police was startled, when analyzing one Friday evening's performance, to count takings of only 4,600 francs, even though the auditorium had been filled. After a closer look, he realized that only 20 out of 150 orchestra seats had been paid for, 300 out of 600 pit seats, 26 out of 150 balcony seats, and not a single one out of 200 seats along the sides. The emperor intervened many times to try to remedy the situation and even paid for his own box himself, but the problem remained unsolved.

Under Louis XVIII and Charles X, the situation became even worse, as the aristocracy treated the Opéra as their salon. They made themselves comfortable and strutted about as though they were at court. Every evening, people of rank occupied the boxes and balconies without paying, completely oblivious that their right to enter might be contested. Not until the Opéra became a more bourgeois institution under Louis-Philippe did it become more routine to purchase tickets. To attract more members of the middle class, Véron even reduced the number of boxes and made a larger number of less expensive seats available.

℘

Nothing was more hierarchical than the Opéra's administrative system before 1830. Its director was little more than a puppet, knowingly manipulated by the minister or even the sovereign. In cases where the latter did not intervene directly, everything went by the head prefect of the palace (during the Empire) or the minister of the king's household (during the Restoration). Each step led to the sovereign whether it originated with the director or a mere stagehand.

Whatever the director or political regime, the regulations of this great opera house seem stringent today. The singers and dancers of the Opéra could not, under threat of dismissal, perform on any stage in the capital other than the Opéra's—except, of course, by order of the director. They had to exhibit model discipline inside the Académie through unfailing hard work at rehearsals and performances, and they received no financial compensation for performances running overtime or for rehearsals lasting late into the night. After the tenth performance of a new work, or the fifth of a revival, the administration could, without notice, take a role from a lead and give it to an understudy or someone making his or her stage debut. Those affected had no say in the matter. Any mistake in the wings, onstage, or in the pit that disturbed other performers or the audience was severely punished. Finally, those arriving late for a rehearsal were fined one-twentieth of their salary, for a performance, one-tenth.

A sheet summarizing the fines imposed during each month was posted in the greenrooms, and it was not rare for the prefect of police to imprison for several days an artist who, on the pretext of having a cold, obliged the Opéra to change its program. According to witnesses, such a rule was indeed enforced as the number of strong-willed artists rebelling against the administration increased.

The Chorus, Dancers, and Musicians of the Opéra

In addition to the major singers (who will be studied separately), the Opéra had between sixty and eighty chorus members, depending on the period. Among these numbers, three or four singers were distinguished by the quality of their voices and their ability to take on solo parts. The chorus was divided into *premiers dessus* and *deuxièmes dessus* (today's sopranos and mezzos), *hautes-contre* (contraltos), *tailles* (tenors), *basses-tailles* (baritones), and *basses-contre* (basses). They were recruited through competitive auditions with an age limit of thirty-five years.

In general the press praised the quality, unity, careful work, and power of the Opéra choruses. Indeed, impressive lung power carried more weight than vocal technique and could prevail over the advanced years or unprepossessing physical appearance of certain singers. It is evident from reading newspaper advertisements of the day that a "powerful voice" was as important as an "adequate knowledge of music." Nonetheless, the press often praised the choruses, and their singing must have compensated for the total absence of acting during performances.

Concerning acting, the beginning of the nineteenth century was a period of upheaval and progress in the theatrical use of choruses. In the eighteenth century, chorus members did not act. They remained planted like rows of onions, set in two straight lines on either side of the stage, and it was in this impassive attitude that they had to interpret anger, love, or despair, regardless of dramatic credibility.

While the Empire and the Restoration inherited much of this tradition, they nonetheless developed more careful staging for choruses. Until then, only the lead roles had involved acting. In *Le triomphe de Trajan*, in 1805, an entire army could be seen marching on the stage; *La vestale*, two years later, had several processions and crowd movements; and in 1809 a cavalry charge provoked the terrified flight of Mexican women in *Fernand Cortez*. When necessary the choral ranks were reinforced by supernumeraries to make the marching throng look larger, and real soldiers were often recruited.

The beginning of the nineteenth century was rich in new experiences, culminating with Auber's *La muette de Portici* in 1828 and its revolutionary way of using choruses. In this opera, which relates the uprising of Naples against its Spanish oppressors in 1647, the audience saw the chorus participate in the action. For the first time, the singers gestured and moved about the stage, bringing the drama to life in accordance with the most elementary principles of dramatic truth. This well-acted Neapolitan revolt was perhaps an omen, since two years later, in Brussels, the same opera and its celebrated "Amour sacré de la patrie" (Sacred Love of the Fatherland) signaled the start of the Belgian Revolution. From that time on, similar experiments were staged, such as Rossini's *Guillaume Tell* (William Tell) in 1829, or, during the July Monarchy, Meyerbeer's operas.

☙

The Opéra's corps de ballet consisted of about one hundred dancers and was probably the only company that did not have to worry about its success. Since the time of Lully, the passion of the French for ballet was such that the ballet within any opera was the most eagerly awaited moment of the evening, and it inevitably received an ovation. As early as the seventeenth century, foreign composers like Francesco Cavalli had great difficulty gaining support for operas that did not contain ballets. The excessive passion of the French for dance continued until the end of the nineteenth century.

This passion made Wagner curse the bad taste of the French and exasperated Verdi, who was compelled to introduce ballets in his operas to satisfy the whims of the audience.

The dancers of the Académie de Musique thus appeared onstage very frequently, either in ballets or during dramatic performances. All operatic works were required by imperial law to include at least one ballet, a law that remained in force throughout the century.

It goes without saying that this mania for dance (*Dansomanie*, to borrow the title of a ballet composed by Méhul in 1800) meant that audiences were not attracted to the great tragic productions, which were more difficult to appreciate. In 1804 one journalist found it deplorable that "the crowds rush to wherever there is dancing, jumping, or acrobatics," and another stated some time later that

> One sometimes accuses composers and librettists of corrupting taste, but more often it is the public's taste that corrupts the composers and librettists. When one cannot entertain as one wants, it is necessary to entertain as the public wants. It is easy to see that dancing is the privileged spectacle today, and that the Opéra itself is supported almost wholly by its ballets.[4]

The dancing itself was quite a spectacle. A period of dubious taste, the beginning of the nineteenth century was far removed from the ethereal refinement of romanticism. The ballets were little more than a series of colossal jumps, of pirouettes, contortions, and acrobatics, each movement more extravagant than the last. Elegance, grace, and sensuality were not important, only the feat itself counted. At the turn of the century, the Vestris family embodied this sacrosanct art of acrobatic dance with great pride. Gaétan, the family patriarch, confessed in all modesty in his very pronounced Italian accent that he was "the god of dance," and affirmed decisively that he was, with Voltaire and the King of Prussia, one of the three greatest men in the world. His son Auguste was even more instrumental than his father in imposing a style of dance that consisted of jumping as high in the air as possible. Smug with admiration for his son's prowess, Gaétan one day went so far as to state, "If my son touches the ground, it is out of courtesy for his comrades." The reputation of such a family proved difficult to sustain, and Armand and Charles Vestris succeeded Gaétan and Auguste with no great success.

The glorification of ballet was such that opera fans and writers during the Empire deplored the fact that the poetry of Quinault, the music of Gluck, and the voices of Nourrit (senior) and Mme Branchu enjoyed only one-tenth the enthusiasm and applause caused by a simple step danced by Mme Gardel or Mlle Gosselin.

Fortunately, a new generation of ballerinas, led by Marie Taglioni, Lise Noblet, Fanny Elssler, and Carlotta Grisi, brought a blossoming and refinement of choreographic technique during the reigns of Charles X and Louis-Philippe. For these exceptional women, technique, even when highly evident, no longer constituted an end in itself, but rather a means of serving the lightness and enchanting grace of the new genre of romantic music such as Schneitzhoeffer's *La sylphide* or Adam's *Giselle*. Audiences became enraptured by this new style, which spoke to the soul rather than to the eye, and by the incomparable charm of the prima ballerina, the spiritual sister of opera's diva. One consequence of this evolution was seen in the corps de ballet of the Académie de Musique, which, after 1832, showed a marked increase in the number of female dancers, with a parallel decrease in the number of male dancers.

☙

The Opéra's orchestra fluctuated between seventy-five and eighty-five members. Its conductors during the period were Rey until 1810, Persuis from 1810 to 1815, Kreutzer until 1825, Habeneck and Valentino between 1824 and 1831, and Habeneck alone until 1847.

In the almost unanimous opinion of critics and chroniclers, the orchestra was of high quality and attracted the best musicians of Paris. Some of the most popular were honored on the posters publicizing a performance. A poster advertising *La vestale*, for example, announced that "Monsieur Frédéric Duvernoy will play the horn solos."

In 1821 the enthusiasm for certain musicians provoked a noto-
rious incident. On learning of the cancellation of a solo accompaniment to a pas de deux that was to have been interpreted by the violinist Baillot, the audience quickly and heatedly demanded the solo as
it had been announced on the billboards. Berlioz, who was present, related the event thus:

> The musicians, seeing the audience's fury, hastened to leave. En-
> raged, the audience jumped into the pit, throwing chairs to right
> and left, knocking stands over, splitting the timpani's skin. The
> mutinous crowd left only after knocking down everything in the
> pit and breaking I don't know how many seats and instruments.[5]

If the Opéra's orchestra deserved its good reputation, it was due
to excellent sight reading (which was highly admired by foreigners),
to the celebrated quality of the wind players, and to strictly controlled
attendance at rehearsals and performances. Regulations required
the musicians to arrive well in advance to tune their instruments and
prohibited them from leaving their seats during rehearsals or performances.

Retirement came for wind players after fifteen years of good and
loyal service, for the other musicians and for singers and dancers after
twenty years, and for administrative employees and theater stage personnel after twenty-five years.

Scenery and Stage Machinery

Let us be precise: the French word for scenery at the beginning
of the nineteenth century was *décoration*, not *décor*, the latter being reserved for the interior of an apartment or a house. By the end of the
Restoration the two words were often confused, outraging purists,
whose reactions could be found in the press.

> That the inhabitants of Pont-aux-Choux and the Boulevard du
> Temple talk of "the *décor* of the Gaîté and the Franconi" is nat-

ural, for that is the vernacular. In the best royal theaters, however, one should conform to dictionary French and the standards of the well-bred by applying *décor* to an apartment and *décoration* to a theater.[6]

Let us now enter the Opéra during rehearsal and mingle with the crew of stagehands, set designers, painters, wardrobe people, carpenters, woodworkers, and dressers as they busy themselves backstage, in the area known at the time as "the streets of the theater." Whatever their specialty these artisans had steady work, given the numerous new operas and ballets and revivals that frequently necessitated the complete restoration of old, faded, or damaged sets, sometimes within a very limited time. The director Véron sometimes offered the stagehands supper in the dancers' greenroom to keep them at their work longer. During particularly important rehearsals, he would sometimes make the theater staff stay as late as three o'clock in the morning.

The painting and design studio employed six permanent artists, who were joined by a few outside painters for special productions. Each artist was a specialist: one painted curtains and clouds, another architecture, a third landscapes, and so on. For several decades the scenery, following eighteenth-century tradition, was almost exclusively composed of painted backdrops depicting views of huge palaces or landscapes. Great artists such as Dégotty, Isabey, and Cicéri were celebrated for their designing and painting talents, and some of their creations were even exported. Audiences marveled at the famous moonlight in *La vestale*, just as three years later they raved about the dream scene in *Ossian; ou, Les bardes*. Years later the Duchess of Abrantès gave this laudatory account of it:

> Nothing has ever made so great an impression on me as the magnificent scenery in the dream scene of *Les bardes*. One found oneself in the midst of a cloudy world, surrounded by mist, which itself surrounded golden palaces suspended in the air. Le Sueur's admirable music was perfect for the scene, and its sounds descended from on high as if they had, in effect, come from

heaven. Mme Branchu's admirably pure voice seemed to come from the highest airborne palace. Everything in this scene, which I have never seen bettered at the Opéra, made a wonderful impression on me, which the many years that have since passed have not altered.[7]

Among the most enduring painted backdrops of the nineteenth century were the famous "gothic sets" that appeared at the end of the Restoration (putting an end to the long career of "classical sets"). These evolved during the July Monarchy for the operas of Meyerbeer and Halévy, and led to a proliferation of medieval villages, crenelated ramparts, subterranean vaults, and rooms furnished with canopied beds.

At the beginning of Louis-Philippe's reign, painted backdrops were more fashionable than ever. Véron was entrusted with the *décorations* for twenty-two operas and twenty ballets (most of them for works by Gluck, Spontini, Rossini, or Auber), and he was obliged to keep them intact during his entire term as director. In addition to these backdrops and similar ones created during the following years, a new "solid" type appeared. By means of complicated scaffolding, certain elements of the scenery could be solidly constructed on the stage to allow singers and supernumeraries to stand at different heights. This attempt at greater realism (the first step in the direction of modern scenery) met with some criticism, for the effect of perspective disappeared—and with it the illusion afforded by painted curtains—as soon as the characters stood beside temple columns or wooden mountains that were not much taller than they were. Furthermore, such constructions required more time to install than simple backdrops, and this, due to the limited technical means of the time, necessitated unpleasantly long intervals between acts.

The Opéra's stage machinery was both rudimentary and difficult to manipulate and resulted in strange, even dangerous staging. Nineteenth-century stage machinery had progressed little since the eighteenth century, and was still dominated by complicated and noisy winches, counterweights, and cables. Winches creaked, cables stuck, and trapdoors closed with a crash that reverberated across the stage. The stage itself was constructed of planks that could be removed, lowered, or raised.

Stage machinery seemed scarcely to have improved since the baroque operas that had gods and goddesses climbing Mount Olympus, getting stuck mid-way, and begging the stagehands to rescue them at all costs. At the beginning of the century, the stage of the Opéra was once again plagued by the kind of incidents that had been common before the Revolution. The famous ballerina Guimard almost had her arm broken while executing two entrechats when a piece of scenery fell from the flies. On one occasion the singer Andrieu was about to begin singing when the bridge he was standing on suddenly collapsed, throwing the poor man down to the second basement along with two other artists and some chorus members.

The stagehands who laughed at these old stories took another view of the Aubry affair of 1806 on the evening that Mlle Aubry, a renowned Opéra dancer, first played the role of Minerva in the ballet *Ulysses*. At the end of the performance, in the purest tradition of baroque opera, she was to ascend to the heavens in a chariot supported by clouds. At a height of more than six meters, the cloud stopped and the chariot rocked violently, throwing Mlle Aubry to the ground and leaving her with a broken leg, a severe lump on the head, and various other injuries.

This episode, already serious enough, provoked a minor revolt at the Académie Impériale that pitted stagehands and their bosses against one another and caused such quarrels and unrest that the emperor was compelled to intervene. During this time Colonia, the stagehand who had carelessly handled the cable, was imprisoned for twelve days and permanently discharged from the company.

Far from diminishing over the years, such incidents continued, with several sometimes occurring in the same performance. In Act 3 of the premiere of *Robert le diable* in 1831, a support carrying a dozen lit lamps crashed to the floor and barely missed Mlle Dorus as she went onstage. In the same act, Mlle Taglioni, who was lying stretched out on a tomb like a statue, barely had enough time to jump to one side to avoid a poorly attached cloud-curtain when it fell noisily onto the stage. Finally, in Act 5, the singer Nourrit, who had to live in order to marry Isabelle, seemed to be carried away by the heat of the action and fell through a trapdoor in pursuit of the devil. Fortunately, stagehands had not yet removed the padded mattress that had just cushioned the fall of Levasseur, who was playing Bertram. Seeing Nourrit land just after he had, Levasseur asked, "What the devil are you doing here? Has the denouement been changed?" Finally, as if nothing had happened, Nourrit climbed out and pulled Mlle Dorus forward to acknowledge the applause of the audience. Far from being troubled by such a cascade of mishaps, the audience gave the singers an ovation that assured the success of Meyerbeer's opera. All the same, the next day *La Gazette de France* felt obliged to reassure its readers that "no one was killed or wounded."

In addition to accidents onstage came the problem of unrealistic stage settings and costumes. It must be said that the lighting did not help matters. Until 1821, lighting effects could be produced only by argand lamps—sooty, smoky oil-lamps—and a sunrise or sunset could be staged only by raising or lowering the footlights. After 1821, gaslight brought enormous improvements to performances and made it possible to flood the stage with sunshine, fire, or sudden light. An opera like *La lampe merveilleuse* (The Marvelous Lamp) owed its success to the advent of gaslight, with effects that were revolutionary for audiences of the 1820s.

Methods for producing tempests and thunderstorms remained primitive. Small rocks shaken in a metal box imitated rain or hail, tiny pieces of white paper or cotton wool thrown from the top of the flies gave the illusion of snow, and a long, thin wooden board twirled between two ropes evoked the sound of wind. When a so-called storm rumbled, however, the false trees on the stage did not move an inch, and lightning that flashed through one window was likely to be invisible in the neighboring window.

The work of the stagehands and scene painters, however, did sometimes succeed in creating a fine illusion. In *Ossian* the bridge that is supposed to disappear after the hero has crossed it collapsed with such perfection that the audience let out a unanimous cry of fright. But for every success there were many failures, and illusion and enchantment did not always go hand in hand. Cortez announced that he would attack at sunset, but the city was already plunged into darkness; Saul was supposed to disappear in a swirl of flames, but that evening there was only a single firework to create the swirl. The action was scarcely better when, in 1815, someone had the idea of suspending dancers from brass wires so that they could "fly" across the stage. The effect was so pitiable that one critic had no compunction in calling the dancers "as nimble as hams hung in a butcher's shop." In an 1831 production of *La sylphide*, numerous supernumeraries were similarly suspended on wires, but this time the director agreed to award them danger money of 6 francs each. Finally, when Rossini's *Moïse* (Moses) premiered at the Académie Royale, one critic ironically observed that "on 16 April at the Opéra, the Red Sea, which had been happy to let the Israelites cross, did not want to engulf the Egyptians. Precautions have been taken to ensure that next time the Red Sea knows its role better."[8]

In this discussion of stage effects, the popular introduction of live animals onstage must be mentioned. Horses had long been used in the processions of *opéras classiques*, but by 1829 dogs, goats, donkeys, and sheep were blithely being used to add realism to the pastoral atmosphere of the Switzerland of *Guillaume Tell*. Inevitably, this realism was accompanied by ludicrous complications caused by animals which would suddenly refuse to move or which would bleat at inopportune moments.

Costumes were also a risky affair, since if the appropriate costume was not in stock another garment would be used without hesitation. One journalist wondered why the supernumerary who led Eurydice's funeral procession in *Orphée* wore a dress with muttonchop sleeves and four rows of lace. Another time the dancer Deshayes lamented that in a Grecian ballet the women's hairstyle was Chinese, the cupids and zephyrs wore green and black shoes, and Venus and the blond Phoebus had black hair.

If new costumes were to be made for a performance, the designers could count on assuring the audience's admiration through generous use of velvet, silk, pearls, and feathers. In 1835 the wardrobe department spent 30,000 frances on *La juive* to acquire real copper and iron armor where previously they had been satisfied with cardboard. Financial constraints, however, did not always allow such spending, and it was often necessary to reuse fabrics and costumes from preceding years.

The newspaper *Le Corsaire*, during the Restoration, took wicked pleasure in pointing out anomalies and in dispensing witty advice to the Opéra's director:

> Put a little paint on the two last steps of Montezuma's throne and remove the three ink spots that have been there since 1813. Don't forget that the yellow taffeta covering the throne is actually an old covering from Mme ————'s carriage, and her coachman is asking for it back. See to it that the trousers are better distributed among Cortez's soldiers; a few pairs of suspenders would be indispensable.[9]

Producing an Opera

Before an opera could be produced it had to meet a number of formal requirements. First the libretto was sent to the prefect of the palace or the minister of the king's household, who would examine it and decide whether it was worthy of being presented to the selection committee. If so, a jury of ten would study the libretto. The jury consisted of three men of letters, three composers, three leading singers or dancers, and the director, who served as chairman. Others (bookkeeper, administrator, inspector general, chorus master, principal ballet master, head stagehand, and chief set designer) could act as consultants during the jury's deliberations, but none of these could take part in the vote.

If the jury gave a favorable opinion of a libretto, the composer would come in to play his score at the piano. If the jury decided it was necessary to hear excerpts played more fully, the cost of copying parts for a quarter- or half-sized orchestra was paid by the administration. This procedure confirmed the general belief in the superiority of text over music in French opera. Good music could fail because a poor libretto was turned down by the jury, but a good libretto would assure the acceptance of an opera, even if its music was insipid or even catastrophically bad.

Finally, when the green light was given, and sometimes after rehearsals had already started, both the text and music of the opera had to pass the censorship of the minister of general police. This procedure determined whether the opera contained anything morally or politically reprehensible or shocking. Even a simple grammatical error in the title could prove to be a stumbling block; for instance, a ballet entitled *La fête à Mathurine* was accepted only on condition that the title be changed to *La fête* de *Mathurine* (Mathurine's Name-day). Once that formality was over, only the dates of the performances remained to be determined. The prefect of the palace, or his equivalent, would then announce the names and order of the operas to be presented during the course of the year.

This procedure may seem very rigorous to the twentieth-century music lover, but it should be understood that such measures were necessary in an era when musical creativity was at its height. Today's paucity of new operas presents a very different situation. Despite the various barriers already mentioned, the period from 1799 to 1809 (to take a specific example) saw no fewer than twenty-nine new operas, as well, of course, as revivals and ballets. Certainly, not all these productions had equal value, but this bubbling of talent and preponderance of new works promoted and enriched the artistic life of Paris, and permitted the public to pick out the few masterpieces and ensure their triumph.

Depending on the opera, the rehearsal period usually varied from several weeks to several months and approached nearly two years for *grands opéras* such as *La vestale* and *Le prophète*. It was not always the rehearsals themselves that delayed a premiere, but rather the thousand and one problems that arose along the way. The king might give priority to another work, thus delaying the original opera being prepared; multiple corrections by a composer could slow down the work of the copyists; and events such as the cholera epidemic that raged in 1832 caused further complications. Then there were the delays caused by the personal rivalries that dominated the Académie de Musique, and whose victim was always the composer, who was held in poor esteem. An opera could also be delayed by the frequent illnesses and indispositions of singers caused by damp and poorly heated theaters and apartments, or by the resistance of soloists, chorus members, or orchestral players in the face of difficult music.

Mounting an opera became an adventure whose hazards could not easily be controlled and whose scheduling was difficult to determine. Dates initially fixed on paper were rarely respected, and premieres were often delayed by several days or even several weeks.

The frequent performances, numerous rehearsals, and unfavorable acoustics in the Rue de Richelieu auditorium affected the singers' health. In addition, the difficulty of the roles, the artists' often rudimentary musical education, and the permanent company's obligation to present the most difficult operas one immediately after the other, practically without a break, also took their toll. Indeed, the Opéra hardly ever closed its doors, allowing its singers only a few days of vacation during the hottest days of summer.

When the health of the artists deteriorated, rehearsals could be almost completely paralyzed. This occurred one particularly harsh winter when the management of the Opéra-Comique made the unfortunate decision to produce *La jeune prude* (The Young Prude), whose cast was three-quarters female. A drafty theater meant that eight singers were simultaneously unable to perform. In 1819 at the Académie Royale, rehearsals for an opera by Spontini, *Olympie*, came to a complete standstill for two months, putting the director in a critical situation. He was forced to go to the home of each singer (lead or understudy) to explain that it was time to resume work, and that the pretext of having sung the day before or of having to perform the next day was an insufficient reason for not rehearsing. After returning to the theater, he recorded the responses he had received:

> Mme Albert: sore throat, wants however to resume rehearsals of *Olympie*, and promises to know her role in a month.
> Mlle Grassari: had her blood let last Saturday, and daily baths have weakened her considerably. She has just worked for more than an hour on the role of Iphigenia, which she is supposed to perform tomorrow, so now she is too tired to rehearse.
> Mlle Armand: state of health unsatisfactory, but if required she will do the first act, no more.
> Mlle Paulin: told me that she has not been able to study the changes in her role of Statira because the part is with the copyist; moreover, she has an important performance tomorrow, so couldn't rehearse.[10]

The vaudeville comedians did not fail to poke fun at these delays by giving their parody of the moment a title that was a pun on the French *Olympie: O l'impie! ou, Enfin la voilà* (Oh the Impious One! or, Here She Is at Last).

Every era experienced similar problems, and one chronicler at the end of Louis-Philippe's reign lamented that the Paris Opéra could not mount a work in less than twenty-five months, while a provincial theater needed only a few weeks. It is true that under Meyerbeer's direction, productions became so grandiose and complex that they necessitated an astonishing number of rehearsals. It seemed that no expense was too great; for example, for the skaters' ballet in Act 3 of *Le prophète*, the inventor of roller skates, who practiced on the public squares, was hired to start a skating class at the Opéra to train the dancers.

An opera's copyist had an unenviable job, copying, by hand, the music for each instrumentalist and singer from the composer's original manuscript. He had to be an excellent musician, capable not only of untangling the composer's harmonic subtleties, but also of deciphering muddled handwriting. This titanic, fastidious task always had to be accomplished in too short a time, and could be slowed or even stopped by the composer's corrections or by his tardiness in furnishing the last act. The budgeted costs for copying an opera could sometimes triple due to such problems.

The copyist inevitably introduced errors himself. The orchestra suffered most from them, and, as its talent for sight reading was well known and admired by Rossini and many other foreigners, the slow pace of its work in rehearsals could be primarily explained by copying errors, which continually obliged the orchestra to stop. Berlioz related with humor that after he had pointed out to a cellist two mistakes in his part, the cellist took wicked pleasure in not correcting them so that his substitute would also stumble.

∾

Once rehearsals started, the singers who had secured the leading roles could be found working together in the studios, accompanied at the piano by the orchestral conductor or by the composer himself, who would be anxious to specify what was expected from a particular solo or ensemble. At the same time, the members of the chorus rehearsed on benches in the singers' greenroom, directed by their leader. They worked on music and diction and memorized their parts. They were fortunate not to have the added difficulty of dealing with a foreign language, since, by definition, the Académie de Musique interpreted only works in French.

Not far away, the ambience in the dancers' greenroom was quite different. The sound of footsteps, chattering, and bursts of laughter resounded in this large, luxurious, and brightly lit room, where a multitude of mirrors reflected the exercise bars. Equipped with a cane to beat time on the floor, the ballet master supervised the dancers. They worked under the admiring gaze of the honored few who enjoyed the privilege of being admitted to this holiest of places. During the Empire and the Restoration, this was a keenly sought prerogative because it was granted only grudgingly to the intimate friends of the emperor or the king. After 1830, Véron admitted most of the faithful season ticket holders and influential patrons of his theater, as well as politicians, high-placed employees of the ministries, journalists, and celebrated artists—that is, all those who could be useful to him because of their money or connections. A staircase located on the left side of the orchestra permitted access to the dancers' greenroom. The staircase was carefully guarded by an employee supplied with a list of the privileged persons allowed to ascend. Once upstairs, each guest could gaze on his heart's desire, who, as she practiced, would simper and wink languorously at her admirer while waiting for the break in rehearsals. This was known in the time of Louis-Philippe as "the meeting of the lions and the gazelles."

If work was proceeding as expected, the director posted the dates and hours of the stage rehearsals. At first the dancers rehearsed with just a first and second violin, while the singers and choristers had either a piano or, more often, five or six musicians to accompany them. Only later did the orchestra arrive.

Too much importance should not be ascribed to the staging of a production, nor should it be judged according to today's entirely different standards. It is really more appropriate to speak of placing the singers than staging the drama. It is true that the Opéra had a stage director, but during the Empire and the Restoration, as in the eighteenth century, his work consisted primarily of directing the singers' entries and exits and their positions on the stage, and sometimes suggesting attitudes and gestures to underline important dramatic moments. In fact, the singers would arrive at the theater with their own ideas, and scenes had a telltale habit of repeating themselves from one *tragédie lyrique* to the next, as the singers reused the same attitudes and gestures with only slight modifications. No doubt their acting would seem highly unnatural to modern audiences. For example, a tragedy on the stage of the Théâtre-Français called for noble and heroic postures, arms extended at timely moments, domineering or angry looks—in short, a bombastic style that we would have difficulty appreciating today, but that was part of a long theatrical tradition solidly anchored in the seventeenth century.

Composers volunteered frank advice and criticism concerning the staging of their works. Spontini exerted a major influence on the grandiose spectacles in *La vestale*, *Fernand Cortez*, and *Olympie*. Meyerbeer, a little later, was the ruling spirit behind rehearsals of his works, a fact stressed by Charles de Boigne in his *Petits mémoires de l'Opéra.*

> Never will we know the true cost of rehearsals to Meyerbeer in terms of insomnia, anxiety, fear, work, and despair. He saw everything, he thought of everything, he supervised everything: libretto, music, staging, scenery, costumes, songs, and dancing.[11]

As soon as they found themselves onstage, the chorus members became even more stiff and self-conscious than the soloists. They crowded together and measured out their steps to allow other players to enter from the wings. When the action forced them to react, they raised and lowered their arms, simultaneously and symmetrically, as they sang out praise or fear. The press expressed clear admiration and relief at the impressive staging of *La muette de Portici* and the new realism of Meyerbeer's operas, in which stiffness and lack of naturalness yielded to more expression and movement—to a semblance of life.

જી

While the artists and theater staff busied themselves with their final preparations, the public consulted publicity posters and bought tickets. More than 260 locations throughout Paris were covered with bills from different theaters, including the Opéra. Every opera lover knew the street corner where the program for the next few evenings could be found. In addition to practical information, the posters announced the names of the singers and dancers, but rarely that of the composer, who was announced only at the end of a performance.

Tickets were sold at the theater. Boxes could be rented, but since the orchestra did not have numbered seats, patrons could sit where they wished, provided they arrived in good time. It was only after the hiring of Louis Véron in 1831 that the Salle le Peletier, which was completely restored, had numbered seats permitting reserved places.

The Paris Opéra had three kinds of performance: ordinary, benefit, and command. It never gave daily performances. From the time of Lully in the seventeenth century to the beginning of the Restoration in 1814, it opened its doors only three times a week, on Tuesdays, Fridays, and Sundays. During certain periods, and particularly during the Empire, a fourth performance was added on Thursdays to distract and occupy the Parisian public during the long winter evenings. Daylight ended very early at that time, since there was no daylight saving time. Darkness fell at about four o'clock in the winter, and evening performances began at about seven or half past seven, while events such as the coronation of Charles X started as early as half past seven in the morning, requiring distinguished guests to arrive at Reims Cathedral at quarter to seven.

In 1817, in the face of protests from the directors of balls and festival halls complaining of competition from the Opéra on Sundays, the government agreed to change the immutable calendar that had prevailed for more than a century, and the evenings of performances became Mondays, Wednesdays, and Fridays. Both before and after 1817, Fridays remained the fashionable evening for going to the Opéra.

Singers and dancers organized benefit performances. They devised their own programs, invited the artists with whom they wanted to appear, and, after paying all the costs, collected the remaining proceeds. This important privilege constituted a kind of bonus to their annual salary. Unfortunately, the ill-considered growth of such evening benefits during the Restoration meant that many little-known artists earned too little even to pay their costs, and Fétis ironically called the concerts more baneful than beneficial. To avoid the disastrous excess of such soirées, Louis-Philippe declared that no theater could exceed an assigned annual quota of benefit performances.

Command performances were those explicitly requested by the imperial or royal family for an exceptional event such as a marriage or the visit of a foreign sovereign. The certain attendance of the monarch or members of his family made this type of evening an occasion of luxury and elegance, and permitted journalists to employ their consummate art of flattery in masterly fashion.

The Opéra—like the Opéra-Comique, the Théâtre-Italien, and many secondary theaters—also fulfilled a social and charitable function throughout its existence. This was especially true during the Restoration, an era preoccupied by religion and good works. Operatic performances and concerts were organized for the benefit of the poor of a district, the victims of a fire, an orphanage, or even a pension fund. The Duchess of Berry and, later, her aunt Queen Marie-Amélie often honored these charity events with their presence. During the severe winter of 1830, the Théâtre-Italien gave a benefit performance for the needy in January, and in February the Académie Royale organized, for the same cause, a grand ball, which brought together more than five thousand people. Thus, high society had the double satisfaction of enjoying themselves at a sumptuous ball while helping those suffering the poverty that was rife in many quarters. During that same winter, records show that 24,000 people of the twelfth arrondissement lacked bread and clothing. The July Monarchy strove to encourage Parisian theaters in these charitable missions by promoting operatic concerts and recitals to help the families of victims of the July Revolution.

The Opéra-Comique

Above all, let us quash the idea that the Opéra-Comique was a kind of branch of the Opéra, even a "sub-Opéra." Nothing is further from the truth. Although the Théâtre-Italien was, for many years, placed under the responsibility of the Opéra and its director, the Opéra-Comique enjoyed true independence, as much in its choice of repertoire as in the action of its directors. Two directors in particular merit attention: Pixerécourt and Émile Perrin. The first held office after a long and bizarre twenty-two-year period when the Opéra-Comique existed as a company in which each artist had a share in the undertaking.

The decisive turning point for this theater came in 1801, when the two rival companies of the Salle Favart and the Salle Feydeau were combined. Their partnership was launched on the evening of 16 September with a lavish spectacle consisting of one production from the Favart repertoire (Méhul's *Stratonice*) and one from the Feydeau repertoire (Cherubini's *Les deux journées* [The Water-Carrier]). This new and encouraging start did not lead to a triumphant, orderly future. Although audiences returned, not only from one year to the next but from one evening to the next, to hear works that might or might not prove popular, the administration had to struggle against a number of improbable crises. Failures, closures, and reopenings punctuated rich periods of creativity (eighty-nine productions in 1828, ninety-nine in 1825!) like a leitmotif.

In addition to financial difficulties were incidents such as that of the evening of 12 May 1804, when the Salle Feydeau was almost destroyed by the audience on the occasion of the premiere of Spontini's *La petite maison* (The Little House). The performance began badly. The actors seemed ill at ease and could not be heard above the sound of latecomers entering their boxes, and early on several awkward innuendos and responses shocked sensitive ears. The first two acts went from bad to worse, and during the third the tumult from the audience was such that the performers left the stage and the curtain was lowered. Protests, shouting, and the threat of rioting caused it to be raised again. Unfortunately, during the time that had elapsed, the orchestra had left the pit and gone home.

In an attempt to avoid a riot, the management had the chandelier lowered to signal the end of the performance, but the inflamed audience threatened to break it into a thousand pieces if it came all the way down, so the chandelier remained half lowered. The members of the audience were in a frenzy. Some shook with laughter or stamped their feet, some cried "Continue the new play," some yelled "House for sale," while others demanded the overture to Méhul's *Jeune Henri* (Young Henri). Ridiculous and witty suggestions followed in quick succession. To induce the audience to leave, the management announced that Mme Scio was indisposed. The crowd, which was not deceived, refused to depart. A steward came out to reason with them, but he was struck with boards and other missiles. No one acknowledged that the singers and musicians had left, and the auditorium became a battlefield. Rows of seats were broken, those that remained were piled up, chairs were turned over, music stands were thrown about, and objects flew around the auditorium. The audience had never been so well entertained at the Opéra-Comique! Towards half past eleven, the mob finally abandoned the devastated Salle Feydeau, two hours after the performance had ended.

Fortunately, the Opéra-Comique also experienced more glorious hours. At the time of Napoleon's regulation of the theaters, an imperial decree gave this definition of the Opéra-Comique's repertoire: "Any comedy or drama containing songs, light melodies, and ensemble pieces." This definition proved to be somewhat ambiguous, and a tragic work could be performed at the Opéra-Comique as long as it included spoken dialogue. At the very end of the eighteenth century this led to the proliferation of works called heroic dramas, lyric dramas, or even operas, in which the traditional recitative was replaced by spoken dialogue. The change meant that a work that had been refused at the Opéra could be presented on the stage of the Opéra-Comique. The inclusion of dialogue is all that distinguishes a masterpiece of *tragédie lyrique* such as Cherubini's *Médée* (Medea), created for the Opéra-Comique in 1797, from Spontini's *La vestale*, given in 1807 at the Opéra. Interestingly enough, *Médée* ends tragically whereas *La vestale* has a happy denouement. The difference between the two repertoires was certainly tenuous.

The trend towards dramatic *opéra comique* did not last. Little by little the rather somber repertoire of the turn of the century evolved into lighter, more diverting pieces, aimed at an audience that was more middle-class than the Opéra's, and which wanted above all to be entertained. "We laughed, we heard the pretty music of a quadrille and a waltz. It was a charming sight—what more could we want?" asked a journalist. For 6 francs, the cost of the most expensive seat (compared to 10 francs at the Opéra or the Théâtre-Italien), audiences wanted accessible music, romance, and humor.

The Opéra-Comique was enormously popular during the first thirty years of the century, before it was subjected to harsh competition from its two rivals, who triumphed with the compositions of Meyerbeer, Bellini, and Donizetti. While continuing to highlight the great masters of the past (Grétry, Dalayrac, Philidor, and Monsigny), the Opéra-Comique also assured the triumph of current masters (Cherubini, Méhul, Berton, Le Sueur) and had an unhoped-for success with Boieldieu and Auber. *La dame blanche* (The White Lady), introduced on 30 December 1825, played 150 times in the course of one year, and achieved its thousandth performance in 1862. Auber's *Fra diavolo* (Brother Devil) and *Le domino noir* (The Black Domino) were hugely popular, and witty commentators were quick to observe that Auber's *Le cheval de bronze* (The Bronze Horse) struck *gold* for the Opéra-Comique.

The Opéra-Comique profited from a sizeable permanent company that redistributed the different roles of the repertoire each evening. Over the years, the orchestra experienced spectacular growth, going from forty musicians in 1801 to fifty-five in 1831, to just under seventy in 1844. The chorus numbered around forty members, and the dance corps just over ten. Finally, the troupe of soloists proved very stable with about thirty-five members, divided according to a classification used only by this theater: leading female singer-lovers (*premières chanteuses-amoureuses*), leading female singer-peasants (*premières chanteuses-paysannes*), duennas, Dugazon mothers (*mères Dugazon*, named for the celebrated mezzo-soprano Louise Dugazon), men taking women's roles (*travestis*), and secondary singers.

If the Opéra-Comique sometimes seemed to lack panache compared to its two illustrious neighbors, this was because it did not attract such prestigious soloists. At the beginning of the century some soloists did succeed in distinguishing themselves there and making a lasting mark. Such is the case of Louise Dugazon, the tenor Jean Elleviou, and the famous baritone Jean-Blaise Martin, whose name was given to a vocal timbre that combines the brilliance of the tenor with the velvety quality of the baritone over a range of more than three octaves. During the July Monarchy, Mme Cinti-Damoreau, having sung at the Théâtre-Italien and the Opéra, became one of the great voices of the Opéra-Comique when she created the role of Angèle in *Le domino noir.*

The Opéra and the Opéra-Comique cooperated in lending the other institution members of their companies when sudden defections threatened to jeopardize a series of performances. It is clear, however, that the talents of the tenor Ponchard, or of Mmes Rigaut, Prévost, or Boulanger—however much appreciated by the Opéra-Comique's audiences—could not stand up to a comparison with the stars, renowned in France and abroad, of the Opéra and the Théâtre-Italien. Even the press devoted fewer columns to the Opéra-Comique and its performers than to the two more prestigious opera houses, which continued to attract the best Parisian society.

Hector Berlioz. Courtesy Orsay Museum.

CHAPTER 3

Major and Minor Periods
of the Opéra

To be honest, the first half of the nineteenth century was not the most remarkable period in the history of the Paris Opéra. It did not have the kind of reputation the post-1850 era gained through the likes of Gounod, Massenet, Bizet, and Saint-Saëns, nor did it have the exceptional prestige enjoyed by the Théâtre-Italien, which from 1820 to 1850 experienced its finest hours of glory with Rossini, Bellini, and Donizetti.

Yet this half-century was not insignificant, and major works did appear during this pivotal period between the operatic standards of the eighteenth century and the more modern genre of the end of the nineteenth century. During the first decades of the century, opera evolved slowly but constantly, and, as the old *tragédie lyrique* yielded its place to romanticism and *grand opéra*, a new style of singing and dancing evolved.

The quality of the numerous works created during the four regimes of this period varied greatly. Not only was the music unequal, but the Académie de Musique itself passed from periods of euphoric activity to long periods of emptiness. In spite of a marked decline after 1810, during the Empire the Opéra experienced a period of glory;

during the Restoration it seemed to be slumbering but went on to experience a spectacular ascent during the years 1825 to 1830; and during the July Monarchy, despite a few triumphant years it languished after 1840.

The success of some operas definitely compensated for the failure of others, and those outstanding works allow one to gloss over the great number of *pasticcio** operas and topical works that certainly do not deserve to be remembered. Though there were some great popular successes during this half-century, few opera-goers now know the names, never mind the works, of Catel, Le Sueur, Spontini, Cherubini, Auber, Halévy, and Meyerbeer. Berlioz, on the other hand, whom everyone now knows, was greatly disliked in his own time and generally ignored by his contemporaries.

Should we criticize an epoch that seems to have produced only minor works of little significance today? Or, conversely, are we to blame for not learning from the great works of the first half of the nineteenth century, accusing them instead of being academic or facile? Perhaps they did contribute, in their own fashion, to the flowering of opera, and should be seen as fascinating landmarks in the history books.

Pasticcio *Operas*

The beginning of the nineteenth century was not overburdened by good judgment or purism in matters of opera; a fact that shocks some and amuses others. Few periods have known so many remarkable concoctions, that is, works re-created by "arrangers" who cut, trimmed, and revised librettos, changed characters, and added arias according to their own tastes. Kalkbrenner, Lachnith, and, later, Castil-Blaze had the distinction of being among these butchers; the butchered were most often classical composers such as Mozart, Haydn, Gluck, and Grétry, or contemporary romantic composers such as Weber. What is most astonishing to today's music lover is that these potpourris and arrangements were incomparably successful with Parisian audiences. One positive result was that these arrangements, however bad many of them were, succeeded in gaining new appreciation for previously unrecognized composers.

As early as 1801, the trafficking of Mozart's *The Magic Flute* saw its rebirth as *Les mystères d'Isis* (The Mysteries of Isis). The libretto was changed from beginning to end, some characters disappeared, others were added, and the opera itself was almost entirely sabotaged. In it were found excerpts from *Don Giovanni, The Marriage of Figaro, La clemenza di Tito* (The Clemency of Titus), and even pieces by Haydn. Reading an enthusiastic review by the famous journalist Geoffroy, it is difficult to believe it describes *The Magic Flute.*

> What purity of melody! What simplicity! What pious, somber, and melancholy character in the marches and ceremonies of the priests! What pathos in the scenes with Isménor, Myrrhène, and Pamina! What finesse, gaiety, and grace in the scenes with Bocchoris and Mona. The musical highpoint is the moment when Bocchoris, about to be put in chains by black slaves, plays his magic instrument. The first notes, the melodic sounds of harp and harmonica, gradually calm the hideous monsters, until finally, unable to resist the charm of the melody, they dance around Bocchoris and throw themselves at his feet in an attitude of admiration and ecstasy. This scene, which rested on the music, had a tremendous effect, and the audience loudly demanded an encore.[1]

Les mystères d'Isis delighted both Parisians and foreigners. Curiously enough, Mozart came out remarkably well from this performance, since the arrangers had the modesty to remain anonymous. When Napoleon inaugurated the Decennial Prize and had the list of operatic performances between 1799 and 1809 drawn up, it showed *Les mystères d'Isis* as the most frequently performed opera of the period, with sixty-eight presentations.

In 1803, the oratorio *Saul* was staged at the Opéra, and it enjoyed one of the greatest successes of the beginning of the century. In fact, this work was nothing more than an amalgamation of pieces by Handel, Mozart, Gossec, Cimarosa, Paisiello, and Philidor, bound together by Kalkbrenner and Lachnith. This "admirable" production was unanimously praised by the press, which lauded the "morsel of such pure taste that it is impossible not to experience new pleasure at every sound." The nature of the work permitted journalists to flatter composers such as Mozart or Gossec, yet criticize others. According to one of them,

> Cimarosa is on the list of composers who made some sort of contribution, but, for the sake of his pride, he would have done better not to have mentioned it. Also included was a chorus by Hindel [*sic*], an English composer who should have stayed at home. The melody that David sang to calm Saul's agitation was a felicitous choice, as it quite sent one to sleep. They say it is by Philidor.[2]

In 1805, Mozart's *Don Giovanni* was tackled in French, as *Don Juan*, with a libretto that had been completely reworked by Thuring and Baillot. Although the music was based on Mozart's original work, the pianist Kalkbrenner had produced only a very mediocre arrangement. The public came principally to hear music by Mozart, but only the overture remained intact and in its original place. The rest was utterly transformed. The opera began with a long recitative written by Kalkbrenner, followed by one sung by Leporello, and finally an invocation to the night sung by Don Juan. The masked trio was interpreted by three police agents, the cemetery scene took place at an inn, and as the finale, an eruption of Mount Vesuvius destroyed Don Juan's palace. Mozart's orchestration was fairly well respected and was almost the only element in this venture to survive without damage. Although it was given about thirty performances, *Don Juan* was far from being a smash hit. Audiences were scornful of it and liked only the lyrics and the staging. *Le Journal de Paris* stated that Mozart had no "particular talent for composition," and *Le Journal des Débats* concluded that *Don Juan* had "too much music." The public had to wait until 1811 to experience the original Italian version of *Don Giovanni*. In 1807, *The Marriage of Figaro* produced only a mediocre effect, and the following year *La Gazette de France* asserted that this opera, in terms of its dramatic worth, represented "the bare bones of our *Mariage de Figaro* [the play by Beaumarchais]." A little later, *Le Journal de l'Empire*, comparing Mozart's opera with Paisiello's *Il barbiere di Siviglia*, maintained that Mozart had not made Figaro funny, that the opera was boring, and that Figaro was cold and insipid. According to the article, only Paisiello had spoiled nothing in Beaumarchais's work, because he had allowed "spirit and thought" to prevail over "song and sound."

During its run at the Opéra-Comique in 1809, *Così fan tutte* was criticized unmercifully by an indifferent, indeed frankly hostile press. Geoffroy's opinion was typical:

> Mozart has composed the whole thing in the awful modern genre of *opera buffa**. It has no dramatic expression, is completely lacking in truth and character, and is stuffed with snippets of muddled ensembles and a never-ending chaos of quartets, quintets, sextets, and so on. This is merely strange at first but quickly becomes tiresome, and in the middle of all this there are only two or three arias and even these are weak, practically indistinguishable, and insignificant.[3]

More than once during both the Restoration and the July Monarchy, the temptation to "rearrange" certain operas of the past proved too strong, and this trend for *pasticcio* operas manifested itself as often at the Théâtre-Italien as at the Opéra and the Opéra-Comique. A little of one composer, a soupçon of another, and what emerges is the opera of a third, developed according to the taste of the day. In 1821 audiences declared that they had never heard anything as exquisite as the second version of *Giulietta e Romeo*, which in 1810 had known a measure of success at the Théâtre de la Cour with the castrato Crescentini. Now, in addition to Zingarelli's music, audiences heard a charming aria by Rossini and a finale in canon form by Portogallo.

These contributions added a certain beauty to the opera, the main attraction of which had previously been the castrato's incomparable voice. In 1831 the Opéra-Comique produced a *pasticcio* entitled *La marquise de Brinvilliers*, whose score was signed by nine important contemporary composers. Similarly, in 1846, the Opéra presented *Robert Bruce*, allegedly by Rossini, but which opera fans will not find in any biography of the maestro. In fact, it was simply a potpourri of excerpts from *La donna del lago* (The Lady of the Lake), *Torvaldo e Dorliska*, and *Bianca e Faliero*, to which Rossini gave his blessing without having added a single note.

One of the most discussed, praised, and, at the same time, despised works was the arrangement of Weber's *Der Freischütz* (The Charmed Bullet), revised and "improved" by Castil-Blaze under the new title *Robin des bois* (Robin Hood). This production, the action now situated in England rather than Germany, premiered in 1826 at the Théâtre de l'Odéon, just before Weber passed through Paris on his way to London (to the great joy of young followers of romanticism, who were already enamored of his music). This led Berlioz (one of the young purists of the time), who was furious at the massacring of Mozart, Beethoven, and Gluck, to viciously attack Castil-Blaze in his *Mémoires*. He gave the following description of *Robin des bois*:

> The whole audience received the premiere with hisses and laughter. The waltz and the "Hunters' Chorus," which had immediately attracted attention, incited such enthusiasm the next day that it was necessary merely to *tolerate* the rest of the score for crowds to flock to the Odéon. Later, the song of the young girls, in Act 3, and Agatha's prayer (half its original length) *gave pleasure*. After which it was noticed that the overture had a *strange verve*, and that Max's air did not lack *dramatic intent*. With familiarity, the devilries in the hell scene became *comic*, and soon all Paris wanted to see this misshaped work; the Odéon made money, and M. Castil-Blaze, having ruined this masterpiece, earned more than 100,000 francs.[4]

As with Mozart and *Les mystères d'Isis*, this astonishing version of *Der Freischütz* managed, little by little, to lead audiences to Weber's music. They began to find great beauty in it, and certain passages even became hackneyed. The "Hunters' Chorus" had such success and was rehashed so many times by those who particularly liked it that the following newspaper advertisement appeared: "Wanted: servant who does not sing the chorus from *Robin des bois.*"

Spontini Honors the Empire

From the end of the Consulate through Napoleon's reign, important musical activity occurred at the very heart of the Académie de Musique. From 1800 to 1815, sixty-five works were performed there, including nine *tragédies lyriques*, fifteen pantomimes or ballets, twenty-two operas, four oratorios, three opera-ballets, four divertimentos, four ballets, one lyric drama, and one interlude.

Among the most important productions, six came from the pen of three composers: Catel with *Sémiramis* (1802) and *Les bayadères* (1810); Le Sueur with *Ossian* (1804) and *La mort d'Adam* (1809); and Spontini with *La vestale* (1807) and *Fernand Cortez* (1809). (Cherubini's masterpiece *Médée* was written in 1797, and, furthermore, is classified as an *opéra comique*.)

The incontestable master of this period was Spontini. He made a definite mark on Paris during his stay in France from 1804 to 1820, not only through his music, but also through his tenure as director of the Opéra-Italien. He became the most revered operatic composer, and it is certainly deplorable that, despite his success during his lifetime, Spontini is little known to music lovers today.

Almost immediately after he arrived from his native Italy (where he had achieved great success with his *operas buffas*), Spontini conquered the Théâtre-Italien, the Opéra-Comique, and the Académie Impériale in quick succession. He was fortunate to have not only great talent, but the support of a protectress, the Empress Josephine. The premiere of his opera *La vestale*, on 15 December 1807, constituted the apogee of his triumphant career in Paris. At the end of the performance, conforming to tradition, Spontini appeared on stage to receive the enthusiastic applause of a crowd that included the empress herself. The audience also clamored for Gardel, who choreographed the ballets, and Caroline Branchu, who created the role of Julia. That evening saw the start of *La vestale*'s long career of over two hundred performances, which made it the greatest operatic triumph of the Empire and the beginning of the Restoration. The emperor saw it twice, and foreign monarchs begged to see a performance during their visits to Paris, sometimes obliging the Opéra's management to change its program in order to accommodate their wishes. *La vestale* became the reference against which other operas were measured, and it came to symbolize the highest achievement of French opera before 1830.

La vestale's libretto is very simple: during a grand victory ceremony, Julia, a priestess of Vesta, sees a young Roman officer, Licinius, whom she used to know. She agrees to receive him secretly one night in the temple where she is charged with keeping the sacred flame alight. During their brief and passionate meeting, the flame goes out and the mob comes running. Although Licinius manages to escape, Julia is arrested and condemned to being buried alive, the traditional punishment for having failed in this duty. At the last moment, divine lightning strikes the sacred altar, relighting the flame. Julia is saved and united with Licinius.

Stylistically, the opera reflects the neoclassical grandeur and heroic action that characterized the art and culture of the Empire. With its processions of centurions, lictors, priests, and vestal virgins; its temples and forests of columns; and its musical qualities, *La vestale* represented a peak of perfection and achievement for the 150-year-old genre of *tragédie lyrique*. Even Spontini's *tragédie Olympie* (1819) did not achieve the heights of the first. *La vestale*, however, is not without weaknesses: the ensemble lacks life, the opera has touches of academicism and some rather weak duets, and it suffers from the kind of *deus ex machina* that lost its credibility with the end of the vogue for baroque illusion. These imperfections are easily compensated by a simple and effective plot; a rich, complex, and sometimes audacious orchestration; new ideas for the use of massed choruses; strong, well-placed characters who clearly direct attention toward the protagonist; and the virgin Julia, on whom all dramatic and musical interest rests, as with Medea and Norma.

In 1809 Spontini presented his second masterpiece, *Fernand Cortez*, in Paris. Although on this occasion it was taken off almost immediately (for political reasons that will be discussed later), in 1817 the Académie de Musique restaged it in altered form, beginning a run of 250 performances that was no less prestigious than *La vestale*'s. With this opera the scenario changes entirely. For the first time the audience is plunged into an operatic story that relates a specific historical event: the conquest of Mexico by Cortez and his struggle against King Montezuma and the Aztecs. Unlike *La vestale*, *Cortez* is a collective opera, an opera of the people in which the hero and his companion—though they love each other—sing not a single love duet. Attention focuses instead on the larger historical picture by means of the local color of the choruses, the "barbaric dances," the spectacular action of the Spanish armies, and the cavalry charge. Fourteen horses took part in this scene, almost as many as actually used by Cortez. (The Académie de Musique frequently employed horses in their *tragédies lyriques* and other operas on ancient or mythological subjects. The Opéra usually contracted the Franconi Circus horsemen, who would then attend specific rehearsals and all performances. Needless to say, audiences and press quickly wearied of this gimmick. They started to talk about "franconi operas" to allude to an opera that was too grandiose or pretentious, and whose stage effects and success depended too much upon the use of these animals. One wit suggested writing on the door of the Académie de Musique "Opera by foot and by horse.")

Far from being pretentious, stage effects such as the burning of the Spanish fleet, beautiful melodies such as the unaccompanied prayer by the Spanish soldiers, the originality of a military march in 3/4 time (probably the only one in the history of the Opéra), and the emotional yet heroic life that sweeps the score from one end to the other, make *Fernand Cortez* an extraordinary opera, and one that played an essential part in the evolution of musical performance art during the first half of the nineteenth century.

Spontini exercised a surprisingly important influence in his century. On the French side, he had a direct and major influence on Berlioz, who all his life declared his great veneration for Spontini. Berlioz considered himself his disciple and sprinkled his press articles and *Mémoires* with commentaries and analyses of Spontini's works. He also wrote numerous letters to his mentor in order to state, with his usual zeal and sense of theater, his admiration. He concluded one with the words "Adieu, dear Master. There is a religion of beauty, and I am a believer. If it is a duty to admire great things and to honor great men, I feel, in shaking your hand, that it is also a happiness."[5]

In addition to Berlioz, a number of other composers, such as Auber, Rossini, and Meyerbeer, wrote for the Académie de Musique. They were all able to profit from the innovations of a historical drama such as *Cortez* to perfect *grand opéra*, the musical genre that linked these composers. Much later, in 1873, a journalist of *Le Ménestrel* spotted the connection between Spontini and a good number of his successors:

> Suppress *La vestale* and *Fernand Cortez* from the history of music and you abolish all contemporary dramatic music. Without doubt we would have had *Le barbier* and the wonderful operas of Boieldieu, Hérold, and Auber—certainly not gifts to be disdained—but would we ever have known *Guillaume Tell* or *Les huguenots*?[6]

Spontini's influence spread beyond France, and the German composer Weber openly expressed his admiration for certain passages in *La vestale* and *Olympie*. Wagner, in his book *My Life*, relates that when they met, he invited Spontini to direct *La vestale* in Dresden. Furthermore, Spontini's melodic style can be linked directly to later Italian bel canto composition. Bellini knew *La vestale* from Naples and Donizetti had it produced in Palermo. It is impossible to underestimate the relationship between *La vestale* and *Norma*: both use choruses in the same way, have a particularly strong central female role, and have the same powerful emotion in the heroine's melodies. More lyrical than Medea and more dramatic than Norma, Julia remains one of the greatest operatic characters of the first half of the century.

Auber and Rossini to the Aid of the Restoration

Apart from the second version of *Fernand Cortez*, the revival of Salieri's *Les danaïdes*, and the unsuccessful staging of Spontini's *Olympie*, the majority of operatic productions during the reign of Louis XVIII foundered in a stagnant pool. Audiences demanded not learned compositions but facile, diverting pieces interspersed by ballets. It was the great era of *Le rossignol* (The Nightingale), *Cent ans en un jour* (One Hundred Years in One Day), and *Zirphile et fleur de myrte* (Zirphile and the Myrtle Flower). These were works that were well received at the time, but that did not make a lasting contribution to music. Journalists issued frequent attacks on these low-quality works, such as the following by Castil-Blaze concerning *Le rossignol*: "Iroquois, and even idiots, would have booed the warbling of such a nightingale, but Parisians were delighted and enchanted by it."[7]

The Opéra, like the Opéra-Comique and the Théâtre-Italien, followed a policy of staging "hit revivals" to refill its coffers during slow times or when public opinion was low. A quick revival of Gluck's *Iphigénie*, Grétry's *La caravane du Caire* (Cairo Caravan), or *La vestale* would be enough to ensure good box office receipts. In the same way, first Grétry's *Richard coeur-de-lion* and later Boieldieu's *La dame blanche* always attracted good audiences to the Opéra-Comique. At the Théâtre-Italien, the two works guaranteed to generate a profit as soon as they were put on were Cimarosa's *Le mariage secret* (The Secret Marriage) at the beginning of the century, and later, Rossini's *Sémiramis*. The French became completely besotted by Rossini, known as the Swan of Pesaro after his Italian hometown. It is clear that though Spontini and Rossini contributed to the financial stability of the large subsidized theaters, the latter nonetheless relied on the popularity of the great eighteenth-century composers, and this led to the director, Choron, being told that the Opéra was "in effect static, with only the appearance of movement."

Fortunately, after 1825, during Charles X's reign, a reversal of fortunes again brightened the Académie Royale's reputation. The two composers responsible for this were Rossini and Auber. Esprit Auber, who is relatively unknown today, figured highly among the musical personalities of his century, since, as well as being a prolific composer, he was director of the conservatory, chapel-master under Napoleon III, and a member of the Institute. Most of his output of about forty works took the form of *opéra comique*, including some true masterpieces such as *Fra diavolo, Le cheval de bronze* (The Bronze Horse), and *Le domino noir* (The Black Domino).

Auber's greatest operatic achievement was *La muette de Portici*, which opened on 29 February 1828 and played five hundred times before the beginning of the twentieth century. Broadly speaking, the libretto tries to recreate the 1647 insurrection of the Neapolitans against their Spanish oppressor. Among those in revolt, the two leading characters are the young Masaniello and his sister Fenella, whose mute role is entirely danced. When her brother goes mad after an attempt to imprison him, Fenella, watching the revolt being crushed by the Spanish viceroy's son, throws herself into the crater of Mount Vesuvius. In spite of some weak melodies and the somewhat artificial virtuosity of the main arias, which quickly dated *La muette*, the opera remains thrilling in many respects.

The originality of a mute role had great value in that it not only banished the normally all-powerful prima donna, but it increased the importance of the orchestra by having it provide a commentary to Fenella's action. Dance became not merely a diversion but a major part of the drama's development. At *La muette*'s premiere, the ballerina Mlle Noblet truly conferred *nobility* upon this role and replaced the acrobatic technique that had been in force at the beginning of the century with the charm, grace, and expression of the new romantic dance style.

Furthermore, as discussed in Chapter 2, this work introduced *direction* worthy of its name. This is attributed to M. Solomé, who directed a chorus that became a main protagonist in the action, contributing moments of life, intensity, and color at crowd scenes in the marketplace and during the rebellion.

Finally, following the precedent set by *Fernand Cortez, La muette* became the second successful historical opera. It was another opera that depended upon crowds as much as soloists, and that set the common man against a backdrop of heroic and revolutionary spirit. Auber employed the new romantic device of stimulating the audience's imagination by transporting it, albeit artificially, across the world. Just as Boieldieu tried to recreate a Scottish atmosphere in *La dame blanche*, and Rossini a Swiss mood in *Guillaume Tell*, Auber conjured up China in *Le cheval de bronze*, Portugal in *Les diamants de la couronne* (The Crown's Diamonds), Sweden in *Gustave III*, and Spain in *Le domino noir*. The poor early imitations of local color gradually gave way to the introduction of genuine national or folkloric themes, beginning with the saltarello in *Benvenuto Cellini*. More than one composer recognized Auber's contribution to dramatic music, and Wagner, to cite one of them, drew inspiration from *La muette de Portici* for *Rienzi*, his first opera.

Was it merely a coincidence that *La muette*, with its theme of insurrection, was produced in Brussels at the time of the start of the Belgian revolution? Similarly, it was playing at the Opéra at the time of the Parisian uprising in July 1830 that brought about the abdication of Charles X and the end of the Restoration. The theme of popular revolt passed from revolution by the Italians in *La muette* to revolution by the Swiss in *Guillaume Tell*. This opera by Rossini, based on Schiller's novel, was one of the last great works of the Restoration. It is not surprising that the climate of latent riot fed on such works, and, inflamed by the productions at the Opéra, Parisians waited only for the legendary last straw. It came with the July 1830 publication of royal regulations suppressing freedom of the press and dissolving the newly elected Chamber. Insurrection followed.

એ્ર

Rossini, an experienced operatic composer with over forty works to his name, ended his operatic composition with *Guillaume Tell.* The abrupt halt, at the height of his glory and at the age of only thirty-seven (he lived to be seventy-six), has been weighed and pondered in every way by biographers and musicologists, who have nonetheless failed to reach any definitive conclusions. Among the most plausible explanations is a desire by Rossini to dissociate himself from new works, and particularly from *grand opéra. Guillaume Tell* represented his first and last attempt at this genre, yet it contributed much to modern opera and bel canto.

Rossini remained nostalgic for the century of the Enlightenment and for the beginning of the nineteenth century, that great era of *opera buffa, opera seria,* and the incomparable art of the castrato. He never recovered from the disappearance of these singers and confided to Wagner, when the latter visited him in March 1860, "You have no idea of the vocal charm and the consummate virtuosity which—since they lack one thing and have been generously compensated with another—these courageous beings possessed."[8] The disappearance of the sopranists marked a real break in Rossini's life, and when he requested "twelve singers of the three sexes: men, women, and castratos" for his *Petite messe solennelle* in 1863, he knew very well that the era of the sopranists had ended, and that he would not obtain what he wanted. By means of a little irony and a little nostalgia, he sought merely to attract the public's attention to these unforgettable singers. In a century dedicated almost exclusively to romanticism, Rossini had little in common with its spirit and its music, and he himself explained that his abandonment of operatic composition was due to a new decadence in singing and the disappearance of *opera buffa* and *opera seria.* Living in an era that no longer corresponded to his musical ideals was painful to Rossini, and he dealt with his dilemma—to continue writing unfashionable music, or to compose fashionable music against his will—by yielding his place to composers such as Bellini or Donizetti, who belonged to the nineteenth century more than he. In doing so, Rossini manifested his great honesty to himself and to his contemporaries.

The fact that *Guillaume Tell* was not a huge success may have helped Rossini in his decision. Following several years of success at the Théâtre-Italien, Rossini had also succeeded in improving the slightly tarnished image of the Académie Royale by adapting two of his best Italian operas, translating them into French and revising them slightly. The operas were *Le siège de Corinthe* (The Siege of Corinth), adapted from *Maometto II*, and *Moïse en Égypte* (Moses in Egypt), adapted from *Mosè*, an *opera seria*. He added to these two works *Le comte Ory*, an opera written specially for Paris and close to both *opéra comique* and *opera buffa*.

With *Guillaume Tell*, Rossini had written something completely new: a very French opera that was both historic and grandiose, but without the gentle cavatinas and fiery crescendos of his preceding operas. The composer who wrote the *Barber* in fewer than twenty days and *Sémiramis* in scarcely more needed a year of labor and effort to complete an opera that was as strange to him as to the audience. One can imagine his disappointment at the reserved reception given by Parisian audiences. Though the premiere, a fashionable gala event, was enthusiastically applauded by an audience containing all the princes, dukes, generals, and ladies of society that Paris possessed, the press and audiences at later performances were less enthusiastic. They were disappointed at the somewhat unorthodox yet dull story, which was rather long (five hours!), and had neither the charming melodies of *La muette* nor the amazing stage effects that made Meyerbeer's works so successful. It was not long before the opera had to be heavily rewritten before it could be presented, and other works gradually usurped it until a change in audiences' tastes caused it to be resuscitated during the Second Empire. This was one more reason why Rossini preferred to retire gracefully, and though he remained quite the éminence grise of Parisian operatic life, he never wrote another page of opera.

Meyerbeer and the Post-1830 Period

The July Monarchy found its savior (the word is not too strong) in Meyerbeer. Without his creative contribution it is probable that Auber's *Gustave III* and Halévy's *La juive* would have been the only prominent operas created in Paris between 1830 and 1850. Meyerbeer was not a prolific composer, but the three works that he composed in Paris (*Robert le diable, Les huguenots,* and *Le prophète*) were performed so frequently and received so enthusiastically by audiences that they masked the general decline of the Académie Royale after 1840.

Meyerbeer and the director Véron had the good fortune of making their Opéra debuts at the same time. For the composer it was a propitious moment: the Opéra was in full ascent, spectators came in droves, and, unusually, the management proved both dynamic and prudent. As for Véron, he took over his duties the day rehearsals for *Robert le diable* started, and this work proved to be the greatest operatic event of his term as director. From the outset, before even knowing the public's reception to it, Véron doubted the musical value of the work and wanted to compensate for its presumed weaknesses by means of an unusual production. The chief attraction was to be the convent scene where, in front of a magnificent backdrop painted by Cicéri, damned nuns climb out of their graves and dance a bacchanale! This breathtaking scene and other "effects" dominated the five acts, and Meyerbeer felt that Véron gave too much importance to visual aspects, to the detriment of the music. "This is all very nice," he said to him during rehearsal, "but you do not believe in the success of my music, and you are seeking a visual success instead."[9]

Doubts again assailed the principals the night before the grand opening but quickly dissipated the next day. The brilliance of the mise-en-scène and the new, rich music (influenced as much by Rossini as by Weber), amazed and astounded the enthusiastic audience, and the very French genre of *grand opéra* was born. Broadly speaking, this treats a historic or fantastic subject whose dramatic strength rests on imposing staging in a large area with choral masses and crowd movements. The colossal aspect of the spectacle helps to mask the poorness and redundancies of certain musical passages. In a way, *Robert* represented the blooming of a musical genre that *Fernand Cortez*, *La muette de Portici*, and *Guillaume Tell* had germinated.

This accessible, brilliant music, full of pretty melodies and lavish choruses, immediately seduced Parisian audiences, who did not like overly intellectual works. Sumptuous scenery and costumes figured strongly, as did ingenious devices such as the use of a megaphone to reinforce the diabolic tone of a chorus. Artists and intellectuals raved about *Robert le diable*, hailing it as a new masterpiece from the romantic school. George Sand praised it, Wagner, Verdi, and Gounod drew ideas and musical themes from it, and journalists were, for once, unanimous in their enthusiasm. "This is almost a political event," *Le Corsaire* reported in its fourth article on Meyerbeer's work. "The salons are calling a truce on talk of politics and the nation to discuss *Robert*. Pianos are opened again as amateurs with good memories try to recall certain melodies."[10]

Robert le diable's unprecedented success seemed never-ending. Less than three years later, it had reached its hundredth performance and had appeared on the programs of seventy-seven theaters in ten countries. Not only did it gratify the bourgeois taste of contemporary audiences, but Meyerbeer's new approach had other positive effects. First of all, it permitted the Académie Royale to compete with the Théâtre-Italien, where the reigning Maria Malibran and Giulia Grisi were giving the theater its finest hours. Moreover, it influenced numerous nineteenth-century composers, who were enchanted by fanciful dramas. The bitter struggle of an innocent (Robert) torn between the influence of a demon with a human face (Beltram) and the love of a pure, virginal woman (Isabelle) is surely linked (beyond the medieval context then in vogue with the romantics) to the scenarios of *La damnation de Faust* and *Tannhäuser*.

As early as 1831, the romantic movement had inspired a definite taste for the Middle Ages in French audiences, who welcomed any extravagant scenic effect. Clever derivations of the masterpieces appeared in order to satisfy this appetite for grand productions, and music was largely relegated to a secondary status. Castil-Blaze deplored this practice with his customary bite:

> The end of the connoisseur. The Parisian public judges music according to the production's scenery, costumes, caparisoned horses, satin, armor, and any other luxurious trapping. Without these pompous accessories, any musical talent would be meaningless to such an incredibly unappreciative audience.[11]

Audiences were not disappointed when two new masterpieces were rapidly produced to meet their requirements. Halévy's *La juive* premiered in 1835, followed a year later by *Les huguenots*, Meyerbeer's second work for the Paris Opéra. These two works are similar not only musically but in their librettos, as both deal with the religious wars that pitted Catholics against Jews and Protestants in the sixteenth and seventeenth centuries. They also have identical, typically romantic epilogues, in which a man kills a young woman of the "enemy" religion only to learn, soon after, that she was his own daughter. Even the production costs of the operas were similar: 150,000 francs for the staging of *La juive* (an exorbitant sum at the time), and 160,000 francs for *Les huguenots*, which required twenty-eight rehearsals, even though regulations provided for only two weeks of work. It was without doubt money well spent, since the two works became the biggest hits of the Paris Opéra during the July Monarchy. The premiere of *La juive* brought in 60,000 francs, and the boxes were sold out for the first twenty performances! The presence in the title role of Cornélie Falcon, the great diva of the moment, was partly responsible for this success. Meyerbeer's achievement and the importance played by the money at his disposal led to the following witty remark by Heinrich Heine: "This man will be immortal as long as he lives! And even a little longer, for he has paid in advance!"[12]

Unfortunately, these triumphs represented the Académie Royale's final hours of glory before one of its worst periods of stagnation. A real crisis lay behind the successful facades of Meyerbeer and Halévy. The works of these two consigned the other great works of the repertoire to oblivion, and, with the tacit agreement of the authorities, smothered the creativity of talented younger composers, who were forced to live unrecognized and ignored.

What is more, in September 1835 Louis Véron quit his post as director, and was replaced by Duponchel, his right-hand man. As one socialite put it, Véron had "the secret not only of making the Opéra indispensable, but of enriching himself through it when every predecessor had been ruined." A great era ended, and the new management had to survive a difficult period lasting several years, softened only by the success of *Les huguenots*. The Académie de Musique mounted no more lavish productions, and, lamentably, it barely managed to survive, with audiences increasingly consisting of cohorts and claques*. The decline under Duponchel became a free fall with the incompetent management of Léon Pillet, who, far from attracting composers, discouraged the most popular ones. Meyerbeer, for example, refused to compose for the Paris Opéra. It took much coaxing before he agreed to leave Germany, return to Paris, and prepare the premiere of his third major opera, *Le prophète*. The work opened on 16 April 1849, even though revolution had already ended Louis-Philippe's reign.

As with *Robert le diable* and *Les huguenots*, Meyerbeer turned to Eugene Scribe for another libretto aimed at plunging audiences into the religious conflicts of the sixteenth century. Halfway between oratorio and *grand opéra*, *Le prophète* premiered with all the ingredients for a resounding hit: the admirable voice of Pauline Viardot, unsurpassable visual effects (the skaters' ballet, the coronation scene, the explosion of the citadel), and a colorful orchestration that successfully masked a high-flown score that was markedly inferior to that of *Robert*. Henceforth Meyerbeer enjoyed legendary status, dominating the period 1830 to 1850, and remaining popular for the rest of the nineteenth century, especially after the posthumous production of *L'africaine* in 1865. It could be said that he brought salvation to a failing Académie de Musique. Though he did not know it, Meyerbeer passed the baton to Giuseppe Verdi, who entered the Théâtre-Italien in 1845 with *Nabucco* and the Opéra in 1847 with *Jérusalem*. With Verdi—and with Gounod, Massenet, Saint-Saëns, and Wagner—a page in the history of the Opéra turned, leaving behind a couple of generations of composers who today are strongly criticized and accused of having written facile, pretentious music unworthy of today's "well-informed aficionados." This prejudice should be fought, and we should be grateful to those recording companies and opera houses that are restoring the thrilling testimony of nineteenth-century musical sensibility.

Berlioz; or, The Unloved

We have just skimmed through a half-century of outstanding successes at the Opéra, from *La vestale* to *Le prophète*. To mention all the failures of the same period would be impossible. One composer, however, who had little or no success at the time he was writing, touches and even astonishes today's audiences. Théophile Gautier maintained that his name should have been linked with those of Victor Hugo and Eugène Delacroix. The artist in question was perhaps France's only true romantic composer, Hector Berlioz.

Though this is not the place for Berlioz's biography or a musicological study of his works, this extravagant character cannot be ignored on the grounds that he was treated by his contemporaries as an object of sarcasm, intrigue, and fiasco. Given the musical universe described above, it is easy to understand why Berlioz's work was unacceptable to audiences obsessed by things Italian, by immediately accessible melodies, and by breathtaking scenery. In his newspaper articles Berlioz had criticized the clique of musicians currently in vogue. They formed, according to him, the antithesis of the school of Gluck and Spontini. Audiences were well aware of Berlioz's opinions, so the originality and "modernism" of his compositions were not unexpected. As a self-respecting romantic idealist, Berlioz did not seek to please at all costs. On the contrary, "to please" suggested to him lowering his standards to satisfy the taste of a "barbaric" and uncultured public, and Berlioz refused to make concessions for what he considered to be undeserving audiences. His music was original, unusual, and sometimes shocking; it revealed true genius; and was comprehensible only to the initiated.

Thanks to the support of the Bertin family, who owned *Le Journal des Débats* and whom Berlioz knew well from supervising the premiere of their daughter Louise's opera *Fausto*, the Académie Royale agreed to mount the composer's first operatic work on 10 September 1838. The opera was *Benvenuto Cellini*, more *opera buffa* than *opera seria*, and it traced an episode in the life of the famous sculptor against the background of the Roman Renaissance. Berlioz had a terrible struggle to finish his score before the prescribed date, and his troubles continued with the start of rehearsals. He could never have imagined how he would be jeered, satirized, and humiliated, and this torture, related in his *Mémoires*, lasted about three months.

> The actors tormented me at rehearsals with their lack of enthusiasm and evident distaste for the work; Habeneck was constantly bad-tempered; veiled rumblings of discontent circulated the theater; and I had to put up with stupid observations by illiterate people who could not understand a libretto that was such a departure from the usual flat, careless rhymes from the school of Scribe. And of course, I had to pretend to ignore these manifestations of widespread hostility.[13]

Berlioz certainly had plenty to be discouraged about. One evening he surprised two musicians in the act of playing, in the finale of Act 2, "J'ai du bon tabac" (I've Got Some Good Tobacco) instead of their actual parts. The same attitude prevailed onstage. At a verse from the libretto that began, "The cocks are singing," the artists roared with laughter, crying, "Why cocks? Why not hens?!" Trying to rehearse the famous saltarello from the carnival scene, Berlioz encountered only complaints, ill will, false starts, and sluggish tempos. These problems were compounded by a stormy relationship with the conductor,

Habeneck, and the contempt of the director, Duponchel, who did not even deign to attend rehearsals.

These difficult rehearsals caused Berlioz's health to suffer, and the premiere of *Benvenuto*, far from being ignored, become an impatiently awaited event in Paris, and provided material for the press for several weeks. The journalists of *Le Journal des Débats*, *La Gazette Musicale*, and *La Quotidienne*, all Berlioz supporters, took up the cause of this young hope of French music. This in turn led to the scorn of his numerous critics, who accused the journalists of an "abuse of publicity." "Let us not forget," cried *Le Journal des Débats*, "that French opera does not have any musician other that Meyerbeer (who is German) from whom it can hope for a first-rate work."[14] *Les Échos Mondains* reported that "the salons are full of talk of the dress rehearsals for M. Berlioz's opera. All those who have attended agree that the music is as rich in orchestration as the effects are grandiose."[15] Théophile Gautier, who was among those spectators, reported on the "rich, tight, dense, extremely complicated but original and audacious orchestration."[16]

Did this somehow encouraging turmoil serve as a prelude to a triumphant premiere? Did *Benvenuto* not symbolize, better than any other opera, true musical romanticism with all its truculence, panache, and even humor? Did it signal the end of the somber and tragic hues of earlier works? Unfortunately not, as the Opéra's audience was unprepared for the boldness of Berlioz's writing, and especially for the turbulent romanticism and the lush orchestral and choral scores of the superb carnival scene. Romanticism as practiced by Walter Scott, with gentle melodies and a high-flown orchestration, went down well, but if the audience had to judge the art of a Berlioz or a Hugo they had more trouble. The new generation of artists faced difficult times, and Hugo's *Esmeralda*, for example, set to music by Louise Bertin, would be a stinging failure.

Thus the premiere of *Benvenuto Cellini* became one of the greatest fiascoes of the century. Poorly prepared, cheaply staged with third-rate scenery, directed and sung by artists who, with the exception of Mmes Dorus-Gras and Stoltz, had no faith in it, the opera was doomed even before the curtain was raised. Curiously enough, the evening did not begin too badly, for the audience, recognizing Berlioz's symphonic talent, gave the overture an ovation. In fact, his *Symphonie fantastique* had been well received by Parisian society, and even though Adolphe Adam dismissed it as noisy and confused, many composers, led by Liszt and Paganini, admired it.

The situation deteriorated quickly after the overture. Baffled by the libretto and shocked by its burlesque overtones, the audience took less than half an hour to decide that the work was worthless. No one made any attempt to appreciate the qualities of the score. The audience punctuated the rest of the performance with whistles, laughs, hen-clucking, imitations of Polichinelle's voice, and other untimely interruptions, though the opera was performed in full. Berlioz's friends had turned out in force, but even their frenetic applause could not be heard over the general tumult. It was impossible that Berlioz would be called to the stage, and even the traditional announcement of his name, as composer, was in doubt. His army of supporters stormed and cheered to try to counteract the tumult of boos and hisses. Someone came out to announce the names of the authors (those not only of Berlioz, but of the librettists Léon de Wailly and Auguste Barbier), but the words disappeared without trace in the general uproar. *Benvenuto Cellini*, quickly rebaptized as *Malvenuto*, had needed twenty-nine rehearsals, but had only three performances before closing. The opera experienced its first triumph only when Liszt, who had defended it untiringly, conducted it in Weimar in 1852.

The Fashion for Parodies

Along with the great repertoire works discussed in this chapter, operatic parodies enjoyed huge popularity throughout the century. Those of the beginning of the century have been forgotten, but the parodies of the second half of the nineteenth century have survived, thanks to the development of operetta, a new genre at the theaters of the Second Empire. Hervé's *Le petit Faust* (Little Faust) and Offenbach's *Orphée aux enfers* (Orpheus in the Underworld) remain the models of the genre.

Between 1800 and 1850 many parodies were written. They would enjoy a little glory then gradually fade, as the operas to which they were linked lost their impact. Several theaters, the Vaudeville among them, made a specialty of these works. The parodies consisted of long spoken texts broken up by musical verses, and, in order to have any real impact, had to be written quickly in order to follow the opening of the parodied opera as closely as possible. The talent of authors who could rapidly assimilate all the details of a full-scale opera is obvious. They had to know the plot, the characters, and the key moments perfectly, and derive the maximum humor from them.

Parody appealed not only to more popular audiences, but also to Opéra-goers. In the case of the more famous parodies, all Paris fought over tickets for the Théâtre du Vaudeville or the Théâtre de la Porte-Saint-Martin to enjoy an "arranged" version of an opera that had been graciously applauded some days earlier in the Salle Richelieu or the Salle le Peletier.

Each regime had its successful parodies, and the boulevard authors' inexhaustible enthusiasm for writing them makes it difficult to list them in their entirety. A few couplets, a verse, or even a single retort could sometimes cause the success of a parody and attract the Parisian crowd purely by word of mouth. During the Restoration, an operatic parody of Salieri's work *Les danaïdes* had the whole capital racing to the Théâtre de la Porte-Saint-Martin. Much of the work's success was due to the talent of the actor Potier, who played Danaüs. After distributing tiny knives to his fifty daughters and ordering them to massacre their respective husbands, Potier cried out in an inimitable voice: "Go, my little lambs!" The dramatic heart of Salieri's opera collapsed with a single line.

The piece entitled *Marino Faliero* (Faliero of the Sea) (destined to provide the inspiration for Donizetti's opera of the same name) spawned a celebrated parody with the savory title of *Mérinos Béliéro*.

During the July Monarchy the parody *Titi à la représentation de "Robert le diable"* (Titi at a performance of *Robert the Devil*) enjoyed equal popularity. Its verses captured the astonishment of the "average Parisian" when confronted by the ostentatious staging of Meyerbeer's work.

Let us look more closely at two parodies of an opera discussed earlier in this chapter: Spontini's *La vestale*. Less than a month after the empress attended its premiere, the Théâtre du Vaudeville presented *La marchande de modes* (The Purveyor of Fashion), a parody destined to become one of the greatest successes of its kind. In it, the principal situations and characters from the Opéra production reappeared, transposed to the popular context of a fashion boutique.

The virgin Julia becomes Julie, the little shopgirl working in the store belonging to M. Crépenville (alias the Grand Pontife), and managed by Mme Létoffé (alias the Grande Vestale). While following the unfolding of the original *tragédie lyrique* step by step, the parody does indulge in a little criticism. At the very start, M. Crépenville gives this spicy analysis of the original opera:

> *Froid sujet, sans art, sans grâce;*
> *froides amours et froide audace;*
> *enfin, un morceau de glace*
> *bâti sur un peu de feu.*
> *Une soi-disant vestale*
> *soupirant en la-mi-la*
> *en plein forum nous étale*
> *ses ardeurs et caetera.*
> *Puis vient un fils de Bellone:*
> *le pouponne, le couronne;*
> *puis un ami le sermonne*
> *et ne fait rien que cela.*
> *Un caveau, du pain et de l'eau,*
> *éclairs et brouillards,*
> *quatre ou cinq pétards.*

Un chiffon brûlant, un peuple hurlant;
et puis, tout en haut,
Vesta montrant son réchaud.

Cold subject, without art, without grace;
Cold love and cold audacity;
Finally, a piece of ice
Built on a little fire.
A so-called virgin
Sighing do re mi
Reveals to us in public
Her passion, and so on.
Then a son of Bellone appears:
Babies her, crowns her;
Then a friend lectures her
And does nothing but that.
A burial vault, some bread and water,
Lightning and fog,
Four or five fireworks.
A burning rag, screaming crowds;
And then, from on high,
Vesta displaying her burner.

Trying to explain the scene in Act 2 when Julia remains alone in the temple, he adds:

On ordonne à la religieuse d'entretenir le feu:
S'il s'éteint la malheureuse n'aura pas beau jeu.
À son devoir elle s'apprête, n'osant dire tout haut,
Qu'elle a bien d'aut'feux en tête que l'feu du réchaud.

The nun is ordered to keep the fire burning:
If it goes out, the wretch will not have a chance.
She prepares to do her duty but does not dare say out loud,
That she has other flames on her mind than the temple fire.

At this point the drama commences. Julie remains alone, not to maintain the sacred fire, but to guard the boutique. Licentius arrives and, from outside the store, sings her a love song accompanied by a hurdy-gurdy. Unable to resist, Julie finally opens the door, and the two lovers declare their adoration.

Alas, Julie and Licentius are caught in the act by Crépenville. Although the young man manages to escape, the little dressmaker is condemned to a diet of dry bread and water. Like the virgin in the last act of *La vestale*, she is deprived . . . of her quilted overcoat, and confined to the attic with a bonnet on her head. Her friends solemnly come to offer their "dreadful curse":

Trempe ton pain Julie, trempe ton pain dans l'eau claire,
Trempe ton pain dans l'eau claire à défaut de vin.
Si l'on met a l'eau fraîche, toute fille qui pèche,
L'eau claire, à la fin, sera plus chère que le vin.

Dip your bread Julie, dip your bread in the clear water,
Dip your bread in the clear water for lack of wine.
If every girl who sinned was given fresh water,
It would eventually become more expensive than wine.

Everything turns out for the best when Licentius, surrounded by his associates, arrives, saves Julie, and threatens to burn the shop down, causing panic among the dressmakers. Forced to yield, Crépenville consents to the love of the young couple, to the great joy of the whole assembly.

Amused by this parody, but also a little shocked by the liberties taken with Jouy and Spontini's fine subject, the audience particularly appreciated the dramatic turn of events in the last verse.

De cette bagatelle que vous daignez accueillir
L'auteur que l'on appelle, n'a pas droit d'applaudir.
Vous voulez qu'on le signale; dans ce cas on vous dira
C'est l'auteur de La vestale *de l'Opéra.*

Of this bagatelle that you deign to welcome,
The author who is summoned has no right to applaud.
You want him pointed out; in this case you will be told,
He is the author of the Opéra's *La vestale*.

Indeed, displaying the utmost humor (and humility), the author of *La marchande de modes* was no other than Étienne de Jouy, the librettist of *La vestale*. This unexpected stroke enthused Paris and delighted journalists, who congratulated the writer "for his dramatic talent in *La vestale* and levity in *La marchande de modes*." The author certainly had the great merit of not taking himself seriously and of accepting with good grace the transfer of the antithesis of his own opera to the Théâtre du Vaudeville.

✃

La vestale spawned a second parody, which was less famous but still highly satirical. The songs and dialogue of this vaudeville by Antoine Desaugiers achieved great success, and the music was even published. The piece, in three acts, is nothing more than the narrative from Spontini's opera, accompanied by clichés.

At the beginning of the work, the main character, who is returning from the Opéra, observes, "If we had to cover up the sins of our beautiful women, I believe that we would have more young girls under the ground than above it." In Act 2, when Julia is condemned and dressed in a black, sacklike garment, the orchestra "plucks out a march fit to accompany the devil to his grave." Then in Act 3 comes the curse: "I see six tombs, seven, eight, nine, ten; it's as cheerful as a De Profundis." As Julia descends into the tomb she grumbles, "To be so mistreated for so little!" Immediately, a thunderbolt flashes, burns the virgin's veil, and reassures the crowd. "Long live the Eternal Father who with his thunder settles the matter," they cry, while Julia whispers, "Ah, my god, I have escaped very nicely!" The parody concludes with an uplifting finale that quickly paints the moral of the story: "The couple gets married, and every virgin asks when it will happen to her. Hallelujah."

Opera As Propaganda

If the principal operatic masterpieces discussed thus far belong to the greatest hours of the Paris Opéra, topical operas belong incontestably to the worst. These works, which artificially highlighted some current political event, shared various traits. They were hastily written, had a dull, trite libretto, shamelessly flattered the sovereign and his dynasty, and had insipid, careless music that was the result of an uninspired collaboration by several musicians.

The Empire and the Restoration continued the long tradition of such operas, either by commissioning these works of propaganda or by accepting them as a homage. Since its origins with Lully, French opera had been linked to the monarchy. The relationship could be manifested by the setting of a baroque opera, which would represent a reflection of the court, or by an opera's prologue, which would glorify the king. Louis XIV, who reigned from 1643 to 1715, doted on topical operas and amused himself by singing excerpts from the prologues that he thought praised him best. Neither he nor the court missed the obvious allusions in prologues such as this one from *Isis*:

Publions en tous lieux, du plus grand des héros, la valeur
triomphante.
Que la terre et les cieux retentissent du bruit de sa gloire
éclatante.

Let us proclaim everywhere the triumphant valor of the
greatest of heroes,
Let the world and the heavens retain the evidence of his
brilliant glory.

Later, Voltaire and Rameau collaborated to celebrate the victorious battle of Fontenoy in 1745 with *Le temple de la gloire* (The Temple of Glory).

The Revolution, in turn, adapted the genre of the topical opera by opening it up to a wider audience as a means of advancing Republican ideas and as ammunition against the institution of the monarchy. It is curious that the leaders of this revolutionary period, when every work became inflammatory and any piece in which an aristocrat had a sympathetic role was banished, did not suppress Gluck's *Iphigénie en Tauride* because of the line, "What cursed monster has, against so great a king, dared to raise his arm?"[17] In fact, the revolutionary years, though characterized by their hatred of the *Ancien Régime*, still saw productions of the *opéras classiques* associated with the earlier period.

The Opéra and the Opéra-Comique presented an abundance of patriotic pieces, unremarkable works that would run for only a few evenings. Gossec's *Offrande à la liberté* (Offering to Liberty), represented one of the first examples of the genre, another was the astonishing *Congrès des rois* (Congress of the Kings), written by a dozen composers (among them Grétry and Cherubini), and ending with the escape of kings and queens disguised as revolutionary extremists and crying at the tops of their voices "Long live the Republic!"[18]

The Empire had no reason to discontinue these political works, since they could only help to reinforce the heroic image that Napoleon cultivated so carefully. The emperor himself ordered the most successful and the most celebrated of them to honor his victories at Jena, Friedland, and Eylau. *Le triomphe de Trajan* opened in October 1807, two months before *La vestale*, and represented the archetype of the genre during the Empire and the Restoration. Persuis's insignificant music was redeemed by a veritable fairyland of scenery, costumes, and solemn processions, which received a standing ovation from the awe-struck audience.

No means were spared to honor the emperor in *Trajan*. The Roman Forum was reconstructed onstage, and as a finale to Act 2, an immense parade of six hundred soldiers and thirteen horses—from the inevitable Franconi brothers—accompanied the victor's chariot. To accommodate such a crowd, the Opéra had to be enlarged with a temporary gallery of wood covered with canvas that led to the narrow Rue Lully and facilitated the passage of the hundreds of supernumeraries and horses. The expense of building this construction, on top of the expense of the scenery, personnel, and hundreds of costumes created for the occasion, raised the total cost of the work to an unheard-of amount.

Unlike most of the works of this kind, *Le triomphe de Trajan*, though admired because of its splendor and as a sign of political tact rather than because of any inherent merit, had a large number of performances. It was even performed, with some revisions, during the Restoration—an astonishing turn of events for an opera conceived as a grandiose tribute to Napoleon, whom the Bourbons held in such contempt. *Trajan* remained the only topical opera to have an honorable career and to overcome the obstacles of being written for a specific regime.

A different fate awaited the opera *Fernand Cortez*, written in 1809. Once more Napoleon was behind the project, and once more he asked Esménard, the librettist of *Trajan* and official poet of the Empire, to write a work to further the imperial cause. Cortez, the glorious conqueror of Mexico, who succeeded in breaking the fanaticism of the Mexican priests, would symbolize the French emperor, the future conqueror of Iberia who would soon make the Spanish people and their clergy bow before him. The premiere of the opera, in the presence of Napoleon and the kings of Saxony and Westphalia, celebrated the image of a regime at the summit of its political and economic success.

No one could have foreseen the turnaround in the situation in Spain during the following weeks. Setting out to do a quick job there, as he had in so many other countries, Napoleon found himself in an unexpected situation. The land of Cervantes became the only country to make a courageous stand against Napoleon, and his military campaign became disastrously bogged down.

Spontini's opera quickly became as subversive vis-à-vis the emperor as it had initially been favorable. As long as Napoleon was preparing to conquer Spain, subdue its population, and crush its Inquisition, the noble symbol of Fernand Cortez, hero among heroes, constituted welcome propaganda to unreservedly sanction the emperor's actions. However, from the moment this same emperor saw himself forced to turn back in his conquest, and thus changed from hero and liberator to vanquished military chief, all allusions to Spain became seditious. To applaud Cortez, who has the line "the universe belongs to heroes," was to insult Napoleon, at least in Napoleon's eyes, and the opera that he had commissioned seemed to have turned against him. The minister of police temporarily banned *Cortez*, and it was given only twenty performances in eight years before its revival— its revenge even—during the Restoration.

Trajan and *Cortez* were the emperor's two main operatic contributions, but they had nothing in common beyond his intervention. While the first was merely a luxurious showcase for an empty score, the other took a more modern approach than the usual topical libretto and proved itself as a first-rate composition destined to exert great influence on future operatic works.

The blending of music and politics during the Empire was not limited to these two examples. In 1806 Spontini branched out with an Italian cantata, *L'eccelsa gara* (The Illustrious Debate), first presented during a gala soirée at the Théâtre de l'Impératrice. Apollo and Minerva descend together from the Elysian Fields to ask the greatest poets of Greece and Italy to celebrate "the hero who presides over French destiny." Homer speaks first, then Virgil asks how it can be possible for him to describe everything Napoleon has done to achieve order, peace, and happiness in Europe. Tasso, in his turn, wonders how he should praise the hero who has restored religion to temples and morality to nations. The press described the principal scene in the unfolding of the cantata as being "subtle and ingenious praise." This competitive discussion between the poets clearly fulfills the premise of the work's title. Apollo puts an end to the contest by declaring that a gathering of every divinity in Parnassus would be necessary to sing the merits of such a hero. At that moment a statue of Napoleon appears onstage, and as the chorus launches into songs of praise to the emperor, laurel wreaths are thrown at the statue. Obviously, a work of propaganda did not necessarily involve either finesse or moderation. . . .

The ruling powers, moreover, were not always the instigators of these patriotic pieces, which would appear and reappear when required in order to celebrate a particular event. When the Grand Army returned to the capital in November 1807, celebrating Parisians could choose between the Opéra, where the inevitable *Le triomphe de Trajan* was showing, the Théâtre-Français, where a historic drama entitled *Gaston et Bayard* was playing, and the Gaîté, Vaudeville, and Variétés theaters where one could see *Le retour de la Grande Armée* (The Return of the Grand Army), *Ils arrivent les pages et la colonne de Rosbach* (Rosbach's Pages and Followers Arrive), and *Les bateliers du Niemen* (The Boatmen of the Niemen River) respectively.

After the many ventures of the Empire's more glorious years, the regime was dying. During the Hundred Days period from Napoleon's return to Paris on 20 March 1815 to his second abdication, on 22 June, the regime had to turn once again to opera to bolster the morale of a population whose territory was being invaded more and more every day. The opera was *Bayard à Mézières* (Bayard in Mézières), a strange *opéra comique* written jointly by Cherubini, Catel, Boieldieu, and Nicolo.

The most popular work of this genre was *L'oriflamme*, named after the orange-red flag used as a standard by the early kings of France. The opera opened on 1 February 1814 at the Opéra, and the Duchess of Abrantès described the premiere as a "national convocation of high society." The boxes had been sold long before the performance (a rare event in Paris at that time), and imperialists and royalists sat side by side, having come with the same nationalistic impulse to make the work a great success. *L'oriflamme*, a patriotic martial piece, constituted a perfect example of a potpourri opera, and was mounted in six days by Méhul and Paër. The overture was from Méhul's *Adrien*, the pastoral section came from Paër, the combat hymn from Kreutzer, and the finale from Berton. The press—or rather the few surviving dailies—unanimously saluted the "quality" of this work, and reported on the audience's massive enthusiasm.

Aside from the press, there remains little record of public reaction to these insidious propaganda operas. It is tempting today to believe that their saccharine-sweet, barely credible paeans of praise would make the spectators, who were quite capable of drawing intelligent conclusions about the merits of such stagings, smile or even laugh. Sadly, we have to accept that this was not the case.

We must not forget that eighteenth- and nineteenth-century audiences were much more receptive to the verses of a libretto than we are today, and that they participated more actively in the unfolding of a spoken or sung work. Moreover, they often supported the regime in power through regular attendance at both general productions and lavish premieres. At the beginning of the Empire, it is a certain fact that the populace hung on Napoleon's every word, that they marveled at the sight of him, and that at the theater the least allusion to the sovereign brought about uncontrollable applause. The audience brought the house down when Dido, in Le Franc de Pompignan's tragedy, declares that "empires are made for those who know how to found them," and they went wild when they heard the following verses from Racine's *Phèdre*:

> *Partons, et quelque prix qu'il en puisse coûter,*
> *Mettons le sceptre aux mains dignes de le porter.*

> Let us be off, and whatever the cost,
> Let us put the scepter in hands worthy of carrying it.

The audience of the Opéra-Comique went into raptures during *Stratonice* when the soprano exclaimed to the emperor, who was present in his box, "We are not indifferent to the pleasure of your presence," and spoke further of "a man, a genius, sent by the gods." No less astonishing was the participation of the audience when, in *Le triomphe de Trajan*, Lainez sang, "Let us pray that the gods achieve their plans, let us ask them to grant Trajan his life." At this point the whole hall jumped up and turned toward Napoleon, crying, "Let him live, yes, let him live!" while Napoleon thanked the delirious audience with a nod of his head.

Negative reactions remained the exception, both because of the displeasure they would immediately have provoked in the auditorium, and the near impossibility of expressing these sentiments in such an authoritarian regime and in a theater as close to the ruling powers as the Opéra. The novelist Lavater conveys the futility of disapproval very clearly when the hero of one of his novels is the victim of dreadful boredom during a performance of *Trajan*.

> When he heard a timid hiss, he realized happily that there was a kindred soul in the crowd, and instinctively responded with a shrill catcall. Suddenly, as though the Empire were in danger, one hundred, two hundred, a thousand heads rose up from the orchestra, the balcony, the boxes, the back of the theater, the front, and shouted in unison, "Throw him out!"[19]

If this kind of individual rebellion was rare, another form of protest, this time collective, came into play if an opera contained political innuendo. For example, in 1825 the audience applauded frantically during Cherubini's *Les deux journeés* after the tirade, "When will the misfortunes of France cease?" It was seen as an allusion to the highly criticized policies of M. de Villèle, leader of the ultra-royalists during the Restoration, and president of the Council from 1821 to 1828.

☙

When the Bourbons came to power, topical operas did not disappear. Insignificant works were given productions that were only slightly less ostentatious than those of the Empire. It must be said that the hero cult that had been so fitting during the recently abolished Empire was not appropriate during the Restoration. It was unthinkable to compare the gouty Louis XVIII to the dashing Napoleon. To compensate for this difference, the Bourbons engaged their ingenuity in resuscitating former heroes of their dynasty, such as Louis IX and Henri IV, and in pulling from oblivion such illustrious unknowns as poor Pharamond, king of France in the fifth century, who began to appear in every concoction, theatrical as well as operatic.

Operas glorifying the monarchy were generally given official presentations in front of the royal family and the entire aristocracy, who were delighted to see themselves crowned with lilies—for lack of laurels—on the principal Parisian stages. One should not criticize too harshly the composers who agreed to collaborate on these useless works, destined to historical oblivion and far removed from opera dedicated to dreams, escape, and the ennoblement of persons and deeds. It is evident that when writing on commission, the working parameters of composers and librettists were extremely narrow. To refuse a commission was to be quickly banished from the select circle of those in favor, while to accept brought riches and honors. The choice was easy.

The Bourbons immediately turned to opera to mark their return to power with fitting solemnity. In all probability Spontini and Jouy finished the music and libretto of *Pélage; ou, Le roi et la paix* (Pélage; or, The King and Peace) in about two months. The opera tells the story of Pélage, the brother of Rodrigue, king of the Visigoths. In 714 Pélage had to flee the Saracens, and he spent twenty-three years outside Spain before liberating his country and recovering his crown and throne. One could not hope to find a clearer parallel to the Bourbons, who recovered the throne of Louis IX after spending many years exiled in England and other countries.

Jouy divided the opera into two acts. In Act 1, he introduces an assembly of Pélage's partisans and illustrates their devotion to saving the country and restoring their king. Napoleon, represented as "Our kings' oppressor," is denounced throughout. At the end of the act, the liberation of the homeland is announced and hailed with songs and cries of joy. Act 2 opens with an immense celebration given in the capital of Asturias, a former kingdom and province in northwestern Spain, for the return of the king "whom we cherish and admire." This act, though even weaker than the first, at least included a large number of ballets and divertissements that spared the audience the preceding act's long, laudatory pledges. The huge festival of peace contained a little of everything. A "heavenly daughter" descended on a cloud of gold, while the spirits of the arts, agriculture, and commerce emerged from the earth and climbed toward the throne. Then, in a sort of magic tableau, portraits of Louis IX, Louis XII, and Henri IV appeared in the form of celestial spirits. The scene embodied the Restoration's new approach: instead of drawing on antiquity as in the Empire, it called directly on its own royal past.

Today one can scarcely imagine such a mixture of puerile vanity and unmeasured folly, but it delighted audiences then and flattered the royal family, which was represented at the premiere by the Duke of Berry. Spontini was completely indifferent to the plot and it is obvious that he found himself unable to endow it with the least spark of genius. The divertissement was lifeless and the ballet was perfectly unintelligible. Even the press, which was usually so quick to flatter, had to recognize the weakness of *Pélage*. As *Le Journal des Débats* reported,

> We must, on the whole, be indulgent. The poem lacks action, but one can see the faithfully outlined reconstruction of both our past misfortunes and our present felicity. With more time, M. de Jouy would have been able to do much better. The music of *Pélage* is sad and monotonous, and only one aria received several encores.[20]

Performed with the ballet from *Le laboureur chinois* (The Chinese laborer), *Pélage* was staged only five times before sinking into oblivion. The libretto, now in the National Archives, has been abridged to four unfortunate pages and just three scenes.

Another example of this type of topical work appeared in 1816 on the occasion of the Duke of Berry's marriage. Using a libretto by Brifaut and Dieulafoi, four composers—Berton, Kreutzer, Persuis, and Spontini—shared the writing of the score of *Les dieux rivaux* (The Rival Gods). This historical-mythological work added luster to the event being celebrated by reviving memorable moments of the baroque era. The commitment to do as much as possible to highlight the great events of the era was a constant characteristic of the Restoration. The regime refused to admit that what had been swallowed during the reigns of Louis XV and Louis XVI could not be stomached at the beginning of the nineteenth century. The ostentation of *Les dieux rivaux*, an allegorical presentation, added another link to a long chain of pompous and antiquated performances, of which Charles X's Reims coronation proved the apogee. It is significant that these topical operas and ballets delighted audiences during the Restoration and were among the clearest manifestations of the attitudes that were to undermine the regime, if one considers that to attempt to manipulate the masses is not an act of wisdom, but often a dangerous provocation.

The worth of *Les dieux rivaux* can be judged from a synopsis of the work. In the first tableau, Cythère's flowers and greenery, her mysterious groves, her gentle brooks, her myrtle, and her garlands disappear. Cupid's torch is extinguished, his bow and quivers are broken; sad nymphs wander about desolately; and one-eyed giants occupy Cythère's palace. Everything changes in the second tableau when Jupiter's messenger announces the return of peace and a king. Cupid is charmed and astonished, and asks the messenger how the king can achieve this divine influence. The messenger responds, "Through his virtue, Louis proves to mortals that a wise man on the throne is one more god on Earth." With these words, the scene is transformed. The giants disappear, Cupid recovers his powers, the nymphs draw near, and Cythère recovers her eternal bloom. Gods appear and quarrel about which king of France has the most merit, but Jupiter halts the uproar. Cupids and graces rise above a group of lilies, Minerva extends her hand, and the image of Louis XVIII starts to shine on a shield on top of a pile of arms. At this point in the premiere, the opera assumed its real meaning as it abandoned its mythological bent and returned to historical matters. As Mme Branchu intoned the lines, "Here is the king, faithful people of France," the electrified audience cried, "Long live the king," threw their hats in the air, waved their handkerchiefs, and jumped to their feet and cheered. Jupiter and the gods, satisfied with their work, slowly climbed toward Mount Olympus.

The triumph of the premiere, attended as it was by the monarchist elite of Paris, proved to be deceptive. The government and those surrounding the king soon reached a consensus, and the complete fiasco of the second, public, performance obliged the director, Choron, to take measures.

> It was agreed last Sunday that, in order not to jeopardize it, if the work could not support a second performance we would postpone the third until His Majesty condescended to honor it with his presence. As the last performance of *Les dieux rivaux* produced only 2,142 francs, it is evident that by continuing the performances we risk a deserted auditorium. It is thus prudent to postpone the opera in order to avoid presenting His Majesty with a complete failure.[21]

Les dieux rivaux was truly a disaster, and even the Duke of Berry, according to rumor, found it so boring that he sought to have the work removed from the theater. Its fate was characteristic of topical operas. They enjoyed great success at the premiere, thanks to the pomp and ceremony that surrounded them, onstage as in the auditorium, then they were subjected to the sarcasm of a population that was no longer fooled, before being consigned to oblivion. The fear of such a fate did not prevent Charles X from giving his blessing to a new opera by Boieldieu, Berton, and Kreutzer, produced in June 1825 on the occasion of his coronation. The work invited the French to rejoice in the crowning of Pharamond, a distant predecessor of Charles, and offered a historic retrospective of the monarchy through its principal heroes, before ending solemnly with an apparition of Henry IV on a cloud!

After such "masterpieces," it is understandable that the July Monarchy, having already suffered taunts and plots of all kinds, preferred to avoid endangering itself with these propaganda operas, which were capable of turning popular opinion against the monarchy. Louis-Philippe was rather reserved and wished to present himself as close to the people, and he would never have accepted being presented as so much larger than life in fanciful stagings aimed at furthering his glory. A page was truly turned with the revolution of 1830, which ended a long period devoted to the cult of the personality. Certain works would henceforth celebrate the nation rather than the sovereign, such as Donizetti's entertaining *La fille du régiment*, whose famous "Salut à la France" (Salute to France) was soon being hummed all over Paris. One of Louis-Philippe's few political interventions in the musical and religious domain was the replacement of ceremonies in memory of Louis XVI by other services in memory of the victims of the July Revolution.

Salon scene. Courtesy Éditions Nathan.

CHAPTER 4

Opera Audiences

Prerevolutionary French society had turned the Opéra into a prestigious theater frequented chiefly by the aristocracy, and the elitist reputation that had been associated with the institution during the seventeenth and eighteenth centuries was not easily overcome.

The 1789 Revolution attacked this fortress of privilege by fighting the idea of the Opéra as a "Bastille of music," by expressing the resentments of the common people towards the *Ancien Régime*, and by attempting to attract a popular audience with works celebrating the holidays of the Republican calendar and other revolutionary or patriotic events. In the same way, during the revolutions of 1830 and 1848, rioters invariably headed for the Opéra, not because it sheltered some important person, but because it symbolized the power of the monarchy and the privilege of the ruling classes. The Académie de Musique frequently provided the backdrop for inflammatory discourse, public flag-burning, and for trees of peace which were planted in front of its walls.

All the same, none of the periods of agitation truly succeeded in opening the Opéra to the common people. Although no law barred them from its doors, it is clear that the price of seats, the general atmosphere of luxurious elegance, and the relative complexity of the works presented there scarcely served to attract the masses.

During the Empire, the Restoration, and the July Monarchy, the Paris Opéra remained the domain of elegant high society, dominated by the aristocracy or the bourgeoisie, depending on the ruling regime. Except during the darkest hours of the 1789 Revolution, Parisian audiences never lost their enthusiasm for the *tragédies lyriques* and *opéras comiques* that had brightened the reigns of Louis XV and Louis XVI. Even during the uprising of 27, 28, and 29 July 1830, *Guillaume Tell* was presented on the 28th, and the Opéra reopened its doors with Auber's *La muette* on 4 August as if nothing had happened. In February 1848, the riot that overthrew Louis-Philippe did not prevent the resumption of performances at the Théâtre-Français, the Odéon, and the Palais-Royal from 27 February on, nor those at the Opéra (rebaptized the Théâtre de la Nation), beginning on 3 March with Verdi's *Jérusalem.*

The Opéra was criticized but indispensable, often packed but sometimes deserted, and consistently viewed as prestigious despite persistent competition from the Théâtre-Italien. The Opéra held fast to a loyal public that was well-to-do and highly colorful, though admittedly often more interested in the theater's elegant ambiance than in the evening's performance.

Society and Customs

At the beginning of the nineteenth century, amusement seemed to be the rule of the day for privileged society, intoxicated as it was by the gradual return to an easy and luxurious life following the preceding distressing years of incertitude and anxiety. An unbridled need for amusement and frivolity took hold of the Parisian population, and led to performances that, if nothing else, highlighted the audience's social success.

Fashion was the catalyst for every folly, for the all-pervasive extravagance, for this need for constant change in an effort to attract attention. In 1805, a journalist from *Le Journal des Débats* wrote,

Fashion that formerly changed no more than once every twenty-four hours is now scarcely stable from hour to hour. Until further notice we can state that to be fashionable a woman must have Roman feet, a Greek head, an Egyptian neck, Turkish arms, and a Spanish body.[1]

Incroyables, royalists of the end of the seventeenth century who displayed great affectation in their dress, and *petites maîtresses*, pretentiously fashionable young women, no longer knew what to come up with next. Women required dresses with a heart-shaped opening at the back and a large rosette of ribbons underneath. Evening shoes were pointed and open, while morning shoes had to be rounded and closed—a fashion, it was said, that promoted health and preserved the voice. Men manifested the utmost fastidiousness and haughty snobbery. One astonished journalist noted,

> From the front an *incroyable* and an ordinary man are indistinguishable; it is from the back that you must look. To be fashionable, you must button your coat from the bottom up, not the top down. This results in many folds or pleats, and it can be said that the more pleats a young man has about his figure, the more stylish he is.[2]

The beginning of the nineteenth century was an epoch when one tried to look twice one's age, took pleasure in a stooped posture, walked with tiny steps, and wore spectacles covering half the face. In the same way, the fashionable tried to dress contrary to the season: what better than high boots and warm clothes in summer, or white stockings in winter, when one becomes completely dirty after ten steps?

During the Empire as during the Restoration, fantasy and eccentricity seemed to be constants in Parisian society. Étienne de Jouy, the famous librettist, was astonished on arriving at a friend's home for dinner to find his friend's father in a chestnut wig and an evening-coat of flowered brocade, his friend in a French coat, his friend's wife bedecked in Medici-style finery with an Indian shawl draped over her

arm, daughter in Grecian attire, eldest son dressed like an English-
man, and younger children dressed up like Egyptian slaves. This same
fantastic attitude was applied to every aspect of daily life. Meals became quite confusing, with lunch taken on the Rue du Mont-Blanc,
but dinner on the Rue des Francs-Bourgeois, and a game of whist
begun in the suburb of Saint-Germain followed by dinner at a table in
the suburb of Saint-Honoré. Some people lived like the English, some
enjoyed the triumphs of French cuisine, elsewhere one ate only Italian polenta and ravioli. On the streets one could see French stage-
coaches, English carriages, and German landaus. Fashions dominated
every aspect of life: the fashion of promenading a certain boulevard,
the fashion of rheumatism or myopia, the fashion of pineapples or
spas in summer, the fashion of metal furniture or of chiming clocks
that did not keep time.

During the Restoration, anglomania took hold, and the *mer-
veilleux* (the *incroyables* and others affecting the eccentric fashions of
former times) yielded place to the *dandy*, the *fashionable*, and the elegant *happy few* who began to frequent English clubs. The Club de
l'Union opened in 1828, followed in 1834 by the celebrated Jockey
Club, where the great Parisian bourgeoisie were to assemble for
decades. The extravagances of burgeoning romanticism contributed
to the cocktail of fashion and amusement, strongly influencing the
young intellectuals of the July Monarchy and transforming the language of the *Jeunes France*. For these new romantics, who were obsessed by Shakespeare and Byron, hyperbole became the rule. Mere
footwear became "ineffable" or "monumental," an idea could only be
"colossal" or "phosphorescent," a brotherly reunion between friends
became an "orgy," and if one wanted to surpass oneself, one had re-
course to antiquity ("It's Babylonian! Cyclopean! Sardanapalesque!").
A young romantic loved words for the sake of words, exclamations for
the sake of exclamations. He went to the Café Riche accompanied by
his best friends, burst out laughing at the Opéra if something displeased him, and swore only by the horns of his father, the guts of the
devil, or the virginity of his grandmother.

The image of women changed considerably during these fifty years, from being frivolous, flighty, readily charming, sensual, and seductive during the Empire, to being frail, angelic, and subject to "the vapors" during the Restoration. The ballerina Marie Taglioni launched this fashion, aimed at "awakening the angel in each waltzer," and according to which women had to be ethereal, dressed in muslin and light shawls and in airy clothing decorated with blue, pink, or lilac ribbons. Literature strongly influenced women in their search for an identity, and they all wanted to be another Elvira, Lamartine's beloved. Countess Dash wrote in her *Mémoires* that Lamartine was responsible for great folly on their part: "His verses have caused us to catch colds while watching the moon on lake shores or under trees on cool clear nights."[3] After 1830, things changed again, and women desired to shake off the constraints of their gender. They wanted to surprise, shock, dare, smoke cigars, ride horses. In the stock phrase of the time, they became lionesses.

Only the aristocratic supporters of the Bourbons tried to resist these fads, and they took refuge more and more in the suburb of Saint-Germain, where they lived in an enclosed sanctuary. They mixed with the high society of Saint-Honoré, with whom they had only superficial differences, but refused any dealings with the financiers and other upstarts of the Chaussée d'Antin, and would associate with them only when obliged to at certain official functions. Parisian high society was thus compartmentalized, each clan having its own customs, lifestyle, and codified language.

Fads and Traditions of the Opera-Going Public

Attending the opera during the nineteenth century was a social must. Not to participate in this manifestation of luxury and, occasionally, music signified exclusion from society. For this reason one had always, apart from a couple of periods, to fight to get a box at the Opéra or Théâtre-Italien, use every trick to obtain seats if one did not have a season ticket, and campaign for days on end in order to obtain an invitation to a performance attended by the emperor or the king. To see *Fernand Cortez* or *La muette de Portici* was one thing, *to be seen* when Napoleon or Charles X appeared in his box was something else.

This race for tickets to an opera, play, or ball was not without a certain affectation. It astonished Mme de Genlis to hear women constantly complaining about having to go out, groaning about the heat at the Opéra or the people they had to greet at the Théâtre-Français, or balking at trying on a new dress they would then have to endure, while these same ladies would never dream of missing these soirées.

The well-to-do members of high society generally kept at least one box at the Opéra, Théâtre-Italien, or Comédie-Française, and sometimes one at the Opéra-Comique, which was considered less high class. Successive generations of the same family sometimes kept the same box, being loath to give up its essential strategic position.

During the Empire the new nobility, though they had little interest in opera, regularly attended performances as proof of their new social status. Mingling with this audience were numerous generals, officers, and war veterans, who were happy to go to the Opéra because it gave them the opportunity to show off the wounds so valiantly won on the battlefield. Everywhere, in theaters and at court, aristocrats rubbed shoulders with soldiers. At the end of 1807, free performances were given at all venues to celebrate the return of the Grand Army, for whom the main boxes and the orchestra of the Opéra were reserved. In the same way, when the Imperial Guard attended *Le triomphe de Trajan*, it was difficult to know whether the real performance that evening was taking place onstage or in the auditorium. These occasions gave the elegant soirées of the Académie Impériale a "warriors at rest" military touch that never failed to cause a sensation.

The working-classes were certainly not excluded from these performances, and with the exception of certain command or invitation-only performances, nothing prevented them from procuring a ticket and sitting on the uncomfortable but inexpensive benches at the back of the orchestra, or in the Opéra's highest tiers. The price for such a seat remained relatively reasonable, although it increased rapidly. A seat which cost 50 centimes at the beginning of the century sold for 2½ francs by 1830, and a seat in the balcony cost 10 francs. Raising the price of the cheapest seats sometimes caused unfortunate incidents, such as when the audience in the fourth tier threw hundreds of tickets on the fashionable society of the balcony and orchestra, by way of protest.

The Opéra certainly became a less popular venue during the Restoration, since the regime in power started a branch of it at court. This became a privileged place of almost divine right, where one need not fear unwelcome encounters and where princes and high functionaries could devote themselves to flirtations with ballerinas from the company. The Duke of Berry, who enjoyed many romantic adventures, could not hide a liaison with the ballerina Virginie Oreille. His dalliances with her led, as the author of one memoir delicately put it, to "more than one piece of tangible evidence." Such liaisons with the "young ladies of the Opéra" were quite common in high society, and even the young Dukes of Orléans, the sons of Louis-Philippe, flirted with the two sisters Titine and Fifine, who were Opéra chorus members.

At the end of the Restoration and during the July Monarchy, the aristocracy considered the Théâtre-Italien to be clearly superior to the Opéra. Considered the epicenter of operatic art and the unequaled rendezvous for fashionable Paris, the Théâtre-Italien opened its boxes to the most illustrious names of the nobility, the same people from whom Balzac gained the inspiration for his aristocratic characters in *La comédie humaine*. After 1830, members of the nobility distanced themselves from the Académie Royale, considering it "a national property that was sold by the revolutionaries." They seldom attended and felt ill at ease in the new mix of diverse social classes.

Among the malcontents of the new regime were the Opéra's ballerinas. Gone were the days when admiring lords of the Empire or the Restoration provided financial support to young dancers and spent generously in order to win their smiles (or more!). The new era concerned itself not with ostentatious expenditure, but with economy, profit, and patiently accumulated capital. The new season ticket holders, even the extremely rich, may have had one eye on the pretty legs of these ladies, but the other was on their own bank account, and more than one ballerina henceforth preferred to keep her virtue intact rather than succumb to cheap favors.

Without a doubt, the Opéra of the July Monarchy, while remaining a venue of luxury, opened up more and more to Parisians of all circumstances. Véron wanted to attract the bourgeoisie as much as possible, and he aimed to make a subscription to the Opéra one of the major criteria for belonging to chic and well-bred society. In very little time, the number of subscriptions tripled, and it became necessary to join a waiting list before being able to subscribe. Along with this upsurge in subscriptions, competition to buy tickets was keen and constant. This was the great epoch of ticket scalpers, black market specialists recruited primarily from among the young unemployed.

This black market had no limits. Neither the police nor the director of the Opéra could halt the parasitic business, which displeased many but provided a service for others. The swindlers, who were well known to the ticket office personnel of the Académie de Musique, would bribe servants to use their employers' cards to rent the best boxes. The tickets would then immediately be resold on the black market. On other occasions, a woman conspirator would dress up like a duchess and arrive at the box office in a carriage to buy seats for a whole family. Another stratagem would be to persuade a passerby to go to the box office, pay for a box with six seats, and resell it to the scalper, who would then give the passerby a free ticket for any evening. The scalpers quickly prospered from this work, and before long were able to run a flourishing business. They carried out their work in broad daylight from a pleasant shop with a colored seating plan, just a few steps from the official ticket office.

Audiences included unquestioning opera fans, often young people passionate about music who, regardless of the ruling power, never missed a new production, attended the same opera fifteen times, and sat on the orchestra benches once or twice a week. Less fanatical than the dilettanti of the Théâtre-Italien and of diverse social origins, these music lovers felt truly at home only in the Salle Richelieu or the Salle le Peletier. When they left these places, they loved to gather in little coteries in cafés, where they weighed and debated the merits of a certain singer or musical score. In the same way, the gentlemen of the press went to the Café des Nouveautés, the habitués of the Théâtre-Français to the Café Procope, and those of the Opéra to the Café de la Régence near the Palais-Royal. According to Étienne de Jouy,

> An habitué of the Opéra would never appear anywhere but the Opéra on Tuesdays or Fridays. He would have felt badly about missing the fiftieth presentation of *Les Indes galantes* in order to see the premiere of Voltaire's *Mérope* at the Théâtre-Français, and a particular fan who had not appeared as usual one night in the Opéra balcony would be asked after the next day.[4]

A Parisian's Musical Week

It is difficult to speak of an opera *season* during the first half of the century, since the Opéra, the Opéra-Comique, and the Théâtre-Italien almost never closed, even during the summer. Indeed, even major productions sometimes took place in the middle of summer, for example, Rossini's *Guillaume Tell* premiered on 3 August.

Two points, however, should be noted. On the one hand, winter remained the undisputed season of privilege, and fashionable society members returned to Paris in November after spending the summer in their country residences. The most brilliant social activities occurred between Christmas and Mardi Gras, the carnival period and time of the most beautiful balls. On the other hand, the Théâtre-Italien made an exception to this rule at the end of the Restoration period and under Louis-Philippe. In 1828, its season was interrupted at the beginning of June to allow an English theatrical company to perform Shakespeare during the summer. The following year, a German opera company took over on 1 June. After 1830, the season at the

Italien was permanently fixed at six months, more or less from October to the beginning of April. This shortened season earned the sarcasm of those who thought that a substantial grant to a theater that only worked six months out of the year was very unfair to the other major companies.

The weekly schedule of performances during this epoch was one of the busiest. The Opéra, as noted above, opened its doors three times a week, initially on Tuesday, Friday, and Sunday, with an occasional supplementary performance on Thursday, and, from 1817, on Monday, Wednesday, and Friday (the ultimate fashionable evening), sometimes with a supplementary performance on Sunday. An evening at the Opéra generally included two or three items, since the audience was rarely satisfied with only one operatic work. On the few occasions during the Restoration when this did happen, season ticket-holders and journalists complained about not getting value for their money and about having to leave the theater at only ten o'clock at night. An evening would thus consist of perhaps a three-act *grand opéra* and a ballet, or a one-act opera and two ballets. It took the arrival of immense works such as *Guillaume Tell* or *Robert le diable* (both lasting four hours) before the Académie de Musique would schedule only one opera per evening.

The Théâtre-Italien also gave three performances a week, alternating with the Opéra to avoid competing with it. Its evenings were Tuesday, Thursday, and Saturday. In 1825, a fourth performance, on Monday, was added for a while. Because it did not compete with high society's well-established tradition of going to the Italien on the three other days, Monday became the preferred evening of more modest Parisians, who could relax with their equals rather than having to mix with fashionable society. On the other hand, a lady of fashion took care not to find herself at the Bouffes on Monday, the "commoners' day," for fear of being treated as a madwoman by her friends. Unlike the other venues, the Théâtre-Italien gave only one opera per evening.

Finally, the Opéra-Comique held almost uninterrupted performances, since its program extended over the whole year and played seven days a week, except for a few rest days taken here and there. Generally, it gave several works per evening, such as three one-act operas or two three-act operas, and addressed itself to an audience that was socially inferior to those of the Opéra and the Théâtre-Italian. This, however, did not prevent members of the aristocracy or even the royal family from attending from time to time.

Let us look at a typical week in the 1834 musical calendar. On Monday, Wednesday, and Friday, the Académie de Musique offered Rossini's *Le comte Ory*, Meyerbeer's *Robert le diable*, and Auber's *Gustave III* respectively. On Tuesday, Thursday, and Saturday, the Théâtre-Italien offered Rossini's *La gazza ladra* (The Thieving Magpie), Bellini's *Il pirata* (The Pirate), and Bellini's *I Capuleti e i Montecchi* (The Capulets and the Montagues). The Opéra-Comique further expanded the selection with, on Sunday, Hérold's *Le pré aux clercs* (The Field of Honor) and *Ludovic*; on Monday, Carafa's *Le revenant* (The Ghost) and *Le valet de chambre* (The Valet); on Tuesday, *Le revenant* and Boieldieu's *Le nouveau seigneur de village* (The New Lord of the Village); on Wednesday *Le pré aux clercs* and *Le nouveau seigneur de village*; on Thursday *Le revenant* and Hérold's *Le muletier* (The Mule-driver); on Friday *Le pré aux clercs* and Devienne's *Les visitandines* (The Nuns of the Order of the Visitation); and finally, on Saturday, *Le revenant* alone. As can be seen, old productions were repeated among the new works in order to vary each evening's repertoire somewhat. With so many repeat performances, it is obvious that audiences particularly looked forward to a new work that would renew the repertoire and rekindle their interest. The Opéra-Comique led the way in creativity. To take 1830 and 1831, the Opéra added five new operas (and two ballets) to its repertoire, the Théâtre-Italien added four, and the Opéra-Comique added eighteen.

To these three prestigious venues, two other theaters can be added: the Odéon and the Théâtre-National. Once the home of the Bouffes, the Odéon alternated comedy and opera during the Restoration, particularly translations and French adaptations of foreign works. These included the French version of Rossini's *La donna del*

Iago and Weber's *Der Freischütz,* "arranged" by Castil-Blaze into the
famous *Robin des bois.* Another venue opened its doors on 15 November 1847 as the Opéra-National. It aimed to launch currently unknown young talent such as M. Maillart, whose fine score *Gastibelza,*
inspired by the verses of Victor Hugo, was played at the new theater's opening. The management announced future productions of
works by Jacques Offenbach, who was not yet thirty years old. Alas,
bankruptcy caused the theater to close the following year in the middle of the season. Not until 1851 did the excellent Théâtre-Lyrique
open, going on to achieve fame with the premiere of Gounod's *Faust*
on 19 March 1859.

Finally, it should be noted that interspersed with these operatic
performances were concerts, which began to feature during the
Restoration and developed further under Louis-Philippe. They were
given at various venues around the capital, not only in theaters but
also in the Salles Erard and Pleyel, the Salle Saint-Jean at the Hôtel de
Ville, the concert hall of the Choron Institute, and so forth. Among
the most important were the conservatory society concerts directed by
Habeneck, Baillot's chamber music concerts, Choron's concerts of
religious music, and prestigious recitals by Paganini, Liszt, and
Chopin. Music lovers had a wealth of performances to choose from.

An Evening at the Opéra

Well before the evening of a premiere, thousands of backstage
rumors emanating from the Opéra provided nourishment for Parisian
conversations. Music lovers discussed at leisure the scheduled singers
and dancers, the presumed merits of a new composition, or the
principal staging effects. If the singers or the composer caused the
delay of a premiere, the press would echo the impatience of the public, who made their displeasure known in the foyers of competing
theaters or in the salons. A lengthy delay would quite turn the public
against an opera, hardly a desirable situation for a composer with a
new production.

At around six o'clock on the great day, congestion began to develop in front of the theater on the Rue de Richelieu, and lines of waiting carriages deposited theater-goers under the marquee of the Salle le Peletier. As a general rule, the performance would begin at seven or half past seven. After receiving the attentions of the boot-cleaners at the entrance to the theater, members of the audience would enter an auditorium that glittered from the luxurious decor and from the brilliance of the central chandelier, reflected as thousands of tiny stars in the precious stones adorning the women's décolleté evening gowns. Since 1793 the people at the back of the orchestra, who were often the real connoisseurs, no longer stood during the performance but sat on benches, the result of the Revolution's respect for its *citizens*. First-time visitors were surprised to see dozens of handkerchiefs on the seats: this was the way to save a place for a friend or relative. Anyone without a place saved had to wander about to find a handkerchiefless seat.

Having reached their seats, few members of the audience made any effort to be inconspicuous. The Opéra's golden rule was always "to be seen." "This is a theater of etiquette, of tone," confessed Picard, director of the "Grande Boutique," as the Opéra was known during the Empire. Charles de Boigne observed similarly, "People do not go to the Opéra primarily for its music. Women go to be seen, and men go to ogle the women in the auditorium and on the stage through opera glasses."[5] Members of the audience were in no hurry to sit down, and five minutes before the rise of the curtain, half would still be in the lobby or in the corridors. When the footlights were lit, doors to boxes would be opened noisily and people would lean forward to greet a well-known individual or wave to friends, ignoring all requests for silence. Why settle down quietly when one could attract a little attention?

Maintaining silence during performances was another problem. In this respect, the audiences of the Paris Opéra fell somewhere between those of theaters in Italy, who only kept their places and remained quiet for the great arias, and those of the Théâtre-Italien in

Paris, who wanted to hear every note and who considered silence to be obligatory. Members of Opéra audiences did their best to listen to the work's most important scenes, yet welcomed the first opportunity to be inattentive. Nothing could be more interesting than to watch latecomers, mentally undress Mme de ———'s new escort, or comment on the strange comportment of the Turkish ambassador, who unrolled a mat in the foyer during the interval and prostrated himself in prayer.

In short, members of the audience had poor attention spans and only truly concentrated on the great arias of their favorite singers or during the ostentatious scenes when fifteen horses and three hundred supernumeraries filed across the stage in a grand finale. Without a ballet, a performance became utter drudgery for some spectators, and so this became every opera's indispensable drawing card and the evening's key moment. The ballet attracted even those most hardened Parisians—members of the Jockey Club with no interest in music! Mme de Rémusat, at the beginning of the century, despaired that the only reason some people went to the opera was "to hear" the legs of the dancers Duport or Gardel. Very often, going to the Opéra meant waiting for the ballet and then, in an almost religious silence, trembling at the thrilling sound of the entrechat and the rustle of the ballerinas' dresses.

The Opéra became not only a temple of dance and of intrigues and illicit love conducted in the depths of boxes, but also Paris's most elegant venue, to be graced only in the latest fashions. To attend the Opéra at the beginning of the century was to attend a fashion show. Tiaras, pearls, furs, and cashmere shawls featured alongside long, flowing feathers (known as weeping willows) and yellow dresses, yellow being the only possible color to wear in candlelight. No stylish woman would dream of attending without makeup, and Napoleon himself was fond of it and thought that a woman should always have "good color," unless she was recuperating from childbirth.

This sartorial extravagance should not be dismissed as mere debauchery since, from the time of the end of the Consulate, it con-

tributed strongly to a new expansion in businesses and cottage indus-
tries. Innumerable Parisians lived off others' outings to the Opéra,
and they rejoiced in the return of old standards that permitted them
to take up again their professions of harness maker, carriage builder,
notions dealer, embroiderer, jeweler, furrier, and feather trader.

The Restoration also contributed to the world of elegance.
Opera-goers of the period concocted fashionable outfits and even colors by borrowing ideas from popular operas and novels. Theaters filled
with dresses à la Mary Stuart, hats à la Emma Bovary, and fichus à la
White Lady. Blossoming romanticism led to the invention of extravagant names for colors, including *Nile waters, mignonette seed, smoke
of mutton stew, Mount Vesuvius lava, frightened mouse, amorous toad,*
and *scheming spider*!

The dressmaker of choice during the Empire was Leroy of the
Rue de Richelieu, during the Restoration it was Mlle Victorine. Fashionable ladies visited Janssen the shoemaker during the Restoration,
and during the July Monarchy went to Mme Sauvinet on the Boulevard des Italiens. They bought muslin and organdy evening dresses,
the bodice cut in a "V" and the skirts lifted at the toe of the right foot
and at the heel of the left foot by a bow or a light golden clasp. Hair
was styled à la giraffe and black leather shoes replaced the formerly
popular white satin ones, which were superseded because they had allowed the feet to spread. As for the more classically minded men, they
attended performances in light-colored trousers, close-fitting coats,
silk, satin, or velvet waistcoats, frilled shirts with large checked cravats,
and those two indispensable accessories, a top hat and a gold- or ivory-
topped cane. One Italian expert went so far as to open a school to
teach men of the world the twenty ways to tie a cravat, charging 54
francs for six lessons.

Opéra audiences were known for their imperturbable attitudes
rather than for fanatical or fiercely contentious reactions. The programs rarely lent themselves to the latter sort of behavior, and audiences generally succumbed to a postprandial apathy as, yet again, they
listened to Sacchini's *Oedipe à Colone* (Oedipus at Colonus) or

Gluck's *Iphigénie en Tauride*. Parisian audiences were, nonetheless, capable of frenzied acclamation during an exceptional evening, such as that of the debut of Cornélie Falcon in July 1832. Searching for the ultimate means to extol the Opéra's newest diva, the men in the audience put their handkerchiefs on the end of their canes so that they could shake them higher and with greater enthusiasm.

With the beginning of the romantic movement at the end of the Restoration, young, fanatical opera connoisseurs would call out criticism to those conductors or musicians unfortunate enough to earn their censure. These intransigent purists (champions of Berlioz) held themselves aloof from the more passive, less exacting members of the audience. The composer of the *Symphonie fantastique* described with a certain delectation these spontaneous moments of aggression, which he called "criticism in action." We have already mentioned the entertaining episode when the entire audience, encouraged by Berlioz, erupted at the suppression of a violin solo by Baillot. During a performance of *Iphigénie en Tauride*, the work that inspired him to become a composer, Berlioz himself interrupted loudly when the orchestral accompaniment to the ballet did not conform to the original score. "There shouldn't be cymbals here," he cried. "Who has the audacity to correct Gluck?" One can imagine the hubbub from an audience ordinarily unconcerned by this type of problem. In Act 3, the hotblooded young Berlioz jumped in again during Oreste's monologue, crying, "What happened to the trombones? This is intolerable!" Berlioz related the audience's surprise in his *Mémoires*: "The astonishment of the orchestra and the audience cannot compare with the very natural anger of Valentino, the conductor."[6]

The best time for the audience to express satisfaction or displeasure was the end of the performance, at the traditional moment of naming or calling for the composer and librettist. At the beginning of the century, the composer and librettist of an opera were not named before the premiere, nor even at the start of the performance. No names appeared on the billboards, and if a work was not popular (that is, it was not discussed throughout Paris for weeks in advance), the premiere took place without anyone knowing either the librettist or the composer. The success of an opera thus depended on its own musical or literary value, not on the reputation of the authors. Audiences came for *Ossian, La vestale,* or *Les bayadères,* not for Le Sueur, Spontini, or Catel. The names of the composers were announced for the first time at the end of the performance, when their disclosure could no longer influence the popular verdict. If the work was a resounding failure, it was quite possible that the audience would leave without even knowing who was responsible for the evening's dreadful production. If it was reasonably successful but engendered no particular enthusiasm, the names of the authors were requested and a member of the company or the administration then came on stage to announce them. If the opera was a triumph, the composer and librettist themselves were called for, and they would then immediately come forward to receive the audience's frenzied acclamation. Needless to say, the opera-goers could clamor for only the librettist or the composer if they felt that the other did not deserve their applause, at which point the chosen one would come forward to receive his reward alone. With the passage of time, billboards and newspapers began to announce the names of composers and librettists before a performance, but the custom of calling them to the stage continued.

ଓ

The discussion thus far has centered on ordinary performances, though even some of these acquired a special character if Napoleon, Louis XVIII, Charles X, or perhaps the young and dashing Dukes of Orléans deigned to enhance the glitter of an evening at the Académie de Musique with their presence. Even more prestigious evenings were those crowning a royal or political event. It was at the Opéra that the emperor celebrated his victories at Jena and Wagram, formally presented Marie-Louise, and celebrated the birth of his son by proclaiming him the king of Rome. Louis XVIII sealed agreements with foreign sovereigns there and organized celebrations for the marriage of the Duke of Berry and the birth of Henri, future Count of Cham-

bord. Charles X appeared there to receive public acclaim on the occasion of his coronation. The Orléans family appeared at a performance at the time of the marriage of Duke Ferdinand, the son of Louis-
Philippe.

The regular scene at the theater described above changed somewhat on the occasion of these special evenings. Parisians began to
crowd the approaches to the theaters at five o'clock, in the hope of seeing the sovereign or a member of the royal or imperial family. Two
women in particular commanded the people's attention during these
years. First, the Empress Josephine, who was always a marvel of beauty
and elegance. "In pleasure as in pain," wrote the emperor's valet, "she
was beautiful to look at. You would smile to see her smile, and if she
was sad, you were sad also. No woman more epitomized the expression 'the eyes are the mirror of the soul.'"[7] The other Muse of these
evenings was the young Duchess of Berry, the daughter-in-law of
Charles X. Although she did not have the grace and presence of
Josephine, "the beautiful Creole," she nonetheless possessed delight-
ful delicacy, lightness, and vivacity, and an almost childlike charm.

The interior of the auditorium would be adorned throughout
with branched candelabras on both sides of each box and decorations
made of flowers and silver gauze. The guests of honor sat in the main
box on the court side, or, during grand official ceremonies, in the first
balcony directly opposite the stage. Since the auditorium remained il-
luminated during the performance, the sovereigns must have had a resplendent view of the assembly of opera-goers. The members of the
audience, particularly the women, were adorned in their most stylish
manner, with dresses embellished with gems for the ladies, and for
everyone branches of laurel or lilies (graciously distributed at the beginning of the evening) to be brandished at opportune moments. The
Countess of Boigne, who attended a performance in the presence of
Louis XVIII, observed in her *Mémoires*, "Florists were commissioned
to furnish us with lilies, and we were coiffed, bedecked, and festooned
with them. The men had white cockades on their hats."[8] To increase
their beauty, the women applied liberal amounts of Eau de Ninon,

said to whiten, soften, and smooth the skin, preserve the teeth and eyes, erase freckles, and prevent wrinkles. Who could ask for more?

As during the *Ancien Régime*, no national anthem per se was played for the sovereign. Each reign, however, had its musical customs. During the *Ancien Régime*, if Louis XVI and the queen attended the Opéra, they heard the chorus from *Iphigénie en Tauride*, "Que d'attraits, que de majesté" (What Allure, What Majesty), in honor of Marie-Antoinette. Whenever Napoleon appeared at a performance, the orchestra played Grétry's aria "Où peut-on être mieux qu'au sein de sa famille" (What Better Place to Be Than in the Bosom of One's Family), a piece that Louis XVI had also liked. Napoleon frequently arrived in the middle of an act, whereupon a welcoming fanfare would immediately interrupt the action onstage. At his departure, *Vivat Imperator* (Long Live the Emperor), composed for his coronation, was usually played.

During the Restoration, the audience routinely sang the popular old French song "Vive Henri IV" (Long Live Henry IV). At the beginning of his reign, Louis-Philippe might be greeted by a resounding *La marseillaise* interpreted by Nourrit, later by *La parisienne*, a patriotic song written by Delavigne and Auber that became very popular after the historic days of July 1830. Unfortunately for Louis-Philippe, the enthusiasm of audiences had waned since the time of his predecessors, who would enter the auditorium to thunderous cheers and applause. The emperor would receive bouquets of myrtle and laurel, and during later regimes hysterical audiences waved palms or fleurs de lys fanatically, causing journalists to write of performances in the auditorium surpassing those onstage.

Toward eleven o'clock it would all be over and the congestion of the start of the evening would be repeated, with the crowd eager to see the monarchs climb into their carriages and return to the Tuileries through the capital's dark and narrow streets. After a court that had been sequestered out in Versailles for more than a century, then a decade of revolution, Parisians had never had much contact with the crowned heads of their beautiful city. Discounting Napoleon, whose military campaigns often absented him from Paris, Louis XVIII came to be regarded as the most genuinely Parisian king since Louis XIII.

Auguste Levasseur, Professional Claqueur

It seems shocking today that at certain moments of the Opéra's history one had to pay people to provide ovations for singers and dancers, and thus manufacture their reputations. The existence of claques did not disturb nineteenth-century audiences, however, and though a journalist might periodically vilify "these base recruits who besmirch the audience with their presence,"[9] claques nevertheless con-tributed to the tradition of the Opéra and Opéra-Comique. They added to the vitality of these theaters, and while sometimes irritating, they became a part of the whole, with a role equal to that of the artists and members of the audience.

Though claques were relatively unimportant during the Empire, they flourished during the Restoration and became an openly organized institution during the July Monarchy. Though tolerated and even respected when scattered among the audiences that filled the Opéra during periods of great success, claques became quite intolerable when they provided the only enthusiastic applause during poor periods of low attendance.

The sumptuous start of Louis-Philippe's reign vis-à-vis opera paralleled the career of Auguste Levasseur, who was regarded as the prince of the claque and universally appreciated for his tact, moderation, and honesty. Directors and artists dealt only with him. He assessed projected performances and decided which works or singers would need "encouragement." Rather then financial remuneration, the management gave him seats. He received at least one hundred tickets for an evening premiere, forty to fifty tickets in the orchestra for a current work in need of support, ten to twenty tickets for a successful opera. Neither an intellectual nor a great musician, Auguste understood audiences better than anyone. He gave judicious advice on what he saw, and he attended all the general rehearsals so that he had a firm basis on which to discuss matters with the director on the eve of a premiere.

He asked nothing of the singers and dancers, expecting them to call on his services and occasionally refusing to dispense them. He was fundamentally honest with a theater's director, and once denied a ballerina's request for a supplementary month of his services because he knew that her contract was soon to expire and he had promised the administration that he would remain neutral. He sometimes accepted a bonus, in the form of "monthly subscriptions" from singers or dancers, who also gave him their complimentary tickets. More than one ballerina who triumphed at the Opéra went so far as to reward him with a small allowance.

Auguste divided the tickets he received into two parts. The first, the lion's share, belonged to him, and he would either sell the tickets or give them to friends in return for their applause. The second batch went to his "platoon leaders," who resold them and kept the money. As for his "foot soldiers," their sole compensation was a ticket.

In effect, Levasseur found himself at the head of an army divided into platoons and squads commanded by lieutenants. On the day of a performance they assembled at a neighborhood wine merchant, where the general announced the colors, and gave his orders in the appropriate vocabulary. They needed to "warm up" Act 1 a little, gently "caress" Act 2 to success, and finally "raise" the last act. Having said this, claques not only applauded an artist's debut or masked a tired soprano's high C, sometimes they would remain perfectly silent in order to protest a ballerina's pretentiousness or unreasonable financial demands.

Early on the evening of a performance, Levasseur stationed his troops (who sometimes numbered over one hundred) in the auditorium according to a well-studied battle plan, the aim being to surround the regular members of the audience with hired soldiers. On particularly important evenings, Levasseur called on sub-claques: well-dressed individuals to whom he sold half-price tickets, and whom he incorporated in groups or individually throughout the ranks.

Levasseur became extremely wealthy through this profession, but he remained conscious of his mission and required tact and elegance from his troops in their dealings with a public that was not only distinguished, but thin-skinned and hyper-sensitive. Let one of his troops fail in these essential requirements and he was immediately dismissed and told to try the claques of the despised Opéra-Comique or Vaudeville. The work there was too easy, paltry even, and a few well-timed bursts of laughter assured a work's triumph. At the Opéra the scheme was more noble, the game more subtle, and those who had to "orient" the audience labored under a heavy responsibility. That was why, in Levasseur's mind, an opera's success was his success and a source of pride and glory.

The Opéra Balls

The favorite diversion of Parisians during the entire nineteenth century was the ball. The Opéra was not the only prestigious place to organize them, and thanks to parties given in the Tuileries, at the Théâtre-Italien and the Opéra-Comique, and especially in private salons, more balls were held than ever before. Certain memoir writers during the Empire reported eight to ten thousand balls every year, and Marie d'Agoult claimed to have danced until five or six o'clock in the morning on sixty-three successive nights during the winter of 1825 to 1826.

After being banned during the Revolution, balls enjoyed a renaissance during the Empire. Indeed, the ball became the symbol of a population eager for amusement not only at working-class dance halls, but at the fashionable galas that abounded in theaters and salons during Carnival time. Journalists and memoir writers focused on the salons and their incredible luxury, their originality and gaiety. The spread of this passion throughout the Empire provoked astonished reactions from foreigners visiting Paris. The account of Mouhib Effendi, who was sent by the Ottoman Sultan Selim III to visit the imperial court, is among the most entertaining.

During the winter, everybody, young and old, even the emperor and his wife, indulge in that entertainment known as the ball. At this gathering equal numbers of men and women, the latter half-naked, dance together. This involves putting a woman into the arms of a man, whereupon the entwined couple turn in circles. Sovereigns and subjects dance to the sound of musical instruments. These Christians do not consider dancing to be shameful. On the contrary, they revel in it.[10]

The Opéra balls were among the most famous, though they were less well attended than they had been during the splendor of the *Ancien Régime*, and less popular than private balls. Masked balls were particularly successful, and the emperor frequently attended and enjoyed listening incognito to conversations. During the Restoration, these balls retained their aristocratic appearance, and the Opéra became well established as a branch of the court, and formally elegant guests demonstrated a stilted semblance of enjoyment. The satirical press began to take an interest in the rather special "fauna" attending these innumerable soirées. *La Pandore* wrote,

Everyone there is a type whose portrait has already been painted: the drowsy husband sitting on the bench in front of the clock; the aristocrats in their boxes; the anarchists in the foyer; the independents in the fourth balcony. Everybody knows that the Opéra balls are a Saturnalia for pretty women, and at the same time a rest home for those whom youth has abandoned, or who have never known beauty.[11]

It was, in fact, the period of the July Monarchy that saw the most radical changes in the customs of these events. During Mardi Gras, the great Opéra ball retained its reputation as the ultimate rendezvous for fashionable Paris, the greatest manifestation of luxury and frivolity. However, the once indispensable gentility provided by the presence of the aristocracy disappeared little by little as this ball opened up to a more eclectic, bourgeois population. It even became a means of lev-

eling social barriers and blending the components of a Paris moti-
vated by a shared thirst for pleasure. It became possible to obtain tickets for the Opéra ball without trouble, sometimes even at half price,
and the ensuing noisy and sometimes outrageous atmosphere had
nothing in common with that which had prevailed during the Empire
and the Restoration.

By 1838 the Opéra ball had become totally democratized and
was opened to huge numbers of revelers, as many as 5,000 in 1846.
On the few occasion the aristocracy now attended, they would leave
utterly disgusted. What Countess Dash called "Pierrot-clowns and
Carnival masqueraders" invaded the Opéra, as well as unscrupulous
men who would force the objects of their desires into obscure recesses
known as "lions' dens" and indulge their salacious passions.

The Polish writer Forster described the balls scathingly in one of
his novels:

> The Opéra has surrendered its sparkling premises to all kinds of
> brazen street youths and entertains in its immense space all man-
> ner of masked balls, great and small. Its dancing hall resembles a
> lunatic asylum overflowing with thousands of threadbare id-
> iots.[12]

Newspapers and novels seized upon the Opéra and Tuileries balls as
their principal sources of ridicule against society in the time of Louis-
Philippe.

Maria Malibran. Courtesy Paul Jackson.

CHAPTER 5

Artistic Life

Musical Studies in Paris

Just as the *Ancien Régime* established no true music policy beyond holding performances at court, it created no special schools for
musicians or singers, amateur or professional. Fortunately, private
lessons and church and cathedral choir schools existed to provide marvelous training for young people.

The first attempt at organized musical education came about in
1784, when Louis XVI founded the Royal School of Singing and
Speech at the Hôtel des Menus-Plaisirs. Its manifesto was to provide
music for the king at private audiences, at the court chapel, or at the
Opéra. Unfortunately, although the school received support and
achieved good results at the very beginning of the Revolution, it did
not survive long enough to become nationally known.

Musical education badly needed attention, and the revolutionary period deserves recognition for setting up an institution worthy of
taking on this instruction, that is, the Paris Higher National Conservatory of Music. The new institution absorbed not only the former
Royal School of Singing directed by Gossec, but the national guard's
School of Music (later the National Institute of Music) created by

Bernard Sarrette, the principal advocate of the new institution. Sarrette took over the administrative direction of the conservatory, under the authority of five inspectors: Méhul, Grétry, Gossec, Le Sueur, and Cherubini—the most illustrious names in French music at the time.

The new conservatory held up to six hundred students of both sexes, but no class could be mixed except during rehearsals of scenes where men and women sang together. This rigorous segregation, established in 1795, was reinforced during the Restoration under the puritanical and authoritarian direction of Cherubini, who installed separate entrances for men and women in order to avoid "unfortunate meetings." Berlioz relates in his *Mémoires* how Cherubini himself showed him the door one day for disobeying this "moral decree." Indeed, it was on the occasion of their first meeting.

In spite of this intransigent discipline, the conservatory, situated at that time on the Rue Bergère in the Poissonière quarter, possessed numerous assets, notably the best French teachers available. Men and women received equal salaries, and they instructed attentive students in all musical and dramatic disciplines. Though fewer girls attended the instrumental and composition classes, many more attended the singing classes. A statistic from 1816 records 90 men and 227 women. All students received the instruction free of charge, and from 1795 they represented forty-six French geographical *départements*, reflecting the beginning of the extreme centralization of French musical studies in Paris.

Henceforth, the value and reputation of the Paris conservatory only grew, and no regime could repress it. The Empire preserved it as well as possible, though numbers diminished for financial reasons. Designed originally for six hundred students and about one hundred teachers, the conservatory shrank to about three hundred students, fewer teachers than intended (seventy-four in 1800 and about thirty in 1802), and three inspectors instead of the previous five, plus the director, a secretary, and a librarian. Among the great names of this epoch were Berton (accompaniment and harmony), Lays (voice), Persuis (vocalization and voice preparation), Baillot (violin), Rey (harmony), and the illustrious Garat (voice). The latter greatly amused his students by pronouncing no *r*'s, according to the current fashion widely spread by the *inc'oyables*, among whom he was a leader.

Only the Restoration, unable to tolerate an institution with such revolutionary origins, made any sort of attack on the conservatory. It hastened to restore the title given to it under Louis XVI, that is, the Royal School of Singing and Speech. The unfortunate Sarrette—dismissed with the arrival of Louis XVIII then reinstated during Napoleon's Hundred Days—preferred to resign when Louis returned to power, and he glady accepted a pension of 3,000 francs from the sovereign. In fact, most of the original teachers returned, and the name of the conservatory seemed to be on everyone's lips throughout the Restoration. Cherubini, who had voluntarily removed himself during the Empire (Napoleon detested him), resumed duties and reigned as absolute master over the school. He was at once respected for his musical stature and disliked for his authoritarianism. His class in composition, the most sought after and respected of all, saw most of the future great names of music pass through it. One of them was Halévy, who at the age of fifteen taught in his master's place when the latter visited England.

In 1831 the July Monarchy hastened to reestablish the title and nature of the conservatory, though its size did not change significantly. It consisted at this time of fewer than three hundred students and about forty teachers, among them Le Sueur (composition) Fétis (counterpoint), Pellegrini (voice), Adam (piano), Baillot and Kreutzer (violin), Naderman (harp), and Nourrit (operatic speech). The great innovation of the new regime was the establishment of a choral class to supply the Opéra chorus, which had become a particularly useful outlet since the demise of the royal chapel.

Along with the conservatory (which remains one of the oldest and most stable French musical institutions), two other schools contributed to the training of young French musicians, and specifically of singers. The aim of the Opéra's School of Singing had, since the seventeenth century, been the operatic training of about twenty men and women a year with the aim of allowing them easier access into the Académie de Musique. In fact, this rather unusual school, nicknamed the Shop, acquired a notoriety that did little to help the reputation of the young women of the Opéra. Morals that had been rather relaxed under Louis XIV became positively loose under Louis XV. It became quite normal to have to drag a singer from a smoky cabaret in order to get her to the theater, or to promise a musician six bottles of champagne before he would agree to play to the end of the opera. These and similar escapades, combined with the slack morals of the young women of the Shop, did little to engender a position of strength for the school at the dawn of the nineteenth century. Its stewardship by the singer Lays, whose voice left much to be desired by this time, only contributed to its decline. The school trained more secondary singers than great soloists, and in the face of the wealthier, better equipped conservatory, it never managed to command attention.

The School of Singing patiently put into place by Étienne Choron proved much more of a force. Choron, a great teacher and the author of numerous theoretical works, attempted to advance the art of French singing—a sorely needed enterprise. Frequently opposed to the teaching methods of the era and disappointed with the results achieved at the conservatory, Choron traveled throughout France opening free singing schools in the principal provincial cities and looking for talented youngsters to bring to Paris. His school, called the Royal Boarding School in 1817 and the Special Royal School of Singing in 1820, was located on the Boulevard du Montparnasse. Initially the school had only twenty-two students, of both sexes, who were looked after by the Royal Household during their four years of study. In this way the king could help a school of his own devising to compete with the "tool of the Revolution": the conservatory. Choron aimed primarily to reform church music, to further the great classical tradition of Bach, Handel, and Scarlatti, and to fight what he considered the "vulgar modern genre." Because of the quality of its vocal instruction, the Choron Institute succeeded in becoming an honorable rival to the conservatory, before turning to religious music in 1825, when its student body numbered between sixty and eighty day pupils and about twenty boarders. The July Monarchy subsequently reduced its subsidy from 46,000 to 12,000 francs, thus putting an end to its all too brief career.

"Barking" Style

Vocal instruction was without doubt the area of greatest musical weakness during the period from the end of the eighteenth century to the mid-nineteenth century. As seen above, the conservatory conducted lessons in all disciplines and employed excellent teachers. Its successes with woodwind and brass instruments revealed a high standard of instruction, and foreign visitors to Paris who heard the student orchestra were astonished by the progress of wind instruments since the *Ancien Régime.*

Unfortunately, the same visitors shuddered at the sound of Paris's opera singers and students. The conservatory teachers, among them the famous Garat, were not entirely at fault, for their teaching was based on the long tradition of shouted singing. This style had become firmly established in the middle of the eighteenth century and was nicknamed *la mode de l'aboiement* (barking style). Resembling "sung theater" rather than Italian melody, French opera required singers to force their voices, exaggerating diction and articulation at the cost of vocal beauty and refinement. The utterly different Italian school had, for two centuries, cultivated the art of pure, natural singing, and at the beginning of the nineteenth century this remained the most beautiful means of vocal expression, in France as elsewhere.

Since the eighteenth century, the shouting style of Paris's opera singers had stupefied visiting foreigners. As early as 1752, the German writer Friedrich Melchior von Grimm exclaimed:

Singing is a shamelessly debased term in France, and means forcing sounds out of the throat and smashing them against the teeth with a violent movement of the chin. *We* would call it shouting.[1]

Casanova, after a Parisian performance of an opera by Lully, related that when the singer Le Maure came onstage, she uttered such a loud cry that he thought she had gone mad. Mozart declared in one of his letters that "the singers of the Académie Royale did not sing, they yelled and howled through their noses and throats with all the force of their lungs."[2]

The *Allgemeine Musikalische Zeitung* of Leipzig, famous for its merciless criticism, claimed that this tendency for French *grand opéra* singers to have harsh voices and to shout was the result of an educational credo that overstressed reason. The article talked of their training, saying that it gave

> their voices a shrill, cutting, even imposing character, representative of reason. On the other hand, the voice of an individual dominated by imagination and inclined toward romanticism is expressed with an absence of this quality of reason, and is instead heartfelt and persuasive.[3]

From the time of her debut, Mme Maillard became one of the greatest singers of her time and heir to the roles of the illustrious Mme Saint-Huberty, but her voice quickly lost its charm. After passing through the capital, an astounded foreigner wrote the following about her:

> The more agitated she becomes and the more she howls, the more the bravos and stamping feet resound. Artists with gentler and more subtle talents cannot compete with her, and since salaries are affected by these bravos, young artists are forced to throw themselves about and yell as much as they can. In general, they succeed only in destroying their voices.[4]

That is what happened to Mme Maillard, and by the time she created the role of the *Grande Vestale*, her voice had become "shrill and disagreeable," and she had "the lungs of an ancient Roman." By the age of forty, a singer was finished.

Lays, a celebrated singer and a teacher at the Opéra's School of Singing, retired in 1823 after forty-two years of service. His voice was tired and forced, and he could no longer control it. "Without any voluntary transition," said Castil-Blaze, "he jumps from the weak sound of his falsetto to the thunder of his chest voice."[5] The tenor Lainez, creator of Spontini's great roles of Licinius and Cortez, also succumbed to the barking style. His voice became shrill and quavering (he was fifty-one years old when he interpreted the young, amorous Licinius, passionately in love with *La vestale*'s heroine), but his faults were compensated by such ardent acting and commanding stage presence that he usually electrified his partners and delighted the audience. Concerning most singers, however, the comments of foreign observers remained the same: French singers had good potential, but controlled their voices poorly, forced the sounds, and succeeded only in shouting. This style became known as *urlo francese* (French howling).

Unfortunately, the singers' compatriots remained completely unaware of the problem, they had become so accustomed to such voices. In 1819, when Mme Albert began singing in the true sense of the term, Parisians did not understand her. A disoriented German columnist for a Leipzig newspaper confessed in his article of 28 April,

> The sounds emitted by this woman resembled what Germans and Italians have for centuries called singing. In France, however, particularly in *grand opéra*, this singing is regarded as insignificant warbling.[6]

The results obtained by the conservatory's vocal instructors during the Consulate and the Empire were lamentable. The students followed their own inclinations, and the teachers, themselves warped by the same education, shouted at will and could propose no method that might result in restrained, sophisticated, and expressive—that is, musical—singing. On one occasion, Napoleon, who fled in the face of such howling, went so far as to tell the singers entering the stage that he hoped they were not going to yell as usual.

It is no exaggeration to say that by the middle of the Restoration, France lagged a good half-century behind its neighbors in the art of singing.

Five Great Figures in French Singing

With the evidence of the preceding pages, one might well wonder how the first half of the nineteenth century experienced any moments of glory when saddled with such wretched singers. In fact, in spite of a few inevitable aftereffects, the barking style did not last forever. A new generation of French singers became influenced by the massive influx into Paris of Italian singers and composers, and they quickly began to understand the new style and put it into practice. The previous extract from the German newspaper about Mme Albert in 1819 marked the beginning of the change.

Before examining the careers of some of the great names of this new style of singing, it would be unjust not to look at the case of Mme Branchu. While she was certainly a graduate of the school of bad vocal technique in force at the end of the eighteenth century, she was nevertheless a true icon during the first twenty years of the nineteenth century and deserves a place among the greatest French singers of *tragédie lyrique*. After her debut at the Opéra-Comique, when she still went by the name Caroline Chevalier, she married the dancer Branchu and joined the Opéra permanently as a principal singer, quickly replacing the regular lead, Mme Maillard. According to contemporary witnesses and newspaper reviews, Branchu had a rare gift for *tragédie lyrique*, with her sensitivity, artistry, and spirited singing and acting. Berlioz, who considered her irreplaceable, described her as having the "type of female voice that was full and ringing, gentle yet strong, capable of dominating the chorus and orchestra or softening to the quietest murmur to express timidity, fear, or dreaming."[7] Foreign observers remained unconvinced, and they continued to see her as an inheritor of the guttural, forced "French singing." By the time she left the conservatory, where she won first prize in Garat's 1797 class, Caroline Branchu had already lost the beautiful voice she had had when she entered. In 1803 certain music lovers noted that "the habit of forcing the notes and of shouting in order to be understood or applauded has already destroyed the charm of her voice."[8] Although her singing far surpassed that of other French singers, she certainly sacrificed her voice by straining to sing from her throat and chest, producing sounds that horrified more than one foreign visitor.

Branchu's true greatness lay elsewhere. Her vocal imperfections and unprepossessing appearance were offset by her unequaled talents as an actress. The greatest productions of the Paris Opéra at the time were *tragédies lyriques*. The strengths of these productions lay in the power and nobility of the speeches and in the importance given to the text, with its attendant tragic gestures and attitudes. Branchu was utterly suited to roles such as Iphigenia or Julia. On one point everyone agreed, she was drama personified, the true incarnation of the characters she played, and she could carry the theatrical interest of an opera alone. She could play the same role every evening, and every evening give it a different personality through a new range of tragic tones and nuances. In this, she anticipated the great Italian singer of *opera seria*, Giuditta Pasta, who, according to Stendhal, could play the character of Tancredi a hundred different ways. Like Pasta, Branchu constantly refined her acting, and she could cast a spell over an audience by her mere presence on the stage. Kalkbrenner, who was fascinated by her, went so far as to compose his opera *Oenone* for her. The caustic Geoffroy immediately rebaptized the opera *Mme Branchu toute seule* (Mme Branchu Alone).

Although the term "diva" was unknown at the time in France, Caroline Branchu could well be called the first French diva, as much for her acting talent as for her extreme popularity in France and abroad. Far more modest and discreet than today's larger-than-life, capricious divas, Branchu, whom a contemporary journalist called a "model of private virtue," was above all an impassioned artist and a perfectionist in her work, not merely a star preoccupied by her commercial value.

Caroline Branchu and her partners onstage belonged to the old school. A new generation of singers, born during the Consulate and the Empire, took the art of singing toward new horizons and formed a pleiad of talented artists who would promote the greatest operatic works of the Restoration and the July Monarchy. The group consisted of Laure Cinti (born in 1802), Adolphe Nourrit (1803), Julie Dorus (1805), and Cornélie Falcon (1814). During their brilliant careers all four would endow the French *grand opéra* repertoire with a style of singing based firmly in the Italian school of bel canto. Under the skillful influence of Italian teachers (Pellegrini and Mme Catalani) and composers (most notably Rossini), they would succeed in banishing the previously revered *urlo francese* and bring about the triumph of a technique that was already well established on the other side of the Alps.

Laure Cinti, who Italianized her French name of Cynthie for her debut at the Théâtre-Italien, became the leading prima donna of the end of the Restoration and went on to sing in the first Rossini productions (*Le siège de Corinthe, Moïse,* and *Guillaume Tell*) presented at the Académie Royale. She was the first Isabelle in *Robert le diable* and created numerous leading parts in the operas and *opéras comiques* of Halévy, Auber, and Adam.

Cinti was taught by Angelica Catalani, the first director of the Théâtre-Italien during the Restoration. She was hired when only fifteen by the Théâtre-Italien, and "passed on" to the Opéra. This common practice usually came at the request of Rossini, who wanted to produce his Parisian operas using accomplished singers with a reputation for purity and agility. Mme Cinti-Damoreau (as she became known on her marriage to the baritone Damoreau), whom Chopin preferred over Malibran, enjoyed many years of public acclaim, before the growing success of her rival Julie Dorus-Gras overshadowed her career.

These two women sang the roles of Isabelle and Alice in the first production of *Robert le diable,* but with the part of Marguerite de Valois in *Les huguenots,* which Meyerbeer wrote especially for her, Julie

Dorus-Gras firmly established herself and began to eclipse Laure Cinti. If her acting left something to be desired (as was often the case with singers trained in the Italian school), her voice had a remarkable range, going from a low C to a high D-flat, which allowed her to be at ease in both the dramatic repertoire and the lightest passages. Julie Dorus held a dominant position in the Opéra's company between 1830 and 1845, and during the plot organized against Berlioz's *Benvenuto Cellini*, she was one of the work's few advocates and gave of herself wholeheartedly until the fall of the curtain—and of the work itself.

ↄ

Naming the greatest male singer of the era is simple, since the first half of the century was so thoroughly dominated by the extraordinary tenor Adolphe Nourrit. Every writer of vocal memoirs, critical reviews, and biographies has lauded this singer's human, vocal, and dramatic qualities. A pupil of Manuel Garcia (Malibran's father) and trained between 1818 and 1822 in the Rossini school of singing, Nourrit made a successful debut at nineteen in the role of Pylade in Gluck's *Iphigénie en Tauride*. His performance in *Le siège de Corinthe* in 1826 assured him a triumphant career. From then on he embarked on the other principal roles of the time, those of *La muette*, *Guillaume Tell*, and *Robert le diable*. The development of his voice—supple, clear, brilliant, agile, and trained by the exercises and technique of Rossini himself—concluded the vocal revolution that had been going on for several years. After hearing the performances of Nourrit and his partners in *Moïse*, *La Gazette de France* wrote:

> It was nothing less than an operatic revolution accomplished in four hours by Signor Rossini. Henceforth, *urlo francese* is banned forever, and singing heard at the Opéra will be like singing heard at the Théâtre-Italien.[9]

La Quotidienne had similar praise:

This magnificent performance must go down in our operatic annals, not only because we heard singing of a quality thus far unknown on the stage of the Académie Royale de Musique, but because it gave the final blow to a decrepit system and consolidated a revolution that has been going on for some time.[10]

Nourrit received most of the press's recognition for ridding the Opéra of *urlo francese*, but his merits went beyond this feat.

As well as his vocal qualities and a physique that had the ladies of the first rows swooning, Nourrit possessed extraordinary theatrical gifts. He exposed the Opéra to impassioned acting and an innate sense of gesture, movement, and life such as had scarcely been seen before. Moreover, Nourrit participated actively in the realization of a production. He closely watched the progress of rehearsals, and often suggested modifications or improvements in the vocal parts or in the staging. His opinions were usually respected, and, during rehearsals for *La juive*, when he proposed replacing a chorus with an aria to advance the dramatic action, he and Halévy immediately wrote the words and music respectively. Similarly, a little later, it was he who had the idea of the grand duet at the end of Act 4 in *Les huguenots*.

In view of so much talent, the end of his career is even more pitiful. Nourrit's world came crashing down with the return to Paris of the tenor Duprez, an excellent singer whom Rossini knew from the fashionable salons of 1823. Panic-stricken at the idea of sharing the limelight with his rival, Nourrit lost his voice in the middle of a performance. He fell into what would today be called a depression, and he fled Paris to seek success in Italy, far from Duprez. Alas, Italian audiences loved his voice but had scant interest in his other talents and charms. They never understood the French singer's impassioned acting and dramatic tones. Nourrit foundered without the dual lifelines of Paris and his adoring public, and, despite some brilliant successes in Naples, on 8 March 1839, at the age of thirty-six, he committed suicide by throwing himself from the top of a building.

His death was not the only loss to the art of singing; to a certain extent it precipitated the end of another rising French opera star, Cornélie Falcon. Falcon was a legendary figure at the Académie de Musique during the July Monarchy, and a perfect example of a singer who peaked too young, and whose fall was, as a result, even harder.

After a childhood at a religious boarding school, Falcon studied singing at a very young age with Nourrit, who was eleven years her senior. The director of the Opéra noticed her at the conservatory's graduating examination, and this dynamic businessman launched the unknown singer into the opera market, just as today one launches a commercial product. He arranged for her to play Alice in the forty-first presentation of *Robert le diable* on 20 July 1832, and he embarked on an energetic press campaign to announce the debut of this young, ravishing, and prodigiously talented singer. The *Courrier des Théâtres* alone wrote about the young Falcon on eight occasions, describing her studies, the salary that she would draw, and so forth. The publicity paid off, and when the big evening arrived the audience contained Mlles Mars and George of the Comédie-Française, Mmes Branchu, Malibran, and Grisi of the Opéra and Théâtre-Italien, the composers Cherubini, Auber, Rossini, and Berlioz, plus Gérard de Nerval, Théophile Gautier, Benjamin Constant, Alfred de Musset, and many others. It was truly a gala evening.

Such a prestigious and operatically experienced audience contained all the ingredients necessary to paralyze an eighteen-year-old debutante, and more than one person expected little from the young singer. Scarcely had she commenced the aria "Va, dit-elle, va mon enfant," (Go, Said She, Go My Child) when a murmur of astonishment ran through the theater, followed by a profound silence, then thunderous applause at the end of the performance. Cornélie had conquered her public. Indeed, she could scarcely fail, with her youth, black hair and dark eyes, a warm complexion that gave her a faintly oriental beauty, and the voice of a dramatic soprano—vibrant, full, and clear, going from a low B to a high D, a tessitura still known today as the range of a Soprano Falcon. The crowning touch was a consummate talent for acting such as had not been seen since Caroline Branchu. Everything seemed to indicate a unique career, filled with productions of *La juive*, *Gustave III*, and *Les huguenots*. Cornélie immediately became a legend and, with Nourrit and Levasseur, made up the trio that all France talked about. Every day, sacks of letters and declarations of love from ardent admirers arrived at her dressing room. Cornélie burnt them all, as she had room for no passion other than opera's.

Unfortunately, the brevity of her studies and the precocity of her debut had not allowed her the time to solidify her technique thoroughly enough to deal with the vocal challenges all singers face. Exhausted by singing in the Opéra's huge auditorium and by the astounding vocal requirements of Meyerbeer's works, and shaken by Nourrit's departure, her voice became unreliable and began to grow hoarse nearly every evening, causing her to cancel many performances. Like Nourrit, Falcon also left Paris for Italy, hoping to recover her voice under the sparkling sun of the Bay of Naples, and also wanting to be near her adored tenor, the man who had taught her everything, whom she venerated, and whom, probably, she secretly loved.

Nourrit's death in 1839 inflicted a further blow, a blow that she would attempt to surmount by giving a farewell benefit performance on 14 March 1840 at the Paris Opéra. The audience experienced one of the most distressing evenings of the Opéra's history. All Falcon's admirers assembled in the orchestra and the closest boxes, but they had nothing more to admire. Her voice had some rare moments of beauty, but it was frequently betrayed by muffled, harsh, and uneven notes. Countess Dash relates:

> Suddenly she opened her mouth, and no sound came out. I do not know how to describe what happened next, the cry that escaped from every throat as if we all wanted to give her our own breath. She tried in vain. Her face expressed a sadness that no painting could portray.[11]

Conscious of the tragedy that she was living, Falcon forced herself to continue to the end of the performance before bursting into tears and falling in a half-faint in front of an audience choked with emotion, devastated to hear the destroyed voice of a woman of only twenty-eight years. "None of the audience will ever forget that painful evening," wrote Théophile Gautier soon after.

Like Greta Garbo in the twentieth century, Cornélie Falcon left the stage and disappeared permanently from the eyes of the world, though she lived to be eighty-three. The minister of the interior exceptionally granted her an allowance of 1,500 francs, in recognition of the joy she had given to Parisian audiences. Berlioz summed up her tragedy best in his description of her distress in learning about Nourrit's death, when her long agony truly began.

> Saint-Roch Church was draped in black. An immense grieving crowd surrounded the casket, praying for Nourrit, who could not live. A young woman in mourning hid in a corner of the nave, sobbing painfully. It was Mlle Falcon, an artist who could not die.[12]

The Birth of the Diva

What more can be said about the legendary diva, one of the most fabulous characters in the history of music, who allowed the dazzling legacy of the castrato to extend into the nineteenth and twentieth centuries?

Unaware of the frequent misadventures that would punctuate the lives of divas from that time on, Parisians at the end of the Restoration and the July Monarchy had the wonderful fortune of being at the very source of the diva legend, of experiencing its birth, and the deification of its heroines.

Of course, passionate acclaim for an outstanding prima donna did not suddenly begin in Paris in 1830. Since the beginning of the century, great artists such as Mmes Festa, Barilli, and Catalani for the Théâtre-Italien and Mme Branchu for the Opéra had already acquired some of the attributes of the diva without yet earning the title. A little earlier, between 1780 and 1785, the illustrious Mme Saint-Huberty had become the object of a true cult. To raise a prima donna to the temple of glory, then, was not new, but singers who might once have merely been "perfect" became "sublime" with the new generation of performers appearing at the Théâtre-Italien around 1830.

The Italian term *diva*, which came from the new glossary of bel canto, became established by these singers. The second quarter of the nineteenth century also saw the adoption of the term *cantatrice*, replacing the simple *chanteuse* of the Opéra. Henceforth, France would have the luxury of differentiating between singers of popular music and of opera. The term *prima donna* also came from Italy, and it served as the counterpart to the *primo uomo assoluto*, the term reserved for the great castrati of the seventeenth and eighteenth centuries. Another innovation was to precede the name of a particularly renowned singer with the article *la*, according to Italian custom. Nobody would have spoken of *la* Branchu or *la* Albert at the beginning of the century, but it became perfectly possible to refer to *la* Malibran and *la* Pasta. Only the aristocracy of Saint-Germain refused to use a term they considered too familiar, preferring to continue speaking of Mme Malibran and Mme Pasta.

Not everything came from Italy and the Italians—the rise and significance of the legend of the diva began with Maria Malibran, born in Paris of Spanish parents. What impressed the audiences of the Paris Opéra most strongly as, three times a week, they enthusiastically watched la Malibran with la Sontag or la Pasta with la Grisi, was the delicious new cocktail of beauty, goodness, talent, and modesty typified by Maria Malibran.

The fact that Caroline Branchu had been, according to Lucien Bonaparte, "devilishly ugly," had had no effect on her career, because her audiences' interest had been elsewhere. Now, however, the new cult of the diva imposed criteria of beauty, charm, grace, and enchantment. The early divas (Maria Malibran, Henriette Sontag, Giulia Grisi, Giuditta Pasta, Jenny Lind, Pauline Viardot, Fanny Persiani, and even Cornélie Falcon) fulfilled these criteria perfectly, but by the second half of the nineteenth and beginning of the twentieth centuries the whims, third-rate acting, excesses, weight, and importance attributed to money tarnished the image of many divas.

Thanks to their looks and prodigious voices, which often spanned very extended ranges, the divas produced delirious joy in audiences and press and sparked the imagination of composers. They interpreted a host of roles (thirty-five for Malibran) and demonstrated accomplished acting skills. Fans fought for a scrap of Malibran's dress and would break the dish from which she had just eaten an ice cream in order to share the fragments. Bellini wrote *La sonnambula* (The Sleepwalker) and *Norma* for Giuditta Pasta, Donizetti composed *Anna Bolena* for Pasta and *Lucia di Lammermoor* for Fanny Persiani, and Meyerbeer adapted his *Prophète* for Pauline Viardot.

Finally came a factor over which the first divas had no control, but which added incalculably to the legend: the circumstances of their deaths. Maria Malibran was passionately in love when she died at the age of twenty-eight after falling off a horse; Henriette Sontag died of cholera in a Mexican hotel at the height of her glory; Giulia Grisi died from cold and fatigue in a seedy room on the outskirts of Berlin; Cornélie Falcon, though she lived to be very old, experienced an equally pathetic artistic death when her voice deserted her at the age of twenty-eight.

Why does one talk of *diva*, but never *divo*? Were French audiences of this era so absorbed by their divas that they forgot the great male singers of the Opéra and the Théâtre-Italien? The number of pages devoted to Nourrit, Duprez, Mario, Tamburini, Rubini, and Lablache during the years 1820 to 1850, and the ovations they received in both French and foreign theaters, attest to their popularity. Nonetheless, it is true that most of the great male singers occupied only a secondary place in the hearts of audiences, who were consumed by their passion for the divas. The time was not yet ripe for the god of singing; that would come later, with Chaliapin and Caruso, well after the period in question here.

A Day in the Life of la Malibran

Maria Malibran excited great commentary and passion in nineteenth-century Paris, even before becoming the first great diva of her time. She symbolized a new type of woman, born before 1830, who became increasingly visible during the July Monarchy. Gone was the era of ethereal, angelic, consumptive women confined to the cocoon-like atmosphere of aristocratic salons. The new woman, the lioness, combined charm and ardor, intellect and a taste for sport, art, and the trivialities of daily life. Maria Malibran embodied this new woman, embracing life, relishing speed and entertainment, and putting as much energy into riding a horse and dancing as into practicing endless vocal exercises.

If she had not been out the night before, she would ride her horse early in the morning and cover mile upon mile, dressed in her riding habit, returning in the afternoon just in time for rehearsals. If, on the other hand, she had danced the whole night long, she would sleep until noon (when her schedule permitted it), jump out of bed, set out immediately without eating, and ride her horse all afternoon, caught up in an intoxicating rhythm of excitement and freedom. When it was time to return to the theater, Malibran would nibble a frugal dinner, quickly down two glasses of Bordeaux, and attend to her costume and makeup.

Once the curtain rose, she would give herself over to her character. She would enthrall her audience with the range of her theatrical powers, and delighted spectators would show their devotion by tossing verses and bouquets of flowers onstage.

Her day was far from over. Immediately after leaving the Théâtre-Italien, Malibran would hasten to the home of a friend, where, without the slightest consideration for the fatigue of her voice, she would perform for hostess and guests. She might sing Saul's *romance* from *Otello*, the cavatina from *La gazza ladra*, and perhaps the final aria from *L'italiana in Algeri* before eating supper and waltzing dizzyingly until four or five o'clock in the morning.

It stands to reason that such a life led to dreadful exhaustion. The diva complained of suffering from "stiffness in all her limbs," and once, when she had to cancel an appearance, she begged the administrator, Severini, to excuse her and concluded her letter with the words, "Have pity on this poor, aching wretch."

In fact, Maria complained less than she might have, for she possessed such a strong will, such a commitment to life, singing, and her fans, that she considered the minor ills of her body to be unimportant. Nothing really stopped her. One evening she returned home at about six o'clock, gulped her dinner, dashed to the theater to dress as Arsace, and fainted just as she went onstage. She was carried to her dressing room and revived by smelling salts from one of the numerous phials on her table. The salts were held too near her lips and caused horrible blisters that would have caused the bravest singer to cancel the performance. Taking a pair of scissors, Malibran calmly slashed the blistered skin and, in a condition that can only be imagined, went onstage and carried off a triumph with Henriette Sontag as Sémiramis. It should not be surprising that the circumstances of her death involved the same stubbornness. She refused to take care of herself properly after a bad fall from a horse and exhibited the same will to sing regardless of pain, only to die once the curtain came down.

The Singers' Social and Professional Lives

Though it is hardly possible to trace a specific career path for singers of the beginning of the nineteenth century, certain constants are apparent. Not surprisingly, singers tended to make their debuts at a very young age. Observers frequently criticized teachers for pushing their students and launching them into the professional world at an age when, though they could carry off prizes, they lacked the necessary maturity to tackle the great roles of the repertoire. Singers trained between 1810 and 1830 made their debuts very early, and their young, fresh voices exhibited excellent technique and purity of timbre. Thus Laure Cinti made her debut at the age of fifteen, Pauline Viardot

at sixteen, Maria Malibran and Cornélie Falcon at eighteen, and
Adolphe Nourrit and Gilbert Duprez at nineteen. Henriette Sontag
and Giulia Grisi both made their Parisian debuts at twenty-one, the
first having already triumphed in Germany, the second in Italy.

Although such early debuts were considered normal in an epoch
when one generally started working very young, serious problems
rapidly became apparent. Voices that had been trained in record time
and immediately exposed to large auditoriums quickly became exhausted due to frequent rehearsals and performances that went on
practically without a break over the whole year. Nourrit's triumphant
career lasted only eleven years, Cornélie Falcon lost her voice after six
years, and Rosine Stoltz was booed during a performance because,
after a career of only nine years, she could no longer sustain notes.
Careers as long as Caroline Branchu's (almost thirty years) or Pauline
Viardot's (twenty-five years) remained rare, and, indeed, Branchu's
chest voice weakened considerably well before her retirement.

The folly of these too-early debuts was compounded by poorly
heated venues, long winter rehearsals, and over-elaborate vocal em-
bellishments that ruined the voices of singers with, at the most, four
or five years of training. Finally, such brief training periods prevented
the singers from developing any dramatic skills or knowledge of staging. Many singers with very beautiful voices suffered, even at the
height of their careers, because of their physical awkwardness onstage
and their total lack of dramatic presence. Julie Dorus-Gras and Louise
Leroux-Dabadie, for example, had no acting talent and no concept of
the arts of comedy or tragedy. Only Nourrit and Falcon, as talented
at acting as at singing, proved their skills as complete artists. As for
Italian singers, their lack of naturalness on the stage was a major factor in the animosity of many French journalists and music lovers toward the Théâtre-Italien.

☙

It is notable that during the period in question, singers tended to
live surrounded by other singers, cut off from the rest of the world.

Whether they esteemed or envied each other, the singers living in Paris knew each other well, kept each other company, entertained each other, and even tended to marry each other. Caroline Chevalier started the trend by marrying the dancer Branchu at the end of the eighteenth century. Later, Laure Cinti-Damoreau, Julie Dorus-Gras, and Joséphine Fodor-Mainvielle owed their double-barreled names to unions with the tenor Damoreau, the violinist Gras, and the actor Mainvielle respectively. The baritone Dabadie, creator of the title role of *Guillaume Tell,* married Louise Zulmé-Leroux, who created the role of Jemmy in the same opera. Pauline Garcia married Louis Viardot, the director of the Théâtre-Italien, and Giulia Grisi married the Italian tenor Mario di Candia, an aristocrat of pure stock who gave up his title to pursue a singing profession. The world of dance shared this habit, and the ballerina Carlotta Grisi married her dancing master, Jules Perrot, whereas Félicité Noblet, who created the role of Fenella in *La muette,* married the singer Dupont. Only Cornélie Falcon, bound perhaps by her platonic love for Nourrit, had no amorous liaisons during her career, and was known as the Virgin of the Arts.

The singers and dancers belonged to their own, detached clan and found it virtually impossible to be introduced into high society or acquire the social status merited by their talent. It is difficult to imagine that the heroes and heroines of the Opéra, the Théâtre-Italien, and the Opéra-Comique, who had all Paris in raptures, managed only with great difficulty to enter the salons, other than for occasional private concerts at which they performed. The most marvelous singer, though, was looked upon as merely a sort of wandering musician. The best way to enter the salon of the Duchess of Duras or the Princess Bagration was to belong to the aristocracy, and this was certainly not the case with these singers.

One group of musicians came from illustrious families but, nonetheless, did not belong to the aristocracy. Adolphe Nourrit was the son of the tenor Louis Nourrit, who had been famous in Paris during the Empire; Pauline, Maria (Malibran), and Manuel Garcia were the children of the composer and great tenor Manuel Garcia, creator of the role of Almaviva, and they constituted one of the most prestigious musical families of the nineteenth century. Fanny Persiani was the daughter of the tenor Tacchinardi, one of the jewels of the Théâtre-Italien during the Empire. Finally, Giulia and Giuditta Grisi were the daughters of the illustrious Giuseppina Grassini, Napoleon's favorite contralto during the era of the castrato Crescentini.

These few privileged artists apart, most singers had to be content with much more modest origins. Levasseur, whose wonderful talent was discovered while he was working as a shepherd, was the son of a farmer. Cornélie Falcon was the daughter of a tailor, and Duprez was the twelfth child of a merchant on the Rue Saint-Denis. Rosine Stoltz abandoned her real name of Victoire Noël in order to hide her origins as the daughter of a household of caretakers from the Boulevard du Montparnasse.

In nineteenth-century society such modest origins precluded admittance to an elegant soirée in the Faubourg Saint-Germain or the Chaussée d'Antin. Marie d'Agoult relates how composers and singers occupied a separate rank and attended the soirées as entertainers, not equals. "In spite of the eagerness of salon habitués to see them, they appeared only as inferiors."[13] Some of them, such as Lablache or Malibran, did come to be introduced into high society due to their wealth and personal radiance, but even that act was a hypocritical facade. Malibran saw the doors of nearly every mansion closed to her when it became known that she was pregnant (by Charles de Bériot) without being married. In fact, prima donnas and ballerinas knew that their only real chance of social advancement consisted of marrying a prince or an important financier. Henriette Sontag became one of the lucky few when she married Count Rossi, ambassador to the King of Sardinia.

&

Were the great singers of the Opéra and the Théâtre-Italien rich? The situation at the beginning of the century was quite different from that fifty years later. During the Empire and the Restoration, a popular singer earned a decent living, nothing more. The concept of the diva as goddess, for whom no salary was too high, had not yet developed, and the time was not ripe to spend extravagantly on musicians who, it was perceived, pursued a profession like anyone else. Undoubtedly, singers who caused the whole capital to run to the theaters and whose renown sometimes extended beyond national borders received poor rewards. Mme Branchu, far from having money to throw around, ended her career if not in poverty, at least in extreme austerity. This singer had been the queen of French singing during the Empire and the beginning of the Restoration, but the director of the Opéra refused a request for a benefit performance. Pellegrini's situation was even worse, and the Théâtre-Italien's famous singer, who had helped so many young talented artists, died in such poverty that he had no money left to pay for his funeral.

The situation changed considerably during the July Monarchy, when every performer was popular. The words *art*, *artist*, and *artistic* had never occupied such an elevated place in conversations and this latest Parisian craze even engendered the word *artistism*. The veneration of Malibran started a new kind of cult, and the most famous male and female singers rapidly became idols. They were cheered at theater exits, were followed to their residences, and became the subjects of passionate sonnets and madrigals. In response to such frenzies, salaries began to grow in proportion to the public's enthusiasm.

Around 1830 Laure Cinti and Julie Dorus-Gras received 15,000 francs a year, Nourrit and Giuditta Pasta received 30,000 to 35,000 francs. Gradually the Opéra's director, Véron, began to pay ill-considered amounts, which caused trouble for his successors when receipts at the Académie de Musique diminished. Though France had no inflation, Cornélie Falcon's salary rapidly climbed to 50,000 francs a year, and by 1848 the earnings of Mario and Duprez were around 70,000 francs, though Mario proved incapable of managing such a fortune. If the musicians of the beginning of the century tended to be

underpaid in relation to their fame, those of 1850 were certainly over-
paid, and more than one novel of the period dealt contemptuously
with singers who spent their time "running into debt and drinking
punch." Charles d'Agoult, at the end of the Second Empire, was startled to discover the leap in fees paid to musicians over less than fifty
years.

> The revolution in the financial and social situations of singers,
> male and female, is both inexplicable and astonishing. The divas
> earn easily 300,000 francs a year. The great actor Nourrit used to
> earn 40,000 francs, Mme Malibran and Mlle Sontag about as
> much. Bordogni, Donzelli, and Rubini used to sing in salons
> for 500 francs, which is what one paid the great singers. Now
> Mlles Patti, Nilsson, and others will not utter a note for less than
> 3,000 francs. These ladies are millionaires, but have no more
> talent than Mme Malibran who, with her family, was poverty-
> stricken.[14]

Let us not forget, either, the additional financial support granted
to singers and dancers in every regime. During the entire first half of
the century, it was rare to find a prominent artist who did not receive
aid from the state or the royal family. Most of them secured support
in the form of bonuses or pensions, which in fact constituted the principal means of support given by sovereigns for the arts.

∽

No singer, however popular, was without small failings and idio-
syncracies, and wage extortion seems to have been the common de-
nominator linking many musicians. The great baritone of the Opéra-
Comique, Elleviou, enjoyed such success at the beginning of the
century that he gave himself the nickname "the Emperor" and threatened to leave the stage if he did not receive a 50 percent increase.
Napoleon refused categorically. Many years later, Lavigne left the
Opéra because he felt his salary was too low. After touring the provinces, he finally returned to Paris and was rehired by the management

for a higher wage. Another time, Mme Cinti-Damoreau wanted to go on vacation and only agreed to continue performing in return for a huge sum.

Singers were not the only ones to make these demands. On one occasion, the director had to accede to the demands of two trumpeters who refused to play at a premiere if their wages were not immediately raised. Similar cases abounded, and in most cases the administration preferred to yield rather than lose good musicians.

Besides the question of money, the director had to cope daily with difficulties caused by rivalries among musicians. He had to deal, for example, with a ballerina who entered his office in a rage because her rival's performance lasted five minutes longer than her own.

The closed world of the Opéra was also the scene of goodness and solidarity. An excellent case in point occurred when the great trio of the time (Damoreau, Levasseur, and Nourrit) asked the director to hold a benefit performance, at which the three singers would appear without charge, to raise the 2,000 francs necessary for Pellegrini's funeral. Touched by their request, the director agreed to the requested sum without making any demands of the artists. The same generosity came from the tenor Lafont, who agreed one evening to replace Nourrit at a moment's notice rather than cancel the performance and disappoint the audience. It could not have been easy to be the replacement for a singer of Nourrit's stature.

Good intentions and cooperation did not prevent bitter competition among the leading singers, more than one of whom suffered a decline on the arrival of a new singing idol, thus shortening their careers. Audiences, albeit faithful to their beloved established singers, constantly looked for novelty, young voices, and new, pretty faces, and performances became more and more sensational. This attitude affected every interpreter in every epoch. Mme Maillard, during the Directory, found herself brutally eclipsed by the arrival of Mme Branchu. The same happened to Laure Cinti, whose star began to dim in 1835 with the triumph of Julie Dorus. As discussed, Nourrit completely lost his ability to sing when he learned of Duprez's return to Paris. During *La muette de Portici* (and in the presence of the composer), his voice deserted him when he learned that his rival was in the audience. He was replaced by an understudy in the middle of the performance.

The jealousies and rivalries of the somber period between 1840 and 1847 were unparalelled. This was the time of the singer Rosine Stoltz's autocratic rule in Paris. This woman, who had made her debut at the Monnaie de Bruxelles, reigned not only over audiences, but also over the heart of the Opéra's director, Léon Pillet. Crafty, scheming, and ambitious, Rosine Stoltz used Pillet to keep away any singer, man or woman, who might overshadow her glory.

Julie Dorus-Gras still commanded full houses in 1840, and became the first to suffer from Stoltz's rivalry. The struggle between the two women became intense, vocally and otherwise. During Dorus-Gras's main aria, Stoltz might cross the stage while devouring a plate of macaroni, causing the audience to burst out laughing, thus diverting attention away from her partner's dazzling singing. It is not surprising that under such duress, Dorus-Gras capitulated in 1845 and never again performed at the Opéra.

Léon Pillet invariably acceded to the endless whims of this authoritarian and calculating woman, and he was blinded by his love for the woman he dared to call "Malibran without the faults." He put the finances of the already struggling "Great Boutique" in total jeopardy, not realizing that profits were falling because the public wanted nothing to do with this impossible woman, particularly since her voice was declining. A newly arrived Russian aristocrat made the following unflattering analysis of the diva, seeming to identify her with the great actresses of the eighteenth and early nineteenth centuries:

> Mme Stoltz's singing, or, rather, her shouting, and her vocal and bodily contortions are in the typical French style, a melodramatic genre in which passion is replaced by delirium, anger by rage, and love by something whose name cannot yet been found, as far as I know, in any dictionary.[15]

At the beginning of 1847, the commission for the royal theaters required Léon Pillet to submit to a review of his management as director of the Académie Royale de Musique from 1840 to 1846. He foolishly devoted one-third of his seventy-one page report to a defense of the indefensible Rosine Stoltz, and every day Parisians followed the polemic that raged between the director of the Opéra and the principal newspapers of the capital. Critics and subscribers read the tirades with great delight, and pamphlets circulated from all sides about the Pillet-Stoltz affair. One evening the frenzied audience verbally attacked the singer in the middle of her performance. Furious at being insulted in this manner, Stoltz demanded the support of her protector, who was present in a first tier box. When she saw that he was powerless to calm the crowd, she tore up her handkerchief in a rage and stormed off the stage.

Her final Parisian appearance took place on 22 April 1847, and, curiously, she was applauded. Was this due to a carefully prepared claque, or to the audience's relief at her definitive departure from the capital?

Profession: Composer

One of the guiding forces of French and Italian composers during the Empire and Restoration was a consciousness of the ruling political power. Total independence was impossible, since payment for commissioned works was often only part of a composer's income, and they all relied on subsidies from the sovereign.

The transition from the Restoration to the July Monarchy was relatively easy for musicians, but the sharp division between the Empire and the Restoration proved to be much more serious. Although the switch in regimes occurred without a revolution, it represented a radical change, and the sympathizers of the "usurper" Napoleon had no reason at all to find favor with the recrowned Bourbons.

During the years 1814 to 1815, this meant that composers had to be extemely careful to avoid what would today be called a witch-hunt. Certain people rejoiced in the change of regime, for example, Cherubini, who had never enjoyed Napoleon's support. Others, such as Spontini and Blangini, sought to rid themselves of their reputation as imperialists and engaged in the basest flattery for the sake of their imperiled pocketbooks.

Spontini, who, it should be remembered, had been Josephine's favorite and the principal musician of the imperial regime, had no compunction in writing to Louis XVIII and asking to be appointed director of the king's private music concerts. He also asked to be director of all Italian *opera seria* and *opera buffa*, or, if that were not possible, superintendent of the Académie Royale de Musique. This audacious request was written on 16 April 1814, just a few days after the change of regimes, and concluded:

> I shall spend the rest of my life, Sire, blessing your happy return and your kindnesses, while striving to make myself worthy of them. Indeed, I feel my feeble genius blossoming and increasing at the thought of being able to dedicate my eternally grateful efforts to the highly cherished and long awaited head of the house of Bourbon. I remain, with profound respect, Sire, the most devoted subject of Your Majesty.[16]

Had Spontini gone too far? Not at all. Far from being offended by this former servant of the "enemy" and by his saccharine, insincere praise, Louis XVIII hastened to grant the composer a bonus of 2,000 francs and to accede to his request for the direction of the Théâtre-Italien, though he later entrusted this post to the ambitious Angelica Catalani. Whatever his character, Spontini henceforth stayed out of difficulty, was recognized as official composer, and went on to write topical works, about which no more shall be said. Louis XVIII proved his clearsightedness by refusing to cast aside those who had served the imperial regime, and this became one of the best means of winning over the intelligentsia of the period to his side.

In 1814, Félix Blangini, a second-rate Italian composer who had spent his most successful days in Paris, found himself in a situation similar to Spontini's. He had worked for Jérôme Bonaparte, the king of Westphalia, for several years, but from 1815, he skillfully and opportunistically manipulated the Duke of Duras and the Duchess of Berry with such savoir faire that he went on to achieve a much more glittering career than previously. He began as composer and accompanist of the king's chamber, then accepted the post of professor of singing at the Royal School of Music. When he lost his position there in 1828, he engineered a compensatory pension from Charles X of 800 francs, until 1830. He went from the entourage of Jérôme Bonaparte to that of the Duchess of Berry, with whom he played the piano and harp, and during the July Monarchy he let it be widely known that he was responsible for training the singer Brocard, the teacher of Louis-Philippe's children.

The overthrow of Charles X had little influence on tenured composers, and Louis-Philippe continued to acknowledge those who had collaborated with his cousins. At the same time, Louis-Philippe handsomely rewarded those who had fought to end the Restoration, and Adolphe Nourrit and the writer Hippolyte Bis, co-librettist of *Guillaume Tell*, were among the partisan beneficiaries. Sympathizer or not, each composer generally honored the sovereign of the moment by dedicating a work to him, more out of respect for secular tradition than out of real political belief. Thus Spontini's *Vestale* and Rossini's *Guillaume Tell* were dedicated to Josephine and Charles X respectively, while Bellini's *I puritani* (The Puritans) and Donizetti's *Martyrs* honored Queen Marie-Amélie.

რ

Composers could receive various forms of remuneration, including specific salaries and bonuses. At the Académie de Musique, the composer and librettist received a fixed and equal amount for each work they wrote. Their earnings reflected the number of performances each work received. During the Empire, both earned 300 francs for each of the first twenty performances, 200 francs for the ten that followed, and 150 francs for the final ten. If the number of performances of a given work exceeded forty, the author and composer were paid a bonus of 500 francs and the sum of 100 francs for each additional performance until the opera disappeared from the schedule.

A few slight modifications were made following a decree from Louis XVIII dated 18 January 1816. Henceforth, composer and librettist divided the sum of 500 francs for a major opera and received the same amount for each of its first forty performances. For subsequent performances, they shared 240 francs. If the opera was a short work of one or two acts that required another work on the program, the creators initially collected 240 francs per performance, then 100 francs after the first forty performances. On top of these basic salaries, certain composers received bonuses, usually from the sovereign. During the Restoration Spontini received a supplementary bonus of 1,500 francs for each act (rather than for each opera) that he composed, in addition to his regular salary. Exceptionally, and perhaps reflecting the composer's genius, M. de la Rochefoucauld granted Rossini 10,000 francs for each new opera. In an attempt to tie Rossini to France, de la Rochefoucauld stipulated that Rossini write an opera each year. In spite of this tempting proposition, the composer ceased writing in 1829, and so gained little from the statute.

The system of remuneration outlined above had the effect of rewarding the best and worst works similarly, and only the duration of the run altered the sum. For this reason, the Opéra-Comique's system was often considered fairer, since it was linked to each evening's receipts. If a work was mediocre, audiences were generally smaller, and this was reflected in the authors' salaries. If it was a masterpiece, full houses helped the purse and the reputation of the composer and librettist. This, of course, was an incentive to raise the quality of operas, but it also meant better payment than that offered by the Opéra. Scribe and Boieldieu, the creators of *La dame blanche*, would have been paid only two-thirds of what they actually received if their work had been given at the Académie Royale rather than the Opéra-Comique. Finally, it should be noted that payment for operas constituted only part of composers' incomes, for they also had responsibilities at the conservatory, gave private singing or instrumental lessons, carried out duties at court and the chapel, and received royalties— though these were rather slender.

ℰℐ

As a general rule, composers at the beginning of the century enjoyed a relatively comfortable position, provided they fit the mold. This meant that they wrote music that, though it could be mildly innovative, would immediately gratify the Parisian public and include pretty melodies, dramatic stage effects, and ballets. Life was difficult for the "moderns," the rebels such as Berlioz, who had to submit to jeers and learn to live more modestly. Opera certainly evolved during the first half of the century, but gently and without revolution. The composers' desire to please limited their artistic ambitions just as much as it guaranteed their fortune and honor.

Not only did composers generally earn more than singers, they also slipped more easily into the official circles and fashionable salons of the capital. High society condescended to welcome the creative geniuses of the moment, turning a blind eye to their plebeian origins. Around 1830, during the effervescent time of glorious bel canto performances and magnificent premieres, composers (especially Italian composers) gradually became the symbol of intellectual and cultural Paris. To invite into one's home Rossini, Bellini, or Meyerbeer was to invite a personality who figured in ten times as many conversations as the king himself. Rossini was the darling of Parisian receptions, and the ultimate honor was to be admitted into the maestro's home, where one could see scribbled pages of notes for his last score spread through the disordered rooms.

ℰℐ

Paris abounded with French and foreign composers, and no one could ignore the difficult, sometimes stormy relationships between the very different personalities. During the first twenty years of the century, a certain distrust developed between the French and the Italians, with the latter seen as pretenders, stealing the fire of the former. Spontini experienced hostility towards his principal operas, which, since they were performed at the Opéra and not at the Théâtre-Italien, were seen as direct competition. In the same way, Le Sueur gave Rossini a very cold welcome to Paris because he despised most of Rossini's work and considered it to be pretentious. Even among the Italians jealousies arose. Cherubini was particularly selective and cold, and even in his friendships he was not easy to get along with initially. He looked with little favor on the nomination of Rossini as composer to the king and inspector general of singing in all the royal musical institutions. Paër, for his part, did everything he could to delay the arrival in Paris of Rossini's masterpieces. Soon after his arrival in the capital, Bellini worried about the cold relationship that he had with Rossini, though in fact this relationship improved rapidly. On the other hand, Bellini would always detest, though cordially, his most direct rival, Donizetti.

On the whole, friendship and solidarity generally prevailed over rivalry, particularly toward the end of the Restoration and during the July Monarchy. The Italians were henceforth so fashionable and such a part of the Parisian musical scene that the rancor of the beginning of the century seemed laughable. The 1830s constituted the main period of this musical ebullience, and composers became acquainted with each other, socialized together, and cooperated in the numerous productions put on by the different theaters.

The French composers Auber, Halévy, Hérold, Boieldieu, and Adam continued to dominate the scene. They had a shared appreciation for each other, while at the same time linking themselves in friendship with the great Italians of the time, namely Rossini, Bellini, and later Donizetti, who arrived in Paris in 1823, 1833, and 1838 respectively. Like some of their predecessors, these foreigners slipped easily into French musical life. Cherubini, who had lived in France since 1787, had become almost more French than Italian. Spontini, who married Marie-Céleste Erard, the niece of the inspired inventor of the piano's double escapement mechanism, wrote French admirably. Rossini was so at ease in French that he made all Paris laugh with his ironic humor and his biting comments. Only Bellini, who lived there for only two years, spoke such poor French that (according to Heine) "it made the hair on your head stand on end," and for that reason he was close only to Cherubini, Rossini, and exiled Italian politicians.

During his prolonged sojourns in the capital, the German Meyerbeer entered the circle of composers without difficulty. Like many others, he set out to win the friendship and good graces of the composer of *Il barbiere di Siviglia*, the éminence grise of the musical world. In addition to friendships among composers, of course, was the enriching company of the great intellectuals and artists of the epoch: Musset, George Sand, Nerval, Gautier, Chopin, Lamartine, Delacroix, Courbet, and others.

The composers' solidarity manifested itself not only during happy times, but under the gravest circumstances, such as the occasion of Bellini's death. The entire romantic generation was deeply affected, and, under Rossini's leadership, started a fund to finance the funeral. After having triumphed on many Italian stages, including La Scala with *Norma*, Bellini had arrived in Paris two years earlier, in 1833, seeking new triumphs at the celebrated Théâtre-Italien. Audiences at this theater were enthusiastic, the singers were of the highest caliber, and the salaries were slightly superior to those of the theaters in Italy. Bellini was not disappointed by his journey, and the production of *I puritani* in January 1835 marked the summit of his career. On 3 February Louis-Philippe granted him the Cross of the Knight of the Legion of Honor, and Rossini himself presented it to Bellini on the stage of the Théâtre-Italien.

Bellini was a favorite at the most elegant Parisian salons, where the aristocracy fawned on the delicate, frail young man. Although he appeared at these social gatherings, Bellini hid a rather reserved character. With lodgings in a cramped and uncomfortable apartment, distressed by the competition with his rival, Donizetti, frequently sick, ill at ease in the French language and thus in his dealings with other people, Bellini was alone in the midst of an admiring crowd, an uprooted individual who craved affection and love. The dichotomy of adulation and melancholy accompanied him to his death at only thirty-four in a small house in Puteaux, a death that could have been the result of a mysterious intestinal illness, or murder.

The religious ceremony took place on 2 October 1835 in the Invalides chapel and was one of the most notable occasions of the July Monarchy. The musical program was graciously supplied by the Opéra orchestra and the singers of the Académie Royale, Opéra-Comique, and Théâtre-Italien. A wave of emotion swept over the audience when Tamburini, Rubini, Lablache, and Ivanoff, the greatest voices of the Théâtre-Italien, interpreted a *Lacrymosa* based on an aria from *I puritani.*

The funeral procession that followed the ceremony gave Parisians the unparalleled opportunity to see several generations of composers, musicians, singers, writers, artists, and politicians, in fact, every prominent Parisian figure, gathered in one spot. One hundred and twenty musicians accompanied the casket, and every ten minutes the drum rolls resounded. At the Père-Lachaise cemetery, after speeches by Paër and others, Cherubini, supported by Auber and Halévy, threw the first handful of earth. Some time later, the city of Bellini's birth, Catania, in Sicily, claimed the musician's body and built a tomb for him in its cathedral.

The tragic figure of this great bel canto composer who died too young became a symbol of the romantic movement and strongly affected a whole generation of artists. A year later to the day, the same artists received a second psychological shock with the death of their twenty-eight year old heroine, Maria Malibran.

The Boulevard des Italiens

This pivotal nineteenth-century Parisian thoroughfare experienced rapid development only after 1830. Until then, it was nothing more than a vast, tranquil promenade of no special character, bordered by two-hundred-year-old trees. The nearby Tivoli Garden—in the area of today's Place de la Trinité—offered Parisians a place to relax and stroll, like the Prater in Vienna. They could buy refreshments and dance at little cost to the sounds of the numerous orchestras that enlivened summer evenings and Sunday afternoons.

Since the end of the Revolution, the center of pleasure and licentiousness had been the gardens of the Palais-Royal and its environs. No visitor from the provinces missed the opportunity to explore this unique attraction, even for only one evening. It represented the ultimate in debauchery and gambling and had countless bawdy theaters that had rapidly multiplied at the beginning of the century, before Napoleon's stringent restrictions came into force. With the Restoration the Palais-Royal regained the former crazed animation of its cafés, gambling dens, and wooden arcades occupied by prostitutes. This excessive activity was fostered by the ostentatious life of the Orléans family, who, from fête to fête and from ball to ball, influenced a socially eccentric population thirsting for entertainment. Moreover, the top aristocracy avoided events at the Palais-Royal, where they claimed to know no one, and preferred to be entertained in the elegance, good taste, and privacy of their own mansions.

The year 1830 constituted a clear watershed, for by closing the gambling houses, destroying the prostitutes' wooden arcades, and installing himself in the Tuileries for the entire duration of his reign, Louis-Philippe dealt a fatal blow to the characteristic atmosphere of the gardens of the Palais-Royal that had existed since the eighteenth century.

Thus the center for leisurely walks, carefree behavior, and entertainment was transferred to the Boulevard des Italiens, already the hub of operatic and theatrical life. Henceforth the tone of Paris would be set by the restaurants, reputable cafés, social gatherings, and large theaters of the area, and the salons would pale before the success of the clubs. In all the inextricable maze of the capital's narrow streets, the Boulevard des Italiens was one of the rare places where several people could walk abreast without being jostled or splashed. The once peaceful avenue became the social and cultural heart of Paris from 1830 to the end of the century.

The boulevard's activity began at the Chaussée d'Antin and extended slightly beyond its limits onto the Boulevard Montmartre and up to the Théâtre des Variétés. Beyond this boundary one entered what Musset called the "great Indies," a kind of unexplored territory where a well-bred lady would not venture. Curiously, while carriages and landaus passed each other in both directions, by tradition the promenader strolled only on the north side of the boulevard, known as the left side. This side held the prime places for meeting and socializing for promenaders, artists, and journalists. The Café de Paris, on the corner of the Rue Taitbout, seemed to be the best known and had the best food. On the opposite corner was the ice-cream maker Tortoni, who served punch and sorbets, a popular choice at the end of the afternoon. In the angle of the Rue Laffitte was the Café Hardy, the preserve of the *National*'s editorial staff. A few meters beyond, on the corner of the Rue Le Peletier near the Opéra, the Café Riche made a fortune by staying open past midnight. As the Café Hardy was very expensive and the Café Riche a landmark for night owls, everyone joked that "it was necessary to be rich to dine at the Café Hardy, and hardy to dine at the Café Riche." The unpopular south side of the boulevard had just one "den of iniquity," the Café Anglais, a cosmopolitan rendezvous. In fact, here, as on the north side, patrons generally comported themselves in good taste, for the boulevard during the time of Louis-Philippe had not yet been taken over by the vulgarity that would come with the Second Empire. The licentiousness that had reigned around the Palais-Royal was no longer acceptable, and the concept of the Boulevard des Italiens as a backdrop for social advancement led to a certain snobbism in the desire to be seen there.

Many of the popular singers and composers adopted the Boulevard des Italiens as the main musical district, and the life of many of them took place exclusively within this limited area. Life consisted of spending time in one's apartment, at the theater, or strolling along the royal thoroughfare. Rossini felt quite at home at Tortoni's ice-cream shop, where the sweets reminded him of happy moments in Bologna or Naples. Donizetti spent ten years of his life strolling and observing the crowd on his beloved boulevard. Like Offenbach in the second half of the century, Esprit Auber made a second home of the avenue. His passion for *opéra comique* was equaled by his passion for women, and what better observatory existed than a sidewalk café? From there one could enjoy pretty, low-cut dresses from which peaked a thin trimming of pleated lawn and a delicate ruffle, one could have a perfect view of an elegant woman's lovely figure in a dress of fine cotton or damask. For all musicians, the boulevard incited reverie, facilitated contacts, and stimulated the composition of a few notes written at the corner of a table.

From the temporary domicile of a boulevard café to an artist's principal residence was only a few steps. Tamburini, Falcon, Malibran, and Chopin lived at one end of the boulevard on the Chaussée d'Antin and the Rue de Provence. Laure Cinti-Damoreau lived a little farther, on the Rue Saint-Georges. At the beginning of the Boulevard des Italiens on the corner of the Rue de la Michodière was the strange wooden structure of the Chinese Baths, a fake pagoda with a tower. It served as a public bath, a fashion boutique, and a beauty parlor. It was here, in a small, cluttered belvedere, that Bellini lived during his brief stay in Paris. A little farther away Giuditta Grisi and a couple of singers from the Leroux-Dabadie opera company lived. Just beyond, to the right, was the Rue de Grammont and the Hôtel de Manchester, where Donizetti occupied a tiny room and struggled to write music.

Next was the Salle Favart, at one time the venue of the Théâtre-Italien and where, after 1830, Rossini occupied a small apartment. On the Rue d'Amboise, to the right of this theater, the great singers Rubini and Ivanoff lived in the same building, only a few steps from rehearsals. At the intersection of the Boulevard des Italiens, the Boulevard Montmartre, and the Rue de Richelieu were the homes of Caroline Branchu, Giuditta Pasta, and Meyerbeer, who on his arrival in the capital had lodged at the Hôtel de Paris. Adolphe Nourrit lived on the Rue Rameau next the former Opéra, where the Duke of Berry had been assassinated.

Before 1830 Rossini, his compatriot Carafa, and, on the floor above, the composer Boieldieu all resided in a beautiful private hotel on the Boulevard Montmartre. Unfortunately the building is no longer standing. Rossini once complimented Boieldieu on his very beautiful auction scene in *La dame blanche*, affirming that he himself could not have done better, Boieldieu had this elegant response: "Maestro, the only time I am above you is when I have climbed the stairs to my room!"

One feels a certain sadness in recreating the fabulous concentration of artists around the Boulevard des Italiens. Today it seems impossible to come close to our inaccessible divas and modern composers, who speak more to the intellect than to the heart. Then, one could see Maria Malibran riding sidesaddle along the boulevard and greeting Meyerbeer before turning onto the Chaussée d'Antin, or watch the dashing Bellini leaving his Chinese Baths and plunging into a crowd of business men, society ladies, rakes, and young women of easy virtue to join Rossini at the Salle Favart. Only by imagining these scenes can today's opera lover understand the role of the boulevard. It was the backbone of nineteenth-century Paris, the symbol of an active and artistic capital that enriched itself through opera while exhibiting its success and joie de vivre on this wonderful, alluring thoroughfare.

Anna Sontag as Adina and Luigi Lablache as Dr. Dulcamara in *L'elisir d'amore*. Courtesy Paul Jackson.

CHAPTER 6

Life at the Théâtre-Italien

"Two rivals fought a duel over the last available ticket," related a journalist. "They are both dead: a third person got it!"

The satiric press of the Restoration and the July Monarchy abounded with similar anecdotes about the Théâtre-Italien. Though many were pure invention, fact often proved to be stranger than fiction. Nineteenth-century Parisians were utterly infatuated with the theater, which represented a state within a state and was the invincible bastion of Italian culture's most prestigious contributions: *opera buffa* and *opera seria.*

Nineteenth-century Parisians had the extraordinary luck to live in a city with an Opéra that presented ballets and dramatic or tragic spectacles in French, an Opéra-Comique similarly dedicated to a national repertoire, and an equally prestigious theater devoted to bel canto. From 1801 to 1882, the Théâtre-Italien enjoyed an exceptional repertoire, a peerless troupe of singers, a fanatical public, and the favorable opinion of most of the press. On top of this, the theater was in the neighborhood of the boulevard of the same name that, after 1830, became *the* place to be seen for sophisticated Parisians. The theater could not go wrong.

Every poet and novelist of the first half of the century devoted at least a few lines or pages to an evening at the Théâtre-Italien, to the pleasure of going there and hearing its divine music. Musset spoke for the entire young literary generation when he wrote, "Harmony! Harmony that comes to us from Italy and that came to Italy from heaven!" Similarly, when Balzac has Rastignac say, "My God! What luck to have a box at the Italiens," he was expressing the heartfelt thoughts of an elegant society as eager to make a glittering appearance at this prestigious place as to hear its music. Through crises and changes, through numerous triumphs and rare failures, the Théâtre-Italien remained an indispensable part of French life.

A Lively History

Castil-Blaze wrote a lengthy history of the Théâtre-Italien of Paris from 1548 to 1856 (the date of publication), dividing the study of this illustrious institution into ten distinct periods. The periods were very unequal, some of them extending over several decades, others lasting no longer than a few hours. The first half of the nineteenth century seemed to be a time of relative continuity for the Théâtre-Italien, which reopened on 1 May 1801 after nine years of closure and had only one brief gap in performances from 30 April 1818 to 20 March 1819 before closing definitively in 1882. The nineteenth century saw by far the longest period of performances in the Théâtre-Italien's history.

This apparent continuity in fact masked quite a different reality. Though the prestige of the theater grew, mishaps did occur. Venue and director changed frequently, financial crises were common, and the music suffered painfully stagnant periods. Indeed, it is difficult to describe its role in nineteenth-century musical Paris, because to speak of the Théâtre-Italien is to evoke an institution rather than a specific building. What is more, rarely was a theater so unsettled, with eight successive moves.

In 1801 Bonaparte agreed to the reopening of a Théâtre-Italien (it had been closed since 1792). He approved its establishment under the direction of the indefatigable Mlle Montansier in the Théâtre

Olympique on the Rue de la Victoire. The future emperor soon decided that he did not like this district, a network of sinister and dangerous alleys, and he ordered the transfer of the company (also known as the *Bouffes* and the *Italiens*) to the Salle Favart. It remained there for two years before moving to the Salle Louvois, where it remained until 1808.

In 1808 the Théâtre-Italien moved from the sacred district of operatic art into exile on the Left Bank, in the Théâtre de l'Odéon, before returning to the Salle Favart from 1815 to 1819. This is the location of today's Opéra-Comique, in the third venue bearing this name, the first two having burned down in 1838 and 1877. From 1819 to 1825, the period of its first great triumphs and of Paris's initial infatuation with it, the Théâtre-Italien resettled in the Salle Louvois on the minor street of the same name. Next to it, on the Rue de Richelieu, was the Opéra, and the two were connected by an underground tunnel that proved extremely useful as an emergency passage for firemen. It was during this epoch that the "Louvois audience" became an entity in itself (as did the audiences of Favart and Ventadour later), an assembly of Italian music enthusiasts who thrilled to the rhythm of Rossinian creations. With the growing success of the Italiens, audiences quickly outgrew the auditorium and felt cramped, despite the 1,500 seats. As soon as the company left, the Salle Louvois was demolished, and today a primary school occupies the site.

From the Salle Louvois, the Bouffes returned to a completely refurbished Salle Favart until the fire that ravaged it in 1838. The administrator Severini perished in this fire when he jumped out of a window to escape the flames. For three years the Théâtre-Italien was shunted between the Salle Ventadour and the Odéon, before returning definitively to the newly restored Salle Ventadour. The Ventadour proved to be its last and most luxurious residence, from 1841 to 1882.

Constructed on the king's orders in 1826, this venue stimulated the renaissance of a previously disreputable district. Little by little the public came to like the new situation, but the beautiful theater, which witnessed so many rich hours of Italian opera in Paris, is now an annex of the Bank of France. The Salle Ventadour had a traditional orchestra and parterre, three tiers of boxes (the front ones open, those behind raised and enclosed), and a fourth tier consisting of a single row of boxes. The decor was primarily a magnificent gold and white, the interior of the boxes was dark red, and fourteen statues supported a cupola painted by Domenico Ferri. Parisians and visitors alike valued the Ventadour above all other venues, and it remained the prime site for Italian repertoire until the Opéra's company took refuge in it between the fire at the Salle le Peletier in 1873 and the opening of the Palais Garnier.

&

The management of the Théâtre-Italien also changed frequently, and a remarkable number of directors and administrators passed through the theater due to crises, failures, rivalries, resignations, and returns. Over a period of fifty years, the theater experienced around twenty changes of management, sometimes having just one director, sometimes two co-directors or a director and an administrator, and sometimes three people sharing responsibilities. This was the situation from 1810 to 1812, when Duval was manager of the Théâtre de l'Impératrice, Gobert was responsible for theater, and Spontini was responsible for *opera seria e buffa.*

Of the twenty-two administrators of the Théâtre-Italien, a few stand out. The first, Mlle Montansier (whose real name was Marguerite Brunet) experienced wealth, failure, honors, and imprisonment during her long life. She made an easy transition from actress to director of the Nantes and Versailles theaters, before becoming administrator of the court theaters under the protection of Marie-Antoinette. The Revolution was less kind to her; her construction of the big theater on the Rue de la Loi (now the Rue de Richelieu) ruined her financially and led to a ten-month stay in prison. This allowed the Opéra to be established in place of her company of players. Despite all these vicissitudes, and at the age of seventy, not only did she

get married, but she obtained permission from Bonaparte to reopen
and manage the Opéra-Italien. Although she soon yielded her position to Picard, the future director of the Opéra, Montansier survived
the Empire and saw the beginning of the Restoration before she died
at the age of ninety, the same year that the Duke of Berry was assassinated in front of the theater she had built.

In addition to Picard, Angelica Catalani was one of the better
known successors to Montansier at the start of the Restoration. No
one fought as hard as she to win the privilege of directing the Théâtre-
Italien, but no one fulfilled the attendant duties so poorly. As a singer,
audiences adored her, but she could not bear anyone else to be equally
adored. She discouraged the other artists and left on tour more and
more frequently, jeopardizing the theater to such an extent that eventually it closed completely. Paër followed Catalani, and he endeav-
ored to repair the damage she had done. All Paris knew his title, composer to the king, and his operas *Agnese* and *I fuorusciti di Firenze*
(The Outlaws of Florence), which were frequently staged at the
Théâtre-Italien. The arrival of Rossini infuriated Paër, but he could
not prevent the "Swan of Pesaro" from taking over the management
of the Théâtre-Italien. Every lover of the fine arts, every sophisticate
and intellectual (including Stendhal) had dreamed of seeing the great
Rossini in command of the Bouffes. Sadly, as with Mme Catalani,
Rossini's leadership caused great disappointment, for he showed himself as poor a director as he was inspired a composer, and Parisians
learned that the composition of a cavatina or a duet does not always
prepare one for the meticulous and thoughtful work of theatrical administration. Only the joint leadership of Robert and Severini, from
1830 to 1838, proved itself equal to the fame acquired by the Théâtre-
Italien since the end of the Restoration.

During all these disparate administrations and despite the brilliant success of its repertoire, the Théâtre-Italien never prospered. The
maintenance of the company and the high costs of even the most insignificant production meant the Théâtre-Italien's finances were no
healthier than those of the other major theaters. In a half-century,

bankruptcy struck four times, in 1803, 1818, 1848, and 1852.

After the failure of Mme Catalani, the administration of the Bouffes passed briefly to the government, before coming under the control of the Opéra. The director of the Italiens thus came under the authority of the director of the Académie de Musique. In 1827 Émile Laurent attempted to operate the theater independently (as Véron had done for the Opéra at the beginning of the July Monarchy), but he failed to extricate it from its financial trouble. Until 1830 only the generosity of the royal family and their annual subsidy of 80,000 francs saved the theater from catastrophe.

To support the business and to increase box office receipts, Laurent opened the Italiens to an English theater troupe that included the celebrated actress Harriet Smithson. She soon captivated the Parisian public and went on to conquer the heart of Hector Berlioz. The Bouffes even took on the temporary title of *Théâtre Royal Italien et Anglais* (Italian-English Royal Theater). Soon after, a German opera company performed in the theater, introducing the French to masterpieces of the German repertoire, beginning with Beethoven's *Fidelio*. From 1830 the government of Louis-Philippe continued to support the Théâtre-Italien with an annual sum of 71,000 francs, which meant the theater received the fourth largest state subsidy after the Opéra (790,500 francs), the Théâtre-Français (206,000 francs), and the Opéra-Comique (186,000 francs).

The Company and Its Personnel

At the beginning of the century, a difficult task awaited Mlle Montasier and her successors. They had to form a company equal to the high ambitions of the new theater by attracting to Paris singers who were already renowned on Italian stages. The mission succeeded brilliantly and within a few years, despite bankruptcy in 1803 that threatened everything, the Théâtre-Italien could look with pride on a prestigious company patiently enlarged and improved by Picard, Duval, and Spontini. Well before the end of the Empire, the Théâtre-

Italien regularly attracted an audience that was passionate about Cimarosa and Paisiello's *buffo* repertoire, and popular singers such as Mme Barilli and Mme Festa were treated like royalty.

Spontini, during his direction of *opera buffa e seria* from 1810 to 1812, molded the company into one of Europe's finest. The press considered him solely responsible for its success, as can be seen in the following extract from the *Moniteur Universel* of April 1812.

We have Crivelli, Tacchinardi, Porto, Barilli, Mme Barilli, and Mme Festa. Nowhere else can one find such an assembly. But today, to be worthy of the capital and the magnificence of the government, it is necessary for a group of this nature to be unique in Europe. This is as it should be. However, M. Spontini, the skillful composer who has molded the group and directs it so zealously, does not yet consider its strengths to be sufficient, and so he has once again called upon Italy to contribute. He has spoken to those who are even more famous, he has made Parisian trophies shine in the eyes of the virtuosos of Rome and Naples, and they have been seduced by the glitter. The arrival of several new personalities has been announced, including Mme Sassi.

This company was responsible for the first great epoch of the Théâtre-Italien in the nineteenth century, and it attracted the public in great numbers. During the Empire, attending the theater was a sign of good taste, during the Restoration it became a necessity. This period saw the Italiens' second great epoch, thanks initially to Garcia, Bordogni, Zucchelli, Pellegrini, Mme Pasta, Mme Mainvielle-Fodor, and Laure Cinti, and later the remarkable Henriette Sontag and Maria Malibran. It can be said that the years 1830 to 1840 formed the apex of the Bouffes' history, with la Malibran, Giulia Grisi, and the great male trio of Rubini, Tamburini, and Lablache, followed immediately by Fanny Persiani and Malibran's sister Pauline Viardot.

In order not to be overwhelmed with a tedious list of illustrious names, let us merely observe that at all times Parisians could enjoy in their own city the flower of Italian opera. They saw and heard artists who had already experienced glory in their own country and who used France as an indispensable springboard to an eventual return home.

The Théâtre-Italien employed not only Italians. Stendhal reported that on 13 September 1823 he attended a performance of *The Marriage of Figaro* that included four French singers—rather too many, it seemed, for such an avowedly Italian work. A little later, almost half of the singers in the company were non-Italians. In addition to the Frenchwoman Cinti (whose real name was Cinthie-Monthaland), Mlles Sontag, Heinefetter, and Speck were German; Mme Malibran, Mlle Amigo, and Santini were Spanish; and Inchindi was Flemish. Later, the Russian Ivanoff, the Swedish Schultz, and the Austrian Ungher arrived. The term "miniature cosmos," used by Albert Soubiès in regard to the Théâtre-Italien, was quite appropriate. Despite their various nationalities, all the singers were experienced in the technique of bel canto and at ease in Italian. Indeed, the great advantage of this company was the vocal quality of its members, which endured from one season to the next, even from one decade to the next, and often contrasted with the lack of such continuity at the Opéra.

℘

Throughout the Théâtre-Italien's history, directors and administrators visited Italy to recruit artists judged indispensable to the Parisian stage. Singers signed frequently renewable contracts that allowed both them and the administration great liberty in deciding whether they would stay or leave. Generally, the company's membership changed frequently, and many performers considered themselves to be merely "passing through" Paris, though this did not prevent some of them from going back and forth between France and Italy for more than twenty years.

According to the tradition of Italian theaters, singers were classified not according to their voice (soprano, tenor, and so on), but according to the type of role they interpreted. This originated from the eighteenth-century system whereby the young lover was played by a tenor, the heroine by a prima donna, and the father or wise old man by a bass. The women were divided into the categories *prima donna* (either soprano or contralto), *seconda donna*, and *seconda buffa*, and the men into the categories *primo tenore*, *primo buffo cantante*, and *primo buffo comico*. Later, Rossini, Bellini, Donizetti, and Verdi expanded the role of the baritone, which until then had rarely been heard in traditional opera.

The prevalent cosmopolitan ambience of the Théâtre-Italien was unique among the stages of the capital, for it existed on all levels. Directors, singers, members of the orchestra, set designers, and stagehands came from France and Italy (the singers, of course, from other countries too), and it was not rare to hear the two languages intermingled backstage. This could have produced a friendly climate that would have bound together all the personalities in a unique franco-italian microcosm. Instead it fostered innumerable rivalries that poisoned the atmosphere, created cliques, and provoked, thanks to the temperamental Italians, stormy squabbles among prima donnas or between musicians and directors. The task of reconciling the citizens of this world was not easy. Some, such as Rossini, survived by bowing their heads and ignoring the most outrageous threats. Others never got used to it. The despondent violinist Viotti, who co-directed the theater with Paër between 1819 and 1824, confessed, "I am weary, obsessed, and disgusted by the harassment these ladies subject me to. My patience is at an end."[1] Health and patience were vital in confronting the countless tantrums and whims of spirited artists (most of them from the south) who refused certain roles, demanded others, feigned illnesses if they did not get what they wanted, and broke regulations, all in the certain knowledge that they were indispensable to both administration and dilettanti.

℘

The Théâtre-Italien's artistic staff was much smaller than those of the other opera houses. The theater rarely employed more than seven or eight leads (the stars of the moment) and a few singers for minor roles. Choruses in Italian operas were much less developed than solos and never required more than thirty choristers, whereas the Opéra and Opéra-Comique required about fifty. Reports from the period describe Théâtre-Italien choruses known for "shouted" singing, poor ensemble work, and lack of vocal agility in Rossini's ubiquitous passages of rapid repeated notes.

The Théâtre-Italien's orchestra, with about forty players, was about half the size of the Opéra's. A comparison of the orchestral scores of *Il barbiere* or even *Norma* with that of *Robert le diable* illustrates why this was so. The press and memoirs of the time contain little information on the choruses and orchestra of the Bouffes, which is not surprising since the essential core of Italian opera resides in the splendor of the voice and the technical prowess of the diva or leading tenor. Moreover, commentaries presented quite different pictures depending on whether or not the writer or newspaper supported the Théâtre-Italien and its music. *Le Courrier des Spectacles* had nothing but praise, and regarded the Italiens' orchestra as the envy of theaters in Rome and Naples. On the other hand, Stendhal railed against trumpets that "violated the ears," and an orchestra incapable of nuance or sensitivity, which played *sotto voce* passages "at full strength," and failed to understand that it overpowered the deep, soft voice of a contralto. Stendhal, it should be understood, had nothing but praise for Italian performances in Italy and scorn for those in Paris.

The Repertoire and Stage Direction

From its reestablishment in 1801 until 1811, the Théâtre-Italien traditionally performed a repertoire of only light and popular *opera buffa*, in the style of Pergolesi's 1733 opera *La serva padrona* (The Maid as Mistress), which represented the bourgeois though impudent soubrettes and sly young lovers locking horns with crotchety old guardians. Although dramatic repertoire in the form of *opera seria* held an important place in the history of Italian music, it was reserved for the court, and thus was seen only on the sovereign's private stage. Thus, as we have seen, Napoleon attended *opera seria* performances by the castrato Crescentini at the Théâtre de la Cour.

For those who did not have access to such performances, Cimarosa was the most popular composer in Paris at the beginning of century, and his *Matrimonio segreto* (The Secret Marriage) became a standard. Paisiello, Mayr, and Paër came next. During the development of the Théâtre-Italien's repertoire during the Empire, a lavish premiere took place on 30 January 1811 when Spontini, then the director of the Théâtre-Italien at the Odéon, presented Paris with its first *opera seria* on a public stage since 1662. The opera was Paisiello's *Pirro* (Pyrrhus), a work of baroque inspiration and immense proportions, produced in Naples in 1787, and possessing an overture and a finale, two rare elements at that time.

Spontini had a major role in this great premiere. Firstly, as director of the Italiens, he made the choice of *Pirro*, a tragic work full of grace, feeling, and beauty. Secondly, he rewrote the opera's recitatives to better suit the taste of French audiences in 1811 (his rewriting was remarkably gentle compared to the usual sabotage inflicted on foreign operas). Finally, Spontini himself directed this first *opera seria*, wishing to render homage to Paisiello and to the operatic genre that was so popular in his native country.

No effort was spared to make the opera as perfect as possible while conserving its simple and unpretentious character. Without resorting to exaggerated pomp or dazzling stage effects, the production celebrated voice and music. The choruses were sublime, not raucous, and the singers sang with a smoothness and mellowness that was too rare at the Académie Impériale de Musique. Spontini brought the admirable tenor Gaetano Crivelli from Italy specially for this production. This Parisian debut in the role of the ancient hero allowed him to demonstrate the great Italian tradition of *opera seria*. Paris was conquered and the press praised the successful experiment.

Spontini tried to repeat his success by offering the complete Italian version of Mozart's *Don Giovanni*, but French audiences had not advanced enough beyond the potpourri operas of the beginning of the century. Apart from a few ardent Mozart supporters, Italian opera lovers found nothing in it to enjoy, and the singers themselves were extremely uneasy in roles they found impossible to interpret. The members of the audience liked only the lighter roles of Zerlina and Masetto; the rest bored them immensely. The second performance was better than the premiere, but the auditorium was half empty and someone remarked that the performance would have been perfect if the theater had been completely deserted. The French continued to think of Mozart as a "rather good composer," but the music was considered too serious and the singing too difficult and generally not worth the trouble. Spontini, who revered Mozart above every other composer, took the blow badly, but it was evident that audiences had not matured sufficiently to appreciate his music. Parisians still preferred insubstantial scenes of the East over the subtleties of Mozart.

Years of stagnation followed under Angelica Catalani's leadership. Second-rate operas and uninspired revivals of previous successes contributed to the theater's ultimate closure. The company resorted to a subterfuge common to theaters in crisis: remounting the same opera with different titles until one of the productions achieved success. Thus *La capricciosa pentita* (Capricious Regret) became *L'orgoglio avvilito* (Disgraceful Pride), and finally *La sposa stravagante* (The Extravagant Spouse). In its last incarnation it enjoyed a triumph based on the aria "Suoni la tromba" (Sound the Trumpet), in which Mme Catalani was able to exhibit her famous vocal agility.

The arrival of Rossini's operas (including *L'italiana in Algeri* in 1817), followed by the arrival of the maestro himself had the effect of a whipcrack on the somnolent Théâtre-Italien. From this time on the name of Rossini would be tied to the theater, in that his operas would form the basis of its repertoire. His detractors did not hesitate to attack the excessive attention paid to the "Swan of Pesaro" and the lack of variety at the theater. In 1823, *Le Courrier des Spectacles* made no attempt to hide its annoyance:

> The repertoire of this theater is so static that the public—which, nonetheless, is happy to attend—knows it by heart. We have

written so many articles on what is presented and on the actors and actresses who perform there, that our subscribers already know by heart what we are going to tell them—provided Mlle Demeri does not do anything unexpected.[2]

Rossini's light and serious operas were produced one after the other before the appearance of operas by Bellini and Donizetti after 1830 expanded the repertoire somewhat. Despite the emergence of these two new talents, Rossini retained primary importance. In 1822, works by Rossini filled 119 out of 154 evenings at the Théâtre-Italien and represented 8 of the 16 operas in the repertoire. In 1825, they filled 121 out of 174 evenings and represented 10 of the 20 operas. Much later, in 1839, when Bellini and Donizetti had become the new heroes of the Boulevard, 33 evenings were nonetheless devoted to Rossini, while 29 and 17 were devoted to Donizetti and Bellini respectively. The three of them completely dominated the Italian repertoire in Paris, and were legends in their own lifetimes.

In addition to these three, other Italian composers arrived in France with new works for the repertoire. Salieri, Fioravanti, Zingarelli, Vaccai, and Portogallo achieved some success, Gemelli and Paisiello featured occasionally, and Verdi arrived in 1845 and achieved great success with *Nabucco*. Also performed but far less popular were works by German composers (Gluck, Mozart, Beethoven, and Meyerbeer) sung in Italian, by Spanish composers (Garcia and Martin y Soler), and by the Maltese composer Isouard, known as Nicolo.

Productions at the Théâtre-Italien were not known for their adherence to the original score. Performing an opera in its entirety while scrupulously respecting the score interested neither artists nor audience. Just as Rossini would reuse the same overture in two or three operas, singers would interchange arias to suit their range, embellish melodies with interminable improvisation, or insert pieces by other composers, all in an effort to show off their technical prowess. In the eighteenth century the practice had begun (particularly among divas and castratos) of developing a repertoire of pieces called "trunk arias" (*aria di baule*) and incorporating them into opera. Rossini tried in vain to curb this tradition, especially after the excesses of the castrato Velluti completely altered the role of Aureliano in his *Palmira*. After 1813 he wrote all the ornaments for his arias, but many singers continued to follow their own inclinations. Some Parisian journalists also reacted violently to the misrepresentation of scores by these vocal excesses, though audiences were generally not critical.

The *pasticcio*, that amalgam of pieces by one or several composers, remained fashionable. We have already seen how Zingarelli's *Romeo e Giulietta* was manipulated and altered ten years after its triumph at the Théâtre de la Cour with the castrato Crescentini. Rossini quickly became a favorite target, and in 1826 Pacini incorporated various arias from different Rossini operas to form a *pasticcio* called *Ivanhoe*. In 1848 the potpourri *Robert Bruce* (discussed in a previous chapter) was concocted.

Because the voice formed the essential, even the only attraction of Italian operas, other components suffered. The libretto had a very low status for artists and audience of the Bouffes, since Italian tradition required that music was of primary importance in an opera and the libretto was only a support and never the first thing to be judged. Rossini frequently wrote Act 1 of one of his masterpieces without any idea of how he was going to continue in Act 2. This lack of interest may be seen as a refreshing contrast to the obsession of journalists and musicologists of judging an opera at the Opéra or Opéra-Comique on the strength of its libretto before even taking the music into consideration. These Cartesian judgments could cause a work to fail despite excellent music. Conversely, while the music performed at the Italiens was the basis of its repertoire, this did not prevent critics from deploring the mediocrity and lack of originality of its librettos. The two authors of *L'histoire critique des théâtres de Paris* (Critical History of the Theaters of Paris) observed, "If Italian opera were considered only with respect to its librettos, this theater would not merit a place in our work."[3]

Another weak point in the Italian repertoire was staging, and theatricality was often neglected. As already noted, audiences in Naples were indifferent to the impassioned acting of the French tenor Nourrit, since on that side of the Alps the voice supported a singer's stage presence. The audience wandered in and out of the auditorium, chatted, listened only long enough to go into raptures over the great aria of the castrato or prima donna, and then continued as before. A sublime voice provided immediate gratification, and the audience asked for nothing more. It was of little importance to eighteenth-century audiences that the castrato blew his nose, greeted his friends, or devoured a plate of spaghetti in the middle of a performance. Italian audiences and singers had little interest in dramatic credibility.

This state of affairs was untenable in France, and the audiences of the Louvois and the Ventadour rejected a good many of the idiosyncrasies manifested on Italian stages. That said, audiences also knew that they could find the purity of singing and dazzling vocal technique that they wanted at the Théâtre-Italien and not on other French stages. All this disposed audiences to adopt a certain number of conventions and to dismiss as unimportant weak staging, scenery, and costumes. This attitude echoed the popular maxim, "The bottle doesn't matter, as long as what's in it gets you drunk."

The complicity between audiences and artists at the Italiens greatly amused the partisans of French opera. It was entertaining to watch Henriette Sontag as Desdemona; though she fell to the ground when she was murdered, she got up in order to die more comfortably on a bed. The week Donizetti presented *Don Sébastien de Portugal* at the Opéra and *Maria de Rohan* at the Théâtre-Italien, it could be said that the first was acted more than it was sung, while the second was sung more than it was acted.

Rudimentary lighting did not aid the verisimilitude of an opera, and audiences at performances of *Sémiramis* had the funny spectacle of seeing the characters spend fifteen minutes milling around pretending to look for each other in the dark while the lights blazed. As for the costumes and props, their elegance and ostentation were often in contrast with the action, and improbability abounded. Why adorn Mme Pasta, who played the valorous Tancrède returning from a perilous journey, with a brilliant feather, a golden lance, an azure shield, a purple shoulder-belt, and a tunic trimmed in silver? Why did Laure Cinti in *L'italiana in Algeri* appear in a ball gown and satin slippers with an extravagant feather, having supposedly just left the hold of a ship where she had been imprisoned by pirates? Bordogni's medieval costume as Juliette's father consisted of a dressing gown trimmed in green velvet. In many cases the entrenched baroque tradition of gleaming costumes and multicolored feathers prevailed, indeed, it fulfilled the audiences' fantasies. Théophile Gautier cursed these anachronisms and described "ridiculously dressed" supernumeraries, actors "wearing foolish hats like gilded or painted sponge cakes," and a Babylonian temple like a "huge apple charlotte decorated with marzipan."[4]

Parisians for and against Rossini

If today's technology had existed in 1820, Rossini would surely have become a "media phenomenon." It is difficult to truly appreciate the man's popularity—well before his arrival in Paris he was anticipated like the Messiah and aroused an increasingly fanatical enthusiasm.

Italians had already spent several years humming "Di tanti palpiti" from *Tancredi* and the "Calumny" aria from *Il barbiere* by the time Parisians discovered the masterpieces of the maestro in 1818. From then on, enthusiasm and fascination gradually increased and his arrival and first weeks in Paris (at the end of 1823 and beginning of 1824) were endlessly described in the newspapers. He was fêted like a head of state and could be seen at celebrations and gala dinners. He appeared at a reception at the residence of Mlle Mars (of the Comédie-Française) in the company of the actor Talma, and at a reception held by Countess Merlin for the finest of Parisian and foreign aristocracy.

The crowning point of these festivities and the height of Rossini's glory was the evening of the performance of *Il barbiere di Siviglia* at a benefit for Garcia in the presence of the composer. Parisians practically went to war to obtain tickets, and the victors brought the house down with their cheering. The highlight of the evening itself came after the performance when Rossini was guest of honor at a dinner for 150 at the restaurant *Le veau qui tète*, on the Place du Châtelet. Seated between Mlle Mars and Mme Pasta, he listened with his customary good nature to speeches and toasts and to arias from his own operas. Scribe and Mazières celebrated the event by writing a vaudeville entitled *Rossini à Paris; ou, Le grand dîner* (Rossini in Paris; or, The Big Dinner). The popular song "Rossini, Rossini, pourquoi n'es-tu pas ici?" (Rossini, Rossini, Why Aren't You Here?) sung to a cancan rhythm soon played to great success at the Théâtre du Gymnase.

From then on, the musical life of Paris followed Rossini's rhythm and honored the great man. One evening his presence at a performance so inspired the singers that a collective delirium spread through the auditorium and into the adjacent streets and bars. Everywhere people toasted the composer's health, even kitchen boys, who were overheard crying "Long live Rossini!" After he attended a rehearsal at the Opéra, journalists hailed him as a "citizen monarch" and an "autocrat without affectation or formality" and maintained that more than one artist would be happy "to kiss the hem of his clothes." On 9 October 1826, following the triumph of *Le siège de Corinthe*, the Opéra orchestra, directed by Habeneck, serenaded Rossini outside his window.

In the Paris of this epoch, Rossini was seen not only as a superlative composer but as the savior of the moribund repertoires of the Théâtre-Italien and the Opéra. The Théâtre-Italien, only too happy to extricate itself from insolvency, scheduled almost all Rossini's masterpieces. The Opéra, suffering terrible stagnation during the period before *La muette* and *Guillaume Tell*, adapted the maestro's Italian works for the French stage. Thus *Maometto II* and *Mosè in Egitto* became *Le siège de Corinthe* and *Moïse en Egypte*. At the same time as he revitalized the capital's great stages, Rossini became a cult figure. Fans loved to see him on the street or at Tortoni's on the Boulevard des Italiens, they repeated his witticisms and discussed him in the great salons, where his fee for musical participation at concerts was astronomical. Talking about Rossini was like talking about the weather, an ideal topic of conversation about which everyone had something to say, and which could help one out of difficulty if conversation was floundering.

Works by Rossini immediately became legendary, and he constantly figured in literature, often in the context of the current euphoria at the Théâtre-Italien. Balzac, among others, celebrated the new myth and had a character say to Princess de Varèse about the prayer in *Moïse*,

> Only an Italian could write this magnificent plea by the victims of a vengeful god, this fertile, inexhaustible, Dantesque theme. Handel, Bach, and even you, Beethoven, get down on your knees, you former German masters! Here is the ruler of the arts, here is triumphant Italy!

What does it matter that this is the exaggerated enthusiasm of a fictional character when it perfectly reflects the Italomania to which the French succumbed so quickly?

During the Restoration Rossini exercised his influence on the musical life of Paris publicly, first as director of the Théâtre-Italien, then as inspector general of singing in the royal institutes of music. This weighty title assured him both the complete protection of the sovereign and a "royal" salary. He used his influence to become the intimate adviser to Lubbert, the Opéra's director, and wielded great power in the decisions taken by this theater. The revolution of 1830 and the new regime ended the extravagant salaries paid by the Bourbons, and Rossini took on the role of martyr. The new "pauper" installed himself in a modest attic lodging in the Salle Favart, where the director Robert, the administrator Severini, the inspector Gimel, the cashier Declos, and the two concierges Perray and Leconte also lived.

Taking this pauper's apartment was part of a scheme to protest his fate at the hands of Louis-Philippe, and he in fact enjoyed large incomes from England, his wife's dowry, royalties on performances and published scores, and business enterprises with the Rothschilds and Aguados, important families in nouveau riche society. Despite his poor surroundings, Rossini continued to receive his distinguished guests (including Emperor Don Pedro of Brazil), and served as éminence grise for Robert and Severini, helping them establish themselves and gladly sharing advice and wisdom.

ço

Like any public figure, Rossini could not please everybody, and he caused intense disagreements between his admirers and his critics. The division of the French public can be seen as the inevitable price of success. As the figurehead of modern Italian music, Rossini suffered the wrath of French nationalists (composers, writers, and audiences) who saw him as an enemy, a disloyal competitor of the great classicist Gluck and of Gluck's successors. Did he not take the bread from the mouths of French composers? Everything about him was criticized: his music was facile and repetitive, relying too heavily on crescendos and vocal artifices; the orchestration was crude; and the action was inexpressive. Many of these attacks were unfounded and due largely to jealousy, and they were accompanied by mocking nicknames such as Monsieur Crescendo or Signor Vaccarmini (Signor Hubbub).

These reproaches were compounded by Rossini's disappointing performance as head of the Théâtre-Italien. Though he received an annual honorarium of 20,000 francs, free accommodation, and fees of 10,000 francs per two-act opera and 5,000 francs per one-act opera composed for the Parisian stage, Rossini was a very unsatisfactory director—and the entire capital knew it. Rossini had accepted the post because he was carried away by the events and enthusiasm of the public, rather than because he wanted it. Composing *Il barbiere* in fewer than twenty days or *Semiramide* in five weeks required less effort and worry than carrying out his daily duties as director of music and stage. The maestro had retained the services of Paër and kept him at his side, but Rossini had little enthusiasm for the job and gladly gave up his responsibilities at the end of two years. He achieved little during his tenure, and the repertoire was based largely on his own works. Few new works were performed, with just one minor masterpiece, *Il viaggio a Reims*, a topical opera written for Charles X's coronation. Rossini did little to encourage new talent, and he had no interest in the theater's financial affairs.

The reigns of Louis XVIII and Charles X were marked by the division of Parisian music lovers into two camps. The larger faction displayed fanatical devotion to their heroes, the smaller one used the press to mock and ridicule the same personalities. Before 1830, the newspaper *Le Corsaire* acted as one of the anti-Rossini mouthpieces, and its malicious diatribes entertained more than one salon during evening gatherings. The following is a description of its (invented) *Orders of the Rossinists*, a trophy to be delivered to the "Swan of Pesaro."

> This four-foot-high trophy would be composed of trombones, horns, clarinets, cymbals, fifes, and Chinese hats. At the top, Rossini's bust, one hand holding a hundred trumpets and the other holding Cinderella's slipper, Othello's turban, Figaro's razor, Moses' staff, and Ninette's spoon and fork. At the base, Mozart would be on his back under the scrutiny of this giant, sprawling and struggling under a bass drum. Cimarosa would be holding onto him by the legs, and a magpie would be snatching his wig off, or perhaps putting his eye out if it is proved that in fact Mozart never wore a wig.[5]

Rossini's self-satisfaction, his exorbitant income, and the noise and showiness of his orchestration and perceived overuse of percussion, brass, and high instruments were fodder for constant criticism and mockery. Here are some random examples of the satiric press's most cutting remarks:

From now on, M. Rossini will only compose for twenty francs per note. Meanwhile, our young musicians have to run around after any work they can get. How interesting!

M. Rossini is dreadfully sorry that the bells at the Samaritan have been destroyed. They had been a rival for him to battle against.

It is probably because we don't want to sing that M. Rossini was named inspector of singing in France. M. Rossini is so fond of the highest instruments that he could introduce the whistle to his orchestra. He prefers, however, to wait for audiences to learn this specialty.

Of all the characters put on the stage by Molière, M. Rossini likes *Le bourgeois gentilhomme* best. As we know, Molière's hero loves the marine trumpet.

M. Rossini was recently seen at a masked ball as Orpheus. Such Italian modesty.

Let us note that the polemic about Rossini abated during the July Monarchy when Donizetti and Bellini arrived in Paris and became the new idols of Paris. Both brought their Italian triumphs to Paris: Donizetti brought *Anna Bolena* (Parisian premiere, 1831) and *Lucia di Lammermoor* (1837); and Bellini brought *La sonnambula* (The Sleepwalker) (1831), *Il pirata* (The Pirate) (1832), *La straniera* (The Stranger) (1832), *I Capuleti* (1833), and *Norma* and *I puritani* (1835).

Characteristics and Customs of Théâtre-Italien Audiences

An audience at the Bouffes was a fascinating microcosm of Parisian society engrossed in the repertoire and traditions of the theater. Naturally, the patrons of the Théâtre-Italien also frequented the

Opéra and Opéra-Comique from time to time, in order to keep abreast of their principal works. However, a deep-rooted attachment to bel canto and the appeal of belonging to an elite meant that they felt completely at home only under the chandeliers of the Louvois, Favart, or Ventadour.

Many studies have too hastily linked the Opéra to the middle classes and the Théâtre-Italien to the nobility. The separation was far from being so clear cut, especially during the period before 1830 when all the prestigious venues cultivated an undeniably aristocratic veneer. It was during the July Monarchy that a distinction formed between the two social classes, due to the enormous impact on the middle classes of the *grands opéras* of Meyerbeer and Halévy. Bankers and businessmen certainly occupied the best boxes at the Théâtre-Italien, but they tended to be enthusiastic about the thrilling effects of a spectacular mise-en-scène rather than knowledgeable about the art of bel canto.

This love for Italian music and beautiful, pure singing was accompanied by a tendency to follow the crowd. Parisians were unquestionably sheeplike and would rush to support popular causes. Their judgment was often based on the size of the crowd that attended a performance, and nothing was more thrilling than to obtain tickets for a performance that sold out a week in advance. All activities were subject to the desire to demonstrate that one belonged to the crowd. The ice-cream maker Tortoni, for example, categorically refused to increase the number of his sidewalk tables on the Boulevard des Italiens because he knew full well that fewer, crowded tables attracted customers better than more, potentially empty ones.

The Théâtre-Italien was immensely popular during the great era of Rossini, Bellini, and Donizetti. During the Empire, it was true anybody who was somebody would attend every work by Cimarosa, but this earlier code of conformity was nothing compared to the prestige of belonging to the 1,500 elite spectators at the premiere of *Otello* or *Anna Bolena*.

One of the forces behind the huge attraction to the Théâtre-

Italien of the inhabitants of Saint-Germain or the lords and ladies of English high society was that the theater purported to be a place of refinement and beauty, from the choice of its carpets and fabrics to the luxury of its corridors and staircases. The Salle Favart, for example, resembled an opulent salon where the nobility gathered for an evening of opera. The aristocracy loved to tread upon the soft carpet of the lobby and slowly ascend the two grand staircases leading to the box seats. An evening at the Bouffes was at once a reunion of intimate friends, a tasteful and elegant social event, and, for some, the ritual worship of Italian opera.

The presence of the aristocracy at the Théâtre-Italien was also guaranteed because well-born young ladies could safely attend. It was felt that the love scenes, sung as they were in a foreign language, presented infinitely less danger than those, in French, of the Opéra. The number of elegant young people who filled this theater was another attraction.

Naturally, fashion remained a major preoccupation. Before 1830 audiences of the Opéra and the Théâtre-Italien competed in the search for elegance; after 1830 it became necessary to prove that while the Théâtre-Italien remained a place of good taste and distinction, the Opéra now reflected the vulgarities of common society. An insane chic reigned at the Bouffes that put Italy and honor above everything. Taffeta dresses from Florence or Naples abounded, preferably of yellow fabric with square or diamond patterns. At every performance one saw Italian straw hats with bouquets of wildflowers tied with ribbons or with birds of paradise, one on the right, the other on the left, tails crossing each other in an arc. The architects of the Ventadour displayed mischievous attention to detail, and the copper border of the first balcony had a perforated motif to allow young ladies' pretty feet to be seen (leading, naturally, to even greater affectation in their footwear).

The distribution of spectators through the auditorium adhered to firmly established customs. Most habitués sat in the orchestra, and they represented a group of people who had subscribed for many years and who retained their strategic places from one venue to the next. They reminisced fondly about the most beautiful memories of the preceding seasons at the Odéon, Louvois, or Favart. The orchestra was also the territory of journalists, the suzerains of the press who wielded such influence over singers' careers.

The young, enthusiastic aficionados whose bank accounts could not keep up with their love of bel canto had to be satisfied with benches at the back of the auditorium. They would jump up from their seats twenty times in an evening to acclaim their favorite diva. The best seats were those of the first balcony boxes. The boxes on the left and in the center formed the ultimate refuge for high aristocracy and the *lions de la ménagerie fashionable*, who were recognizable by their curled forelocks and pince-nez glasses. To the right were the young dilettanti of the best Parisian society. The occupants of these boxes in the first and second balconies considered their seats to be an inherited right, and they guarded them jealously.

The behavior of the audiences at this Parisian theater constantly surprised Italians visiting Paris. Comportment was quite different from that in the theaters of Rome, Naples, or Venice, mainly because French audiences listened to the whole opera from the first to the last note. It was as if they aimed to get complete value for money by not missing a single note, and only the intermission allowed a relaxation of mind and ear. Italian audiences never achieved such concentration, and they wandered in and out of the auditorium, socialized, and consumed ices during the performance. A few sublime arias (the reason for their presence at the theater that evening) caused them to take their places. They would listen delightedly, in an almost religious silence, to the castrato's thrilling solo or the prima donna's *aria di furia*, before relaxing once again. Consequently, Italian audiences were less demanding that French ones, and a few bold pieces were enough to guarantee an evening's success. To them the theater was a place for festive entertainment, not a sanctuary.

Since the French were more demanding and listened to every note, they were not satisfied with a few beautiful pieces diluted by secondary arias and overlong recitatives. They required a work that was consistently entertaining, otherwise their enthusiasm wilted and lassitude prevailed. (Of course, audiences at the Théâtre-Italien consisted not only of opera fanatics but also of the type of spectator who could not always suppress a yawn during rather long scenes.)

The resultant atmosphere was very different from the one in Italy. French audiences were infinitely more serious and were better behaved (though they were still capable of noisy enthusiasm after certain great moments). Moreover, Figaro's jokes and Isabella's trickery left the audience largely unmoved, for the simple reason that they understood nothing of what they heard. This represented the great paradox of the Théâtre-Italien; it was the capital's most elite address, yet offered singing in a language incomprehensible to 90 percent of the audience. Certainly, Parisians loved Italian and considered that its unutterable charm and musicality made it the language par excellence of opera. Everyone agreed that *amore* was ten times more sensual than *amour, gioia* ten times more radiant than *joie, addio* a thousand times more moving than *adieu.* Although members of the audience received a program summarizing the content of each scene in three or four lines, and although they regarded the libretto as unimportant compared with the physical pleasure that the music afforded them, they could not follow the singers' words. For this reason many Italian singers felt themselves less invigorated by Parisian audiences, who did not catch their jokes, than by Italian audiences, who would be caught up in laughter or sadness.

To remedy these linguistic shortcomings, classified advertisements announcing private lessons in Rossini's language flourished in the Restoration and July Monarchy press. One could learn, if not to speak Italian fluently, at least to know a few indispensable phrases and to be able to grasp the key moments of an opera, and thus to be fashionable! The following advertisements were typical:

> For some time the study of the Italian language has become so widespread among us that the most insignificant concert has its

dilettanti, and a pretty woman who spends only a little time in society would blush if she could not say *bello, bellissimo* when hearing a *cavatina del gran maestro.* If anyone has still not been initiated into the language *degli amori e delle grazie,* write to M. Raynaud, Rue Gaillon, No. 14, near the Boulevard des Italiens.[6]

And:

The richness of Italian, one of the most beautiful and unquestionably the most harmonious of modern languages, has always assured the interest of those who enjoy literature and the fine arts, especially ladies. This young teacher (M. Marini) has been able to transform normally tedious study into endless amusement through the analytico-natural method.[7]

The audiences of the Théâtre-Italien were generous with their *bello*s and *brava*s in the course of an evening. If they did not always grasp the humor of a situation, they were extremely warm when rewarding the singer or composer taking a bow at the end of a performance. Delirious ovations greeted the heroes and heroines of the day, and flowers rained down from all sides of the theater. The spectators shouted, demanded further curtain calls, and waved their handkerchiefs, conscious that they were privileged to be in the presence of Maria Malibran and Giulia Grisi, Giovanni Rubini and Luigi Lablache. Many aristocrats recorded in their memoirs that it was the only theater where people of their milieu could allow themselves noisy approval and a kind of aristocratic vulgarity.

The end of an evening at the Théâtre-Italien represented for some "the truest picture of an aristocratic world," for others a loathsome meeting place for "Rossinians." The scene after a performance was as colorful as the performance itself, for the audience lingered while leaving the theater in a barely concealed desire to see and be seen. Some engaged in an enthusiastic discussion of Mme Pisaroni's *cabaletta* or Mlle Sontag's ballad, others commented with no less knowledge and with equally minute detail on M. de L——'s conspicuous absence or Countess C——'s extravagant costume. In the constant congestion of the Théâtre-Italien there was always time to gossip. The streets around the theater invariably became backed up, and it was no small matter to recover one's carriage and leave the district. At the beginning of the evening it was not rare to wait half an hour in one's carriage before reaching the steps of the theater, and it took just as long to escape the crowds and clear a passage through the dark alleys at the end of the evening.

The Dilettanti

Although caricatured by many nineteenth-century novelists, the dilettanti nevertheless marked the beginning of romanticism through their amusing, excessive, yet rather touching appearance. Just as popular singers today have their fans, and great opera singers are trailed by an unquestioning entourage of devotees who follow them from festival to festival, buy all their recordings, and send fan mail, Italian singers in nineteenth-century Paris had their dilettanti. Some were connoisseurs and people of taste, others were snobs and fanatics, but whatever their character, they were unlikely to go unnoticed.

The dilettanti came mainly from well-to-do society and generally were young and fashionable. They belonged to the category of people who did not need to earn a living and who could devote themselves, with complete peace of mind, to the pleasures of the spirit. The Théâtre-Italien became their whole life, the air that they breathed. Not only did they occupy the theater's boxes at least once a week (though never on Monday, when it was overrun by the hoi poloi), but they never missed afternoon rehearsals. They shared Heinrich Heine's belief that the world beyond this gilded musical showcase was a "musical Sahara." They despised *opéra comique*, considering it to be an inferior genre reserved for more modest citizens, and they had no respect for the Opéra, where, according to them, the singers shouted and the orchestra produced a deafening racket.

An evening at the Bouffes was so much a part of their life that apoplexy threatened if a white strip across a poster announced a cancellation, or if the director came on at the beginning of a performance to announce the replacement of an ailing singer. For them, the prestige of appearing at the Théâtre-Italien was a secondary reason for attending, since they wished primarily to affirm their exclusive devotion to Italian music and especially to Rossini and his successors. To the dilettanti the Théâtre-Italien presented the best in modern music, the music of young people and of the future, and they considered it far removed from the dusty work of Rameau, Gluck, or Grétry that played at the Académie de Musique. To admire Rossini, Bellini, and Donizetti was an act of intelligence and good taste intended to prove to the French that this was the music of tomorrow; vibrant, sensitive music that reached the heart through sublime voices with faultless tone and technique.

The dilettanti knew no half measures in their enthusiasm, had a predilection for categorical judgments, and an intolerance for contradiction. A married couple with differing opinions about Italian music were destined for divorce. This intransigent attitude at the theater amused their critics hugely. Society ladies and financial bigwigs entered their boxes at the very last moment and with a maximum of noise (in order to be better noticed), but the dilettanti took their places well before the curtain was raised. They could then inhale the theater's atmosphere and concentrate on the event to come, even if it was their twenty-seventh visit to the same opera. Anyone who dared to sneeze too energetically or close the lid of a snuffbox too loudly earned their condemnation.

A somewhat foreboding demeanor masked a genuine knowledge of opera, and the dilettanti knew every note and nuance of certain operas. If they honored Rossini's *Semiramide* above all others, it was partly because they could compare it with three or four other *Sémiramis* by different composers. During the performance every subtlety, vocal inflection, and emotion produced little cries of admiration, groans of pleasure, and assorted looks of rapture that seemed to ask "Did you hear that? Have you ever heard a more divine voice than that?" An aria or duet would scarcely be finished before these fanatics would bring the house down with *bellissimo*s or *bravo*s and demands for an encore. Nothing offended them more than to hear someone cry *bravo* instead of *brava* for a prima donna. Above all they feared an invasion of the barbarians of the Opéra and Opéra-Comique, who were unaware of the good linguistic manners that reigned among the civilized regulars of the Théâtre-Italien.

At the end of the performance these faithful admirers were the last to leave after sustained applause and after throwing bouquets purchased on the steps of the theater on their way in. Little wonder that Parisians enjoyed joking that the Théâtre-Italien had no need for a *claque*, since it already possessed a *clique* of supporters who were as enthusiastic at the umpteenth performance of a work as they had been at the premiere.

Bel Canto in the 1830 Salon

The fashionable eighteenth-century literary and artistic salons survived the Revolution and continued to attract the French and foreign intellectual elite of the beginning of the nineteenth century. The high society of the Directory and the Empire frequented the salons of Mme Récamier and the Duchess d'Abrantès, that of the Restoration the salons of the Countess Merlin and the Duchess of Duras (who gave her name to a variety of dresses, shawls, and hats), and that of the July Monarchy the salons of Princess Belgiojoso (for Italian expatriots), Delphine Gay, and the Countess d'Agoult.

The refined and selective atmosphere of the aristocratic salons of the Restoration quickly diminished after 1830 with the rise of the middle classes and the opening of salons to the very different social spheres of artists and writers. Around this time the inhabitants of the suburb of Saint-Germain began to retire behind their own closed doors and were said, laughingly, to be sulking. The 1848 revolution carried a still more decisive blow to the salons by discrediting them completely and brushing aside this former elegant life.

Until 1830 the salons epitomized an idle society with no concept of work that spent six months of the year in Paris and the other six in the country and had no interests beyond excelling at political, literary, or artistic conversation in the glittering surroundings of a private mansion.

As one can imagine, opera held a choice place in the long winter soirées when counts and duchesses received their friends "at eight o'clock, after dinner," and kept them sometimes until dawn. Above all, aristocratic society was obsessed by Italian opera. The best treat one could offer one's guests was Rossini, la Malibran, and la Sontag singing the most beautiful pieces of their repertoire.

Surprisingly, musicians appeared not as distinguished guests but simply as professionals, brought in to entertain, paid generously, and shown the door once the work was done. As discussed in the preceding chapter, even the most famous singers rarely gained entrance into salon society, and they had more difficulty being accepted than, for example, academicians. If a hostess planned an unrivaled evening she would contact Rossini, who would undertake the musical preparation, the planning of the program, and the recruitment of singers and harp or flute virtuosos. They would all arrive at the appointed hour, execute excerpts from their repertoire, captivating some and putting others to sleep, receive warm compliments from the master of the house and a few ecstatic dilettanti before taking their leave on the understanding that someone would bring their fee the next day. Very few musicians had the honor of lingering in the salon after the concert, taking part in the conversations or dancing, if there was a ball.

The charming, vivacious, and original Malibran proved, as always, the exception, but other artistic heroines were scrutinized mercilessly and their manners compared unfavorably to the impeccable ones of the salon-goers. These few lines by Marie d'Agoult about Henriette Sontag give a glimpse of the climate of the salons,

Spoiled by the Germans, intoxicated by the presence of aristocracy and good breeding, avid for praise, even more greedy for money, and with very little wit, she tried to play the great lady but succeeded poorly. She arrived late for the concert with barely an excuse, sang capriciously, was impertinent or silent toward her admirers—unless they were princes, ambassadors, bankers, or directors of the fine arts.[8]

An evening at the home of Countess Merlin was sought after by everyone, for not only did she maintain a sincere friendship with Maria Malibran, but she also surrounded herself with the dilettanti of the best Parisian society. A concert at her residence with Rossini accompanying Lablache, Donzelli, or the divine Malibran was a gathering of devoted admirers, who, with genuine interest, listened delightedly before enjoying supper or dancing with the artists.

At the opposite extreme was a soirée given by the Bonfils family, who epitomized the nouveau riche of the Chaussée d'Antin. In their luxurious but ostentatious apartments, the Bonfils tried to bring together bankers, stockbrokers, public notaries, and wealthy foreigners, as well as a few barons and countesses to gild the evening with their coats of arms. Though many of their guests did not understand opera and were more concerned with the buffet, the host still called upon the services of the Théâtre-Italien's finest talents. La Malibran and Lablache might start the concert with a duet by Fioravanti, then Lablache, Donzelli, and Zucchelli would sing the trio from Rossini's *La pietra del paragone* (The Touchstone). Malibran would present an aria of her own choosing, and finally Mme Tadolini would join the four singers to interpret the quintet from *Matilde di Shabran* by the inevitable Rossini. Once the concert ended, the atmosphere in the salon relaxed, and the guests could enjoy themselves once again.

Celebrated French composers. Courtesy Paul Jackson.

CHAPTER 7

The Press and Opera

A Half-Century of Evolution

For its newspapers and journals, the first half of the nineteenth century can be seen as a period of crisis that ended with the birth of the modern press. Censorship was a constant threat, yet the press managed little by little to free itself of the restrictions of various political regimes, to modernize technically, and to reach an ever larger audience. Suffocation, revolt, then liberalization were the three main stages in its journey from Napoleon to Louis-Philippe.

It was common knowledge that Napoleon had no sympathy for journalists or writers and believed them to be either ideologues or metaphysicians and thus dangerous to his regime. Their only duty, according to him, was to put their pens to the service of the state, just as a soldier would his sword. Since journalists obviously did not share this reasoning, censorship became the inevitable outcome.

In January 1800 Bonaparte issued a decree cutting the number of political newspapers to thirteen, causing a reduction in subscriptions from 60,000 to 32,000 in just five years. The emperor still felt threatened by criticism and conspiracy and gradually increased his hold on the press. He decided to try "a little suppression," and tackled the principal newspapers. One of these was the renowned *Journal des Débats*, which was appropriated and transformed into the *Journal de l'Empire*. Thanks to censorship and the merger or disappearances of certain papers, only four national newspapers and one regional newspaper for each provincial area remained at the end of the Empire.

The revolt that could not take place under Napoleon exploded during the Restoration, to the extent that it contributed to the regime's fall. This was the point at which the modern press really came into being, initiated by a battery of writers and journalists who were stimulated by their common struggle against censorship. Censorship had earlier been abolished, but it reappeared between 1817 and 1819. It was reestablished after the assassination of the Duke of Berry (an act considered by extremists to be the consequence of excessive liberalism), before being abolished in a grand gesture of generosity at the time of Charles X's coronation. Although it was ineffective, censorship achieved the threefold result of reinforcing journalists in their convictions, influencing writers (headed by Chateaubriand) who initially favored the regime but who ended by opposing it, and causing a rash of clandestine satirical pamphlets. In 1826 the alternative press reached 40,000 subscribers while the official press reached fewer than 11,000. By signing his three 1830 ordinances, the first of which required the muzzling of the press by censorship, Charles X signed his own dismissal.

Louis-Philippe did not begin his reign on such a basis; indeed, freedom of the press constituted the touchstone of his government. This government, though, was supported by only one social class, the bourgeoisie. From 1830 on, censorship was illegal and any political opinion could be freely voiced in the ever more numerous daily papers. Constant insecurity, repeated attempts against the royal family, and the violence of certain opposition newspapers led to the 1835 *lois de septembre* (September laws), which prohibited attacks against Louis-Philippe and his government. In fact, nothing really changed, since what was removed from one medium reappeared immediately elsewhere in one of the numerous clandestine brochures and satiric journals that viciously attacked poor Louis-Philippe. The bitter combat during the Restoration fed an incredible expansion in the number of periodicals and subscribers (42 million printed copies in 1836, 80 million in 1846). With a decline in the price of newspapers and the development of printing techniques came the great epoch of the fathers of the modern press, Hippolyte de Villemessant and Émile de Girardin.

The Music Press

In addition to journals dedicated to music, the major Parisian dailies not only announced the day's performances, but frequently published reviews of the capital's principal productions.

The music press experienced the same vicissitudes as all other periodicals during these fifty years. The importance of specialized papers grew appreciably from one period to the next. During the Empire opera lovers could refer only to the daily *Courrier des Spectacles ou Journal des Théâtres*, which was taken over in 1807 by the daily *Courrier de l'Europe et des Spectacles* and from 1810 to 1811 by the weekly *Tablettes de Polymnie*. The first rapid expansion of the music press dates from the Restoration and the birth of *Le Courrier des Spectacles de Paris* (taken over by *Le Corsaire*), *Le Miroir des Spectacles*, *Le Courrier des Théâtres*, and *La Pandore* (all dailies), as well as *La Revue Musicale*, a weekly put out by Fétis, the Paris Conservatory's famous counterpoint teacher. In 1829 two illustrated reviews were also started: *La Revue des Deux Mondes*, to which Marie d'Agoult contributed, and *La Revue de Paris*. In the latter, Louis Véron, future director of the Opéra, launched the fashion of serialized novels and coined the expression *la suite au prochain numéro* ("to be continued in the next issue").

A new leap forward occurred during the July Monarchy with the appearance of the weeklies *L'Entracte*, *Le Ménestrel*, and *La France Musicale* and the bimonthly *L'Artiste*, and with the transformation of *La Revue Musicale* into *La Revue et Gazette Musicale de Paris*, published every Sunday. All the newspapers subsequent to 1830 survived beyond the influence of the July Monarchy into the Third Republic and, in the case of *Le Ménestrel,* until 1919.

The influx of new journals of all kinds after 1830 was directly related to their low cost, due to the use of cheaper paper. The annual subscription for a daily during the Restoration was between 70 and 80 francs (and 112 francs for the official *Moniteur Universel*), but it dropped to 40 francs under Louis-Philippe. A weekly musical magazine cost only 10 francs a year around 1840, well within the reach of almost every purse.

❦

A typical Restoration newspaper of musical and theatrical criticism was distributed before ten o'clock in the morning and always consisted of four pages. The first page comprised a listing, without commentary, of that evening's programs at the various theaters, as well as the names of the actors, singers, and dancers scheduled for each of them. Curtain time (usually seven or half past seven), being known to every Parisian spectator, was only announced on the occasion of a special performance.

The other pages were varied and would include a commentary— sometimes laudatory, sometimes caustic—on the vaudeville or *opéra comique* the readers had applauded the night before. A column called, depending on the journal, *Variétés* (Varieties), *Mélanges* (Mixtures), *Butin* (Booty), or *Bruits de Coulisses* (Backstage Noises) supplied a mine of information and gossip about the Parisian theaters, their future programs, and the feats and actions of certain actors and singers. The more serious literary reports analyzed the latest staging of a *tragédie* at the Théâtre-Français, or painted a quick picture of the life of an eighteenth-century writer.

A place was always reserved for an open letter to the editor from a reader. Interestingly, the reader was always named, a courtesy that was rarely extended to journalists. Finally, the journal would keep readers informed of the latest fashions, the elegant or eccentric clothing that had been observed that week in the main boxes of the Opéra or the Théâtre-Italien.

Readers wishing to practice some of the music themselves were aided by the substantial improvements in printing technology during the July Monarchy. From that time on, illustrations embellished the articles, and the newspapers offered engravings representing perhaps Rossini or the singer Lablache, or even the complete score of an aria by Bellini, a fashionable ballad, or a quadrille. By then a weekly would often amount to eight pages, but it had, unfortunately, lost the detailed announcements of daily performances, perhaps because the number of theaters had increased so greatly, from eight at the end of the Empire, to fifteen during the Restoration, to over twenty during Louis-Philippe's reign.

Cliques and Rivalries

Only a novice would buy the first available newspaper. Each newspaper, whether musical, theatrical, national, or political, had certain artistic opinions in the same way that each supported different ministers from the Chamber of Deputies. While Empire newspapers remained as deferential as possible and dared not air overly pronounced opinions, those of the Restoration and the July Monarchy held themselves in battle order, always ready to storm the enemy camp.

As always, two parties opposed each other. One hundred and fifty years previously, Lully opposed Italian composers; fifty years previously the rivalry was between the Gluckists and the Piccinnists; at the time in question, the rivals consisted of the partisans of the great French school of the Opéra and Opéra-Comique, and the fanatics of Italian music based at the Théâtre-Italien.

Le Courrier des Théâtres set the tone when it wrote, "We would speak [of the Théâtre-Italien] at greater length if it were a theater for the general public and not a concert hall intended for the pleasures of 1,200 persons."[1] In other words, this paper would not mention a performance at the Bouffes, and it was joined in its exclusive support of French music by *Le Courrier des Spectacles, Le Corsaire, Le Ménestrel,* and *La Revue et Gazette Musicale de Paris.* These journals defended the French (and assimilated) schools of Rameau, Gluck, and Spontini with great fervor, and, when the time came, would side resolutely with Berlioz.

On the other hand, *Le Miroir des Spectacles* understood only Rossini, *L'Artiste* spoke of little but the Théâtre-Italien and had nothing but praise for it, and *La France Musicale* applied its frank and substantial support to Italian music, while treating the Opéra as a "worm-eaten structure." Even *La Quotidienne,* the major current affairs newspaper, barely deigned to show an interest in performances at the Opéra. Naturally, these diverse viewpoints meant that reports of the same performance differed substantially from one newspaper to another. "A mere twenty people in the orchestra" in one became "a packed auditorium" from the pen of a rival.

℘

Little love was lost between the two camps, and, in general, the partisans of the Opéra and Opéra-Comique were infinitely more scathing toward the Théâtre-Italien than the dilettanti of this establishment toward them. Those newspapers favorable to Rossini or Bellini devoted their pages to articles on the talent of Mme Pasta or the inimitable cavatinas of *La gazza ladra,* and they did not concern themselves with what went on "elsewhere." The proponents of French music, on the other hand, attacked their rivals gleefully.

In 1823 *Le Courrier des Spectacles* defended "the only institution that has been with us since the time of Louis XIV," and ironically commanded in one of its articles:

> Be off with you, Gluck and Quinault, Spontini and de Jouy, and all you composers and authors who believed that beautiful French verse was worthy of the premier theater of Paris; yield your position to the Italian system."[2]

La Pandore also used its columns to attack the enemy:

> Who will deliver us from M. Rossini? From this petty musician who rebels against the wise laws of counterpoint? Who will restore the lost songs of the guardians of beautiful melodic doctrine?[3]

In 1829 *Le Courrier des Théâtres* wrote,

> The unfortunate Mme Malibran received only 14,000 francs and change for her benefit performance at the Bouffes the day before yesterday. With her meager salary, that takes this poor woman's earnings to just over 94,000 francs. Could a fund be started to remedy this great misfortune? Our French compatriots can be helped later.[4]

Le Corsaire, which before 1830 blithely attacked the Théâtre-Italien, lost some of its bite after the Revolution. Nonetheless, in 1836 it judged that the Bouffes' star was dimming, and summarized the opinion shared by all music "nationalists": "We retain two theaters, the Opéra and the Opéra-Comique. That is plenty; the third is a parasitic plant sucking the sap from the other two."[5]

Not content with arguing the merits of French and Italian music, the newspapers also became involved in controversy over the performers. Whereas some took pleasure in pointing out Mme Pasta's vocal faults or Mme Malibran's lack of naturalness onstage, newspapers such as *L'Artiste* defended the same venerated artists. While *Le Corsaire* and other newspapers lauded Mme Dorus, *Le Courrier des Théâtres* extolled only Mme Damoreau and attacked poor Julie Dorus, whom they called "as cold as seraglio marble" with "her sour cries."

The most serious controversy between journalist and musician concerned a writer from *Le Courrier des Théâtres*, Charles Maurice, and the tenor Lafont. It began on 5 July 1832 with this inflammatory description of the singer in the role of Masaniello: "The hero of *La muette de Portici* was represented yesterday by an enormous stomach and huge thighs, which were, worse yet, oiled with quantities of sweat, probably to add to the indecency of it all."[6] After reading these lines Lafont rushed to the headquarters of the newspaper for an explanation. He furiously demanded an apology, but the next day the journalist related the singer's visit in these terms:

> A vulgar fishwife, screaming, gesturing coarsely, and using foul language would be a weak imitation of the actor Lafont swearing by all the devils that he is a distinguished personage and anyone writing otherwise will have to deal with him.

The exchange of words took such a virulent turn that the two protagonists had no other course than a duel with pistols, after which, since they missed each other, the polemic ceased and everything returned to normal.

Content of the Articles

On opening a newspaper, the nineteenth-century opera lover expected to find a certain number of indispensable "ingredients," not all of which related to pure musicological analysis. First, especially in the general newspapers, would be an accurate account of an operatic evening. The chronicler would carefully report the details of the ladies' attire, the elegance of their escorts, and the luxury of the theater, plus of course the reactions of the audience and the ovations received by singers or the composer. Prior to 1830 the presence of the imperial or royal family naturally necessitated long remarks about their arrival at the theater, the ensuing clamor and songs, the actions and gestures of the sovereigns, their departure in front of the massed crowd outside the building, and the special lighting used at events such as the coronation of Charles X. Some articles thus gave a glimpse of the evening itself, and the paper presented an analysis of the actual work later.

Once any general preamble was completed, the journalist would give a long, detailed, act-by-act commentary on the libretto, the action, and the main characters' feelings. This section usually constituted about three-fifths of the article, and would be interspersed with laudatory remarks on a noteworthy duet in the second act, or the encore of a particularly popular aria in the fourth. Only in the last column, sometimes in the last few lines, came a brief mention of the performers. This is partly explained by the fact that the opera houses had permanent companies that changed little from one performance to the other, and subscribers had already read all about the artists.

The amount of space assigned to dancers and singers over the years reflects the evolution in audiences' tastes. During the Empire and much of the Restoration, dancers held absolute power and were the ones who caused crowds to flock to the theater. *Le Journal de Paris* of 25 September 1804 advertised the second presentation of *Panurge*, an opera in three acts, at the Académie Impériale. While the composer and librettist were not even named, and all the singers were jumbled together in three lines, one learnt that

> M. Saint-Amand will reappear in Act 2 and dance a pas russe with Mme Gardel in Act 3. M. Duport and Mlle Sa Soeur will dance a pas de deux in Act 3. M. Henry will make his return with a pas de deux in Act 2 with Mlle Clotilde.

There can be no doubt as to where the main interest of such a production lay.

The following year *Le Courrier des Spectacles* announced Grétry's *La caravane du Caire* and Rousseau's *Le devin du village* without naming the singers but specifying that "M. and Mlle Duport will reappear in Act 2 of *La caravane* dancing a new pas de trois with Mlle Hulin, five years old, and they will dance more new steps in *Le devin*." Nearly twenty years later nothing had changed, and *La Pandore* acknowledged sadly, "The singing was poor and the opera was poor! Only the dancing at the Académie Royale de Musique is worth reporting." Even so, the journalist concluded that the Opéra "always dances, sometimes shouts, rarely sings, and often falls."[7]

Although dance remained prestigious in later years, it came to share the limelight with singing more and more. New musical instruction from 1820 to 1830 led to a marked development in vocal technique, and singing triumphed in *La muette, Guillaume Tell, Robert le diable, La juive,* and *Les huguenots.* Advertisements for performances not only put singers and dancers on an equal footing (while also announcing the names of composers and librettists), but substantial reviews of premieres began to appear, reporting on all the artists, whatever their role. An opera's ballet continued to be an indispensable component, certainly, but just one component of the "great spectacle" offered to audiences.

Journalistic Weaknesses

Through the years the journalists retained an incredible anonymity through unsigned articles. At most they were initialed by a single, cryptic, capital letter. Only a few famous names, such as Geoffroy, Castil-Blaze, Fétis, Berlioz, and Liszt, were known to readers and sometimes written out in full. In fact, the writers of many articles were either enlightened music lovers who contributed what they could to theatrical news, or newspaper staff members who wrote on everything, from politics and economics to music, with varying degrees of good nature and skill. In 1829 the editor of *Le Démocrite*, A. Martainville, acknowledged on the first page that he was "responsible for all the articles," but more often total anonymity prevailed, and a reader could remain unaware of the author of the opera reviews for months. This gave the journalist greater room for manoeuver and sheltered him from all kinds of pressures. Sometimes readers never learnt the name of a journalist, such as when *L'Universel* announced on 3 April 1830 that "the person who until now has contributed our articles on the major theaters has just given up his duties."

It was necessary to wait for *La Revue et Gazette Musicale de Paris* to find a newspaper that met the high hopes of music enthusiasts. In each issue, next to the title, it printed the names of its twenty-three illustrious contributors, among them Adam, Berton, Berlioz, Castil-Blaze, Fétis, Halévy, Le Sueur, and Liszt.

Apart from the writers for *La Revue* and those of *Le Ménestrel*, few music journalists showed much knowledge of the subject or had any comprehensive training. Not only did authors of cultural articles plagiarize each other (especially at the beginning of the century), but the articles were more likely to be written by habitués of the theater rather than educated specialists. They often limited their work to the account of a salient moment in the libretto and a brief commentary on the artists' performances. Real musicological discourse, thorough enough to prove that it came from a knowledgeable musician's pen and not just from "somebody in the audience" was a rarity, particularly before 1830. In this regard, it is disconcerting to compare the French musical press of the time with a specialized German newspaper such as Leipzig's *Allgemeine Musikalische Zeitung*. This paper sent some of its best journalists to Paris to attend the major productions of the Académie de Musique and other operatic theaters. This produced remarkable results. The journalist had most likely attended many other productions of the same work and was well acquainted with the score. He analyzed each scene and aria, the conducting, the construction of the choral parts, the dramatic interest of the action, the quality of the recitative, the coloring of the instrumentation, the scenery, and the costumes. He also analyzed each singer's performance with appropriate remarks and spoke about the dancers and the spectators' reactions to them, before concluding with his blunt opinion of the work and the composer. For a production such as Spontini's *Olympie*, far from the most important operatic event of the century, the Leipzig newspaper devoted eleven columns to a musical analysis of the work, and included music showing the key themes of the score. It is clear that in the same era no French newspaper achieved the same level of coverage or knowledge.

Many French periodicals at least recognized their shortcomings and did not promise their readers an analysis for which they were unskilled. The musical critic of *La Quotidienne* noticed possible influences from *Sémiramis* on *La donna del lago* (a common device of the time and detectable by any dilettante), but confessed humbly, "I am not learned enough to confirm the thing, and am only reporting what I have heard."[8] A judicious Martainville wrote in *Le Démocrite*, about the premiere of *Guillaume Tell*.

> We leave to others the task of explaining in technical terms the reason for the effects produced by the principal pieces of this beautiful score, the task of seeking to reveal the composer's secrets. This is work that we do not involve ourselves in. We do not believe that a journalist should speak as a musical professional to his readers, but as an enthusiast of good taste and good faith who communicates to them the impressions he received, which they themselves probably received since, doubtless, most of them are also only amateurs."[9]

A good defense!

When Martainville referred to "others," he was doubtless thinking of the journalists of the specialized press, but, unfortunately, writing for these papers did not guarantee competence. *Le Courrier des Spectacles* wrote that in *Don Juan* "everything appeared to have been composed haphazardly," *Le Corsaire* was content to find "some beautiful things" in *La somnambule*, while *La Gazette Musicale* noted only that "the orchestra performed its duties well," and *L'Artiste* judged *Le prophète* "a little stingy with melodies, but abounding in curious details and pretty instrumental effects." Such reviews were scarcely better than those of general newspapers such as *Les Débats*, which judged that certain excerpts from an opera by Carafa "were very well done because they were finely worked" and that the prima donnas of the Opéra-Comique "gave pleasure," or *La Quotidienne*, which found in Rossini's music "spiritual notes," and a "brilliant treatment."

A lack of musical training was more to blame than true incompetence, and certain journalists were completely at a loss before great new works such as *Guillaume Tell*, *Robert le diable*, and *La juive*, which they confessed they were incapable of explaining, at least before having seen a certain number of performances. It was often necessary to wait for the third or fourth article on a new work to see the critic surface and gain control of the situation.

∾

One fault common to numerous journalists was a lack of imagination. Their minds were too rational, leading to the excessive predominance in their articles of the treatment of text over music. As discussed in a previous chapter, excellent music could fail in France if accompanied by a poor libretto, while a good libretto could support mediocre music. A journalist from *Le Courrier des Spectacles* wrote the following in 1823 regarding a work given at the Opéra-Comique:

> Music alone, whatever the *ultra-dilettanti* say, cannot support a work on a French stage. It protects the work from complete failure at the premiere, it prolongs its frail existence for a few days, but it will end up by disappearing with the work, dealt a death blow by the audiences' indifference."[10]

This stubborn refusal to be influenced by beautiful music or to admit the weaknesses and overemployed conventions of the libretto supporting it remained one of the greatest shortcomings of the era's opera lovers. How could the French appreciate *Don Giovanni* when Geoffroy, in his article in *Le Journal des Débats*, criticized the fact that Don Pedro, who dies in Act 1, already has a statue erected to him in Act 2 when there has scarcely been time to bury him? With such Cartesian reasoning how could poor Mozart be understood, he who dreamt that poetry was "music's obedient daughter"?

La vestale was the greatest triumph of the Empire, yet it had to overcome the prejudices of the press about what was, in fact, a quite acceptable libretto. The critic from *Le Journal de Paris* could not understand how the virgin, Julia, could be involved in such a love story when the vestal virgins of antiquity, according to him, entered the temple between the ages of six and ten, made vows of chastity for thirty years before resuming their liberty between the ages of thirty-six and forty, which could still be considered "the age of love" but surely not "one of folly."[11] The reviewer from *Le Courrier des Spectacles* prided himself on his knowledge of history and wondered how Licinius could conquer the Gauls one hundred years before they were known to the Romans. He ended on a note of idiosyncratic humor by pitying the fate of the unfortunate virgins who let the sacred fire burn out, while regretting the fact that they did not know about phosphoric or oxygenated lighters, with which they "would have got out of the affair without any scandal or bother."[12]

As always, with the passage of time came evolution. Mozart gradually came to be appreciated by audiences and critics until, finally, after 1820, he was praised by them. As for the importance of the libretto, it retained its stature until the July Monarchy, but an opera's music also gained in importance. At the same time, librettos came to be praised for originality and the abandonment of the formerly prevalent academic style. Curiously, dramatic action continued to astonish and even shock if it exceeded the bounds of accepted good taste and propriety. A journalist for *Le Journal des Débats*, for example, admitted that in *La juive* he could not bear the sight of the immense pot of boiling water into which the Catholics wanted to hurl Rachel, and he implored that this scene be kept short.

Style and Humor

Nineteenth-century journalistic style is sometimes difficult for modern readers to tolerate. The French press was certainly very literary, but it also suffered from verbiage, pedantry, and pompous language that may have been acceptable in the nineteenth century but surely would not be today. The political flattery of the years 1800 to 1830 reached incredible heights of inflated style. The following is from an article in *Le Journal des Débats* relating a command performance of *La vestale* and the ballet *Psyché* in the presence of Louis XVIII and his family.

The words "by order" are always a happy omen. They promise the presence of one of our princes, and the hope of beholding one of Henry IV's grandsons is an irresistible attraction that summons a throng of spectators eager to see the inheritors of this adored line. Yesterday not only the king but his whole family honored, nay, embellished, even consecrated this performance with their august presence."[13]

A similar article appeared in the same newspaper regarding the Duchess of Berry.

Young child, you who are the object of so much love and good wishes, you appear to us during political storms as the star that appears as the last sign of hope for a sailor battered by the tempest."[14]

In the strictly musical domain, extravagant language was equally obligatory. To signify the quality of *La juive*'s music, *La Gazette Musicale* wrote that "M. Halévy dipped into the rich source of his inspiration with great success."[15] After attending Meyerbeer's *Le prophète*, *L'Artiste*'s critic praised the staging by speaking of "Jean's Sardanapalesque funeral" and "women twisting under the burning kisses of the fire." Finally, carried away by his enthusiasm, he described "the dreadful clanking, burning beams, streaming flames, anguished desperation, helpless fury—all realistic enough to frighten—sparkling and bedazzling." Why announce the end of the season at the Italiens in a straightforward way when the same journalist could write that "April, when the grass returns to the meadows and flowers to the chestnut trees, has also caused the singing company of the Ventadour Theater to take wing"?[16]

ॐ

It must be said that not every journalist employed such honeyed praise and hyperbole. Many did their work well, especially considering their minimal musical training and lack of proper perspective regarding operatic creations that they first saw at the same time as the audience. In comparison, 90 percent of today's opera critics write about works that they already know, that they have seen one or many times, and that they have heard even more often, thanks to recordings. Their position is very different from that of their nineteenth-century counterparts, who had to quickly analyze new works and be satisfied with one or two presentations to assimilate the dramatic and musical interest, the quality of the libretto, the resourcefulness of the staging, and the talent of the singers.

A caustic tongue and lively wit could often compensate for other weaknesses. Like those of today, nineteenth-century journalists had sharp tongues, and though they knew how to employ sweet words, they had no pity for fading singers, incompetent stage directors, or inadequate backstage staff.

The prima donnas of the Opéra-Comique had their share of critics. "I have said nothing about Mme Saint-Aubin's return," wrote one journalist, "because I did not notice that she has made any progress during her absence."[17] At Mlle Fargueil's debut, *Le Journal des Débats* found her quite charming, but then exclaimed, "What a shame that such a weak, vinegary trickle came from this package of roses!"[18] *Le Ménestrel* could be just as corrosive. "Who claimed that Mme Henri-Potier's voice has declined? What slander! Mme Henri-Potier is nearly always a quarter tone *above* the note."[19]

The musicians of the Opéra and the Italiens did not escape the journalists' pearls: "Mozart will crescendo, and the voice of Garcia and the reputation of Mme Malibran will *degringolando*," affirmed *Le Corsaire*.[20] *Le Courrier des Théâtres* reported that "Mme Dabadie's voice merits a new nickname: ear-splitting."[21] *La France musicale* announced the departure of the irascible Mme Stoltz for Italy, and sincerely regretted that she was leaving "seven years too late." *La Gazette de France* contributed the following unkind words about Mme Damoreau:

> Those who are charmed by her mild voice have a small request to present in her personal interest. Would she please moderate her

passion for liquorice juice. It has an effect on all the organs that becomes obvious when she opens her mouth—an effect that her mirror should have shown her long ago.[22]

Instead of this satiric tone, which cannot have pleased any of its victims, journalists sometimes employed a more direct, infinitely less malicious humor that clearly conveyed their opinions about a theater, a style of music, or a composer. On 1 January 1824, *La Pandore* wrote,

> Until now we have classified the capital's different theaters in a way that we now recognize as faulty. Having regained a proper sense of justice and equality, we will now reflect popular opinion by listing the rank of the theaters according to their true importance.

In a childish hoax, the newspaper placed the Académie Royale, the Théâtre-Italien, and the Théâtre-Français in eleventh, twelfth, and thirteenth (last) positions. This nevertheless spoke volumes about its opinion of the royal theaters. The next day, *La Pandore* reinstated the more usual classification, placing the Académie Royale first, the Théâtre-Français second, and so on.

A journalist at *Le Journal des Débats* dealt humorously with the fanaticism of the dilettanti. After attending a mere fifteen performances of *Otello*, he found Mme Pasta better than ever, and concluded, "Happily, the faithful dilettanti who were attending their 143rd performance share my opinion, so I am not afraid of repeating it."[23]

Rather than harshly criticizing Giulia Grisi and the identical settings of Italian drama, *Le Corsaire* preferred to employ imagination and humor:

> Nothing overburdens a poor woman like the weight of a long and interminable tragedy in which night after night she has to repeat, *io morró, io non posso morir* (I shall die, I cannot die); *io son pazza* (I am crazy); *io son perduta* (I am lost). All these imaginary calamities merely dry the chest and the throat as though

they were real. Constantly grovelling at the feet of a furious father, marching to the scaffold, being stabbed, passing from folly
to despair and from despair to death affects the strongest voices
in the long run.[24]

When, in 1832, the Opéra-Comique once again found itself in
peril, it tried to found a new company that would form a good basis
for a fresh start. *Le Courrier des Théâtres*, though it supported the Salle
Feydeau, wrote on the subject daily with noteworthy wit and imagination. "About the Opéra-Comique's future company, nothing new.
If that means it is not forming, that is good news!" "The Opéra-
Comique's new company is not advancing. Apparently it is going
backwards. At least something is happening." When the new company was finally launched, the paper wrote that "Quite astonished by
its birth, the Opéra-Comique's company has just gone to sleep.
Nighty-night!" And "Lost: a fifteen-day-old baby girl, rather badly
swaddled, and of a somewhat unfortunate constitution. Anyone who
finds her is requested to inform her parents, who had her baptized
with the name New Company of the Opéra-Comique. As a reward,
she will not be expected to sing."[25]

If the press of the first half of the nineteenth century did not always manifest artistic competence, at least humor was in good evidence. This proved again and again to be the best weapon for reviving
the interest and curiosity of Parisians in the diversity of their city's
operatic life.

Adolphe Nourrit. Courtesy Paul Jackson.

Notes

Chapter 1

1. Chaptal 1893, p. 269.
2. Cited in Arthur-Lévy 1892, p. 445.
3. Letter from Napoleon to Fouché, Boulogne, 23 June 1805; cited in Rémusat 1880, vol 2, p. 414.
4. Letter to his brother, 4 October 1805; cited in Rémusat 1880, pp. 414–415.
5. *Journal des Dames et des Modes*, 15 September 1806.
6. Cited in Fleischman 1965, p. 163.
7. Letter to M. de Rémusat, 2 March 1810; cited in Arthur-Lévy 1892, p. 444.
8. Ibid.
9. Letter of 13 February 1810 in *Lettres inédites*, P. Lecestre, ed.
10. Ibid., letter of 3 October 1810.
11. Castil-Blaze 1856, p. 423.
12. Chastenay 1897, p. 74.
13. Cited in Fleischman 1965, p. 247.
14. Chastenay 1897, p. 74.
15. Wairy 1967, p. 345.
16. V. de Broglie, *Souvenirs*, vol. 2, p. 215; letter of 27 September 1821.
17. Countess of Boigne 1908, p. 185.
18. Karr 1839–1840, March 1840.

Chapter 2

1. Bonet de Treiches, Ro 793.
2. Cited in Lanzac de Laborie 1913, vol. 8, chap. 1.
3. Ibid.
4. *Le Courrier de l'Europe et des Spectacles*, 5 Febrary 1808.
5. Berlioz 1969, vol. 1, p. 111.
6. *La Gazette de France*, 5 March 1828.
7. Abrantès 1832, vol 6, pp. 273–274.
8. *Le Corsaire*, 18 April 1827.
9. Ibid., 29 March 1824.
10. Archives nationales, ser. AJ13–111.
11. Charles de Boigne 1857, p. 12.

Chapter 3

1. Geoffroy 1825, vol. 5, pp. 192–193
2. Ibid., p. 252.
3. Ibid., pp. 461–462.
4. Berlioz 1969, vol. 1, p. 115.
5. Berlioz 1852, pp. 185–186.
6. *Le Ménestrel*, 27 June 1875.
7. Castil-Blaze 1855, vol. 1, p. 148.
8. The Rossini-Wagner encounter, March 1860; see L. Rognoni, *Gioacchino Rossini* (Turin: ERI, 1968), pp. 417–418.
9. Véron 1856, vol. 3, p. 150.
10. *Le Corsaire*, 2 December 1831.
11. Castil-Blaze 1855, vol. 2, p. 227.
12. Cited in Bouchor 1946, p. 44.
13. Berlioz 1969, vol. 2, p. 25.
14. Cited in Boschot 1942, pp. 140–141.
15. Ibid.
16. Ibid.
17. Mongrédien 1986, p. 52.
18. Ibid., p. 51.
19. L. Spach (also known as Lavater), *Henri Farel* (Paris: Guyot, 1834), vol. 1, p. 330.
20. *Le Journal des Débats*, 25 August 1814.
21. Archives nationales, 0^3 1645 (32).

Chapter 4

1. *Le Journal des Débats*, March 1805.
2. *Le Journal de Paris*, 2 December 1804.
3. Dash 1896–1898, vol. 2, p. 42.
4. Jouy 1815b, vol. 3, pp. 241–242.
5. Charles de Boigne 1857, p. 106.
6. Berlioz 1969, vol. 1, p. 109.
7. Wairy 1967, p. 207.
8. Countess of Boigne 1908, vol. 1, pp. 342–343.
9. *L'Artiste*, November 1831.
10. Bareilles 1820.
11. *La Pandore*, 2 March 1824.
12. Cited in Matoré 1951, p. 89.

Chapter 5

1. Baron Grimm, Lettre sur Omphale, in *Correspondance littéraire, philosophique et critique* (Paris: Garnier, 1877–1882).
2. Cited in Fleischman 1965, p. 275.
3. *Allgemeine Musikalische Zeitung*, 23 April 1817.
4. J. F. Reichardt, *Un hiver à Paris sous le Consulat* (Paris: Plon, 1896).
5. Castil-Blaze 1855, vol. 2, p. 186.
6. *Allgemeine Musikalische Zeitung*, 28 April 1819.
7. Berlioz 1852, 13th evening.
8. Cited by Mongrédien 1986, p. 19.
9. Cited by Derwent 1937, p. 172.
10. Ibid., pp. 172–173.
11. Dash 1896–1898, vol. 2, p. 158.
12. Charles de Forster, *Quinze ans à Paris*, vol. 2, p. 274.
13. Agoult 1877, p. 303.
14. Charles d'Agoult, *Mémoires inédits*, present property of Count Josserand de Saint-Priest d'Urgel.
15. Balabine 1914, p. 156.
16. Tiersot, 1924.

Chapter 6

1. Cited in Soubiès 1910.

2. *Le Courrier des Spectacles*, 6 May 1823.
3. Argé and Chainaie 1822, p. 155.
4. Cited in Soubiès 1913, pp. 122–123.
5. *Le Corsaire*, 5 November 1823.
6. Ibid., 28 January 1827.
7. Ibid., 5 November 1827.
8. Agoult 1877, p. 304.

Chapter 7

1. *Le Courrier des Théâtres*, 2 September 1831.
2. *Le Courrier des Spectacles*, 19 January 1823.
3. *La Pandore*, 1 January 1824.
4. Cited by Gheusi, No. 61.
5. *Le Corsaire*, 11 February 1836.
6. *Le Courrier des Théâtres*, 5 July 1832.
7. *La Pandore*, 14 January 1824.
8. *La Quotidienne*, 4 November 1825.
9. *Le Démocrite*, 3 August 1829.
10. *Le Courrier des Spectacles*, 17 May 1823.
11. *Le Journal de Paris*, 16 December 1807.
12. *Le Courrier des Spectacles*, 16 December 1807.
13. *Le Journal des Débats*, 10 May 1814.
14. Cited in Imbert de Saint-Amand 1887 p. 241.
15. *La Gazette Musicale*, 15 March 1835.
16. *L'Artiste*, 1 June 1849.
17. *Le Journal des Débats*, 12 March 1805.
18. Ibid., 9 March 1835.
19. *Le Ménestrel*, 12 July 1840.
20. *Le Corsaire*, 30 November 1829.
21. *Le Courrier des Théâtres*, 19 July 1832.
22. *La Gazette de France*, 5 March 1828.
23. *Le Journal des Débats*, 2 May 1825.
24. *Le Corsaire*, 11 Febrary 1836.
25. *Le Courrier des Théâtres*, summer 1832.

Bibliography

1. Opera, Performances, Composers, and Singers

Almanachs des spectacles de Paris. All years. Paris: Barba.

Bailbé, J. M. 1969. *Le roman et la musique en France sous la Monarchie de Juillet.* Paris: Lettres Modernes Minard.

Barbier, P. 1982. *Gaspare Spontini à Paris.* Dissertation, Rennes.

———. 1989. *Histoire des castrats.* Paris: Grasset.

Barzun, J. 1982. *Berlioz and His Century: An Introduction to the Age of Romanticism.* Chicago: University of Chicago Press.

Becker, H., and G. Becker. 1989. *Giacomo Meyerbeer: A Life in Letters.* Portland, Ore., Amadeus Press.

Blanchard, R., and R. de Candé. 1986. *Dieux et divas de l'Opéra.* Paris: Plon.

Blaze de Bury, H. 1865. *Meyerbeer et son temps.* Paris: Michel Lévy.

Bonet de Treiches. *De l'Opéra en l'an XII.* Bibliothéque de l'Arsenal, Ro 793.

Boschot, A. 1942. *Hector Berlioz.* Paris: Plon.

Bouchor, J. 1946. *L'amateur d'art lyrique.* Paris: Heugel.

Bouvet, C. 1930. *Spontini.* Paris: Rieder.

Brunel, P. 1981. *Vincenzo Bellini.* Paris: Fayard.

Castil-Blaze. 1855. *L'Académie Impériale de Musique.* Paris: Castil-Blaze.

———. 1856. *L'Opéra-Italien de 1548 à 1856.* Paris: Castil-Blaze.

Chaalons d'Argé, and Ragueneau de la Chainaie. 1822. *Histoire critique des théâtres de Paris (pendant 1821)*. Paris: Lelong & Delaunay.

Charlton, D. 1986. *Grétry and the Growth of Opéra-Comique*. Cambridge: Cambridge University Press.

Choron and Fayolle. 1910. *Dictionnaire des musiciens, artistes et amateurs*. Paris.

Cooper, M. 1949. *Opéra-Comique*. New York: Chanticleer Press.

Croston, W. L. 1948. *French Grand Opera: An Art and a Business*. New York: King's Crown Press.

Curzon, H. de. 1911. *Meyerbeer*. Paris: Laurens.

Dean, W. 1982. French Opera. In *The New Oxford History of Music*. Oxford: Oxford University Press, 8:26–199.

Derwent, Lord. 1937. *Rossini*. Paris: NRF.

Deshayes. 1822. *Idées générales sur l'Académie Royale de Musique*. Paris: Monge.

Fétis, F. J. 1884. *Biographie universelle des musiciens*. 2nd ed., revised by A. Pougin. Originally published 1860–1881. Paris: Firmin-Didot.

Fleischman, T. 1965. *Napoléon et la musique*. Brussels: Brépols.

Fragapane, P. 1954. *Spontini*. Boulogne: Sansoni.

Geoffroy. 1825. *Cours de littérature dramatique*, vol. 5. Paris: Blanchard.

Gheusi, J. Histoire du Théâtre des Italiens de Paris. *L'Avant-scène Opéra*, Nos. 56–63.

Gourret, J. 1973. *Chant*. Sens: ICC.

———. 1981. *Encyclopédie des fabuleuses cantatrices de l'Opéra*. Paris: Mengès.

———. 1983. *Histoire de l'Opéra-Comique*. Paris: Albatros.

———. 1985. *Histoire des salles de l'Opéra de Paris*. Paris: Trédaniel.

Hagan, D. 1965. *French Musical Criticism Between the Revolutions*. Thesis, University of Illinois.

Heriot, A. 1956. *The Castrati in Opera*. London: Secker & Warburg.

Johnson, J. 1988. *The Théâtre-Italien and Opera and Theatrical Life in Restoration Paris*. Diss., University of Chicago.

Lalo, P. 1947. *De Rameau à Ravel*. Paris: Albin Michel.

Lasalle, A. de. 1875. *Les treize salles de l'Opéra*. Paris: Sartorius.

Lesure, F., et al. 1983. *La musique à Paris en 1830–1831*. Paris: Bibliothèque Nationale.

Merlin, O. 1978. *Quand le bel canto régnait sur le boulevard*. Paris: Fayard.

Mongrédien, J. 1978. L'Opéra à Paris sous la Restauration. In *Bulletin de la Société de l'Histoire de Paris 1976–1977*: 159–169. Paris: Librairie d'Argences.

————. 1986. *La musique en France, des lumières au romantisme*. Paris: Harmoniques Flammarion.

Ortigue, J. d'. 1829. *De la guerre des dilettanti*. Paris: Ladvocat.

Osbourne, C. 1994. *The Bel Canto Operas*. Portland, Ore.: Amadeus Press.

Perris, A. 1967. *Music in France During the Reign of Louis-Philippe*. Thesis, Northwestern University, Illinois.

Pierre, C. 1895. *B. Sarrette et les origines du Conservatoire National de Musique et de Déclamation*. Paris: Delalain.

Poujin, A. 1911. *Marie Malibran*. Paris: Plon.

Reparaz, C. de. 1977. *Maria Malibran*. Paris: Perrin.

Segalini, S. 1985. *Meyerbeer, diable ou prophète?* Paris: Beba.

————. 1986. *Divas, parcours d'un mythe*. Actes Sud.

Siohan, M. 1967. *Histoire du public musical*. Lausanne: Rencontre.

Soubiès, A. 1910. *Le Théâtre-Italien au temps de Napoléon et de la Restauration*. Paris: Fischbacher.

————. 1913. *Le Théâtre-Italien de 1801 à 1913*. Paris: Fischbacher.

Stendhal. 1923. *Notes d'un dilettante*. Paris: Champion.

————. 1864. *Vie de Rossini*. Paris: Michel Lévy.

Tiersot, J. 1924. *Lettres de musiciens écrites en français du XVe au XXe siècle*. Turin: Bocca Freies.

————. 1930. *La musique aux temps romantiques*. Paris: Félix Alcan.

Vernières, J. 1836. Les coulisses de l'Opéra. *La Revue de Paris*.

Véron, L. 1860. *Les théâtres de Paris depuis 1806 jusqu'en 1860*. Paris: Bourdillat.

2. History, Paris, and Society

Ariste, P. d'. 1930. *La vie et le monde du boulevard*. Paris: Tallandier.

Arthur-Lévy. 1892. *Napoléon intime*. Paris: Nelson.

Aulard, A. 1823. *Paris sous le Ier Empire*. Paris: Jouaust.

Bareilles, B. 1820. *Un turc à Paris (1806–1811)*. Paris: Bossard.

Bertaut, J. 1936. *Le roi bourgeois*. Paris: Grasset.

————. 1957. *Le boulevard*. Paris: Tallandier.

Burnand, R. 1843. *La vie quotidienne en France en 1830*. Paris: Hachette.

Dumas, M.-A. 1852. *Histoire de la vie politique et privée de Louis-Philippe*. Paris: Dufour & Mulat.

Gabriel-Robinet, L. 1962. *Journaux et journalistes*. Paris: Hachette.

Guerrini, M. 1967. *Napoléon et Paris*. Paris: Téqui.

Hatin, E. 1861. *Histoire de la presse en France*. Paris: Poulet-Malassis.

Hillairet, J. 1966. *La Rue de Richelieu*. Paris: Minuit.

Imbert de Saint-Amand. 1886. *La cour de l'impératrice Joséphine*. Paris: Dentu.

———. 1887. *La Duchesse de Berry à la cour de Louis XVIII*. Paris: Dentu.

Jullien, A. 1884. *Paris dilettante au commencement du siècle*. Paris: Firmin-Didot.

Karr, A. 1839–1840. *Les guêpes*. Paris.

Lanzac de Laborie, L. 1913. *Paris sous Napoléon*, vol. 8. Paris: Plon.

Le Nabour, E. 1980. *Charles X*. Paris: Lattès.

Mansel, P. 1982. *Louis XVIII*. Paris: Pygmalion.

Matoré, G. 1951. *Le vocabulaire et la société sous Louis-Philippe*. Geneva: Droz.

Mazédier, R. 1945. *Histoire de la presse parisienne*. Paris: Pavois.

Ordonnances de police. 1806, 1807, 1808. Paris: Bertrand Pottier.

Paris ou le livre des cent et un. 1831. Paris: Ladvocat.

Robiquet, J. 1928. *L'art et le goût sous la Restauration*. Paris: Payot.

———. 1946. *La vie quotidienne au temps de Napoléon*. Paris: Hachette.

Vier, J. 1955–1959. *La Comtesse d'Agoult*. Paris: Armand Colin.

3. Memoirs

Abrantès, Duchess d'. 1832. *Mémoires*. Paris: Ladvocat.

Agoult, Countess d'. 1877. *Mes souvenirs*. Paris: Calmann-Lévy.

Balabine, V. de. 1914. *Journal, Paris 1842–1852*. Paris: Émile-Paul.

Berlioz, H. 1852. *Les soirées de l'orchestre*. Paris: Michel Lévy.

———. 1956. *Evenings with the Orchestra*. Trans. by J. Barzun.

———. 1960. *Memoirs*. Annotated, and revised by Ernest Newman. New York: Dover.

———. 1969. *Mémoires*. Paris: Garnier-Flammarion.

Blangini, F. 1834. *Souvenirs*. Paris: Allardin.

Boigne, Charles de. 1857. *Petits mémoires de l'Opéra*. Paris: Librairie Nouvelle.

Boigne, Countess de. 1908. *Mémoires*. Paris: Plon.

Brifaut, C. 1921. *Souvenirs d'un académicien sur la Révolution, le Ier Empire et la Restauration*. Paris: Albin Michel.

Chaptal, Count. 1893. *Mes souvenirs sur Napoléon*. Paris: Plon.

Chastenay, Mme de. 1897. *Mémoires*. Paris: Plon.

Dash, Countess. 1898. *Mémoires des autres*. Paris: Librairie Illustrée.

Genlis, Mme de. n.d. *Souvenirs d'une femme de lettres*. Lille: Maison du

Bon Livre.
Jouy, É. de. 1815a. *Guillaume le Franc-Parleur*. Paris: Pillet.
———. 1815b. *L'hermite de la Chaussée d'Antin*. Paris: Pillet.
Merle, J. T. 1827. *Lettres à un compositeur français sur l'état actuel de l'Opéra*. Paris: Barba.
Rémusat, Mme de. 1880. *Mémoires (1802–1808)*. Paris: Calmann-Lévy.
Véron, L. 1856. *Mémoires d'un bourgeois de Paris*. Paris: Librairie Nouvelle.
Wairy, C. 1967. *Mémoires*. Paris: Mercure de France.

4. Manuscript Sources

French National Archives

Series AJ^{13} Archives de l'Opéra.
Series O2   Maison de l'empereur.
Series O3   Maison du roi: Restauration.
Series O4   Maison du roi: Louis-Philippe.

Periodicals

Allgemeine Musikalische Zeitung (Leipzig)
L'Artiste
Le Corsaire
Le Courrier de l'Europe et des Spectacles
Le Courrier des Spectacles
Le Courrier des Théâtres
Le Démocrite
Le Drapeau Blanc
La France Musicale
La Gazette de France
Le Journal de l'Empire
Le Journal de Paris
Journal des Dames et des Modes
Le Journal des Débats
Le Ménestrel
Le Miroir des Spectacles
Le Moniteur Universel
La Pandore
La Quotidienne

La Revue et Gazette Musicale de Paris
La Revue Musicale
Tablettes de Polymnie

Glossary

Ancien Régime
Literally, "the old order." Refers to the absolute monarchy that reigned in France before the 1789 revolution.

castrato
Also called sopranist or male soprano. The castrato was the idol of Italian opera, especially in the seventeenth and eighteenth centuries. With a range similar to the female soprano or contralto, but with stronger, more flexible vocal technique. The best castratos were remarkable in their subtlety and technical prowess.

claque
Members of the audience hired to applaud a singer, demand encores, and generally try to ensure the success of a production.

Consulate
The government of 1799–1804 led by consuls, including Napoleon.

Empire
The period of Napoleon's military dictatorship, 1804–1814. It ended with Napoleon's exile to Elba.

French franc
Multiplication by 13 will give an approximate current equivalent of nineteenth-century francs.

grand opéra
An epic or historical work of a serious nature, usually in four or five acts. Generally involves active dramatic participation by the chorus and includes a ballet. Examples include *Guillaume Tell* and *Les Huguenots*.

Hundred Days
The period of Napoleon's return to power, March–June 1815. It ended with the Battle of Waterloo and Napoleon's final exile to St. Helena.

July Monarchy
In July 1830 an uprising overthrew the ruling Bourbons and set up the throne of Orleans, a younger branch of the house of Bourbon, with Louis-Philippe as king. Louis-Philippe reigned until the February 1848 Revolution, when he was overthrown and the Second Republic set up.

opera buffa
Comic, often farcical opera that developed as a reaction to the excessive ostentation of *opera seria*. Drew on everyday characters involved in love intrigues, domestic scheming, and infidelities. Examples include *Don Giovanni* and *Il barbiere di Siviglia*.

opéra comique
Franch eighteenth-century light opera, less showy than Italian *opera buffa*. By the nineteenth century it was no longer necessarily comic in nature and differed from *grand opéra* only in that it contained spoken dialogue, whereas *grand opéra* was set to music throughout. Examples include *Fidelio* and *Les deux journées*.

opera seria
Originating in Italy, the main operatic form of the seventeenth and eighteenth centuries. Became highly stylized and complex, containing intricate arias designed to allow the soloists to display their virtuosity. Often consisted of the stylized treatment of mythological or classical subjects. Examples include *La clemenza di Tito* and *Mosè*.

pasticcio
Rearranged operas with altered story lines and introduced elements. Productions made up of contributions by various composers, designed to give the audience maximum gratification without necessarily supporting a plot or even a unified musical theme.

Restoration
The era 1814–1830 when the Bourbon monarchy was reinstated with Louis XVIII, succeeded by Charles X.

tragédie lyrique
A form of French opera that flourished from the seventeenth century to the early nineteenth century. Based on a serious, sometimes tragic, theme. Examples include *Médée* and *La vestale.*

Index of Names

Numbers in bold refer to illustrations.

239